GHOSTS
OF MANILA

GHOSTS
OF MANILA

The Fateful Blood Feud Between

Muhammad Ali and Joe Frazier

MARK KRAM

HarperCollins*Publishers*

HarperCollins books may be purchased for educational, business, or sales promotional use. For information please write: Special Markets Department, HarperCollins Publishers Inc., 10 East 53rd Street, New York, NY 10022.

FIRST EDITION

Designed by Philip Mazzone

Library of Congress Cataloging-in-Publication Data

Kram, Mark.
    The Ghosts of Manila : the fateful blood feud between Muhammad Ali and Joe Frazier / by Mark Kram.
      p. cm.
    ISBN 0-06-019557-6
    1. Ali, Muhammad, 1942– 2. Frazier, Joe, 1944– 3. Boxers (Sports)—United States—Biography. I. Title: Fateful, brutal blood feud between Muhammad Ali and Joe Frazier. II. Title.

GV1131 .K73 2001
796.83'092'073—dc21
[B]   00-053934

01 02 03 04 05 ❖/RRD 10 9 8 7 6 5 4 3 2 1

For Mark, Tracey, Kerry, Raymond, Robert, and Alix, my children—And my wife, Rene

So in the Libyan fable it is told
That once an eagle, stricken with
   a dart,
Said, when he saw the fashion of
  the shaft,
"With our own feathers, not by
   others' hands,
Are we now smitten."

—Aeschylus

INTRODUCTION

"We went to Manila as champions, Joe and me, and we came back as old men," Muhammad Ali once told me. He was standing outside a South Carolina hospital, well into his forties by this point and years removed from that unspeakably hot tropical morning in Manila in 1975. Narrowly, he had beaten Joe Frazier that day in the final act of their heroic trilogy, and yet Ali would look back on it in years to come with a certain uneasiness, only too aware that it signaled what should have been the end of his career. The choice that stood before him at that juncture was a clear one: get out in one piece, or go on in a sport that is unforgiving to old men, especially those with too much pride, heart, and unexamined confidence for their own well-being. Had he bolted the gym door following Manila (as I was certain he was ready to do after eleven years of covering him for *Sports Illustrated*), the denouement might well have been different.

The major thrust of this book is story, not biography; it is a portrayal of what each man was and is now. It is the tale of two men,

Muhammad Ali and Joe Frazier, whose early close friendship is destroyed as their rivalry becomes steeped in ugliness played out dramatically on one of the largest stages in the history of sports. Divided by the heated temper of their times and their colliding views on race, they find themselves caught in a swirl of public love (Ali) and hate (Frazier), one left with a ruin of a life, the other battered to his soul. For five years, from 1971 to 1975, they sucked the life out of each other over three fights, the first and third of which remain as thrilling and vivid as they were then.

Secondarily, this book is intended to be a corrective to the years of stenography that have produced the Ali legend. Cheap myth corruscates the man; the wire scheme for his sculpture is too big. Junk commentary has been slapped on it to the point that a precise appreciation of just who Ali was (and is) has become obscured. Worse, grandstanding compassion over his admittedly tragic current situation has only served to block a clear view of him even more. While myth usually begins in a place of truth—in this case, uncommon boxing skill—it often ends in a place of fantasia, and this is where we find Ali. He has been celebrated for the wrong reasons and has been interpreted by an increasingly uninformed generation of media that was barely born at the height of his career. Ali is already, like Marilyn Monroe and Elvis Presley, condemned to wander television screens for eternity in snippets of file tape, the visual wallpaper of the mythic.

What was he and what was he not? Important world figure is commonly the description that travels with him these days. Unquestionably, he was important to boxing and sports. Of worldly significance? Well . . . countless hagiographers never tire of trying to persuade us that he ranked second only to Martin Luther King, but have no compelling argument with which to support that claim. Ali was no more a social force than Frank Sinatra. Nor was he especially complex, unless you happen to view instant contradiction of utterance as deep. The politically fashionable clung to his racial invective as if it were the wisdom of a seer. Today, such are the times, he would be looked upon as a contaminant, a chronic user of hate language and a sexual profligate.

Ideology drove what most writers thought of Ali, especially Norman Mailer, who settled upon him like a mollusk, and sometimes in revealing transference seemed to want to merge with the champ. Ali played big in New York salons, bigger even than the Black Panthers, who were also viewed as hip avengers for political rightness. What was laughable, if you knew anything about Ali at all, was that the literati was certain that he was a serious voice, that he knew what he was doing; he didn't have a clue.

Two ideologists summon up the thinking then and now—Ken Tynan and R. Emmett Tyrell. Tynan was a superb writer given to large crushes on certain showmen and insurrectionists. In his recently published *Journal*, he watches Ali beaten by Frazier, and etches bleakly. Frazier is Nixon's hatchetman, and Ali's "flair, audacity" is cut down by "stubborn, obdurate hard-hat persistence. We may come to look back on the 60s as the Indian summer of Western imagination, of the last aristocrats of Western taste."

To the far right of Tynan is Tyrell, who regards Ali in a 1997 column as a corrupting rule breaker. Ali tore down the sport by introducing racial prejudice, and destroyed Frazier with utter nonsense and false calumny. Frazier *was* black. Ali remains a figure today because he is "idolized by the ignorant and by mountebanks still making money off him." Bits of truth, minus the politics, fleck to the surface in both views.

Part 1 of this book, revisionist only to those who will not like their mythic perception jostled, begins with Ali and Frazier isolated in retirement. Part 2 deals with the emergence of both men with special emphasis on the manipulation of Ali by the Muslims. Part 3 reexamines their three bitter fights, especially the dead reckoning in Manila. More than twenty-five years later it still stands out in sharp relief as an utterly brutal, fateful affair. Fateful, because Frazier, convinced that Ali had stolen his black identity, seemed to sentence himself to victimhood; and because Ali, who soared on the wings of unsurpassed talent, spent his last ounce of it in that furnace heat— and he knew it. Men of far less abilities would peck at his remains five years beyond when his art was transcendental; sadly, it would cost him his health. I once asked his former wife Belinda how we should remember Ali. She said, "Remember him as a great fighter."

Legacy has become a pulverized, empty word of late, rather odd considering that America is not noted for much historical memory. In particular, the word seems out of place with sports heroes. Few leave anything behind for long for the next generation—just a line of numbers. Besides the thrill of watching Ali work, whatever his lasting impact on sports might be is altogether mixed. He did lead the way for black athletes out of the frustrating silence that Jackie Robinson had to endure. On the minus side, he also changed the climate of sports, from their promotion to the atmosphere in which they are conducted. His influence in games today can be seen in the blaring, unending marketing of self, the cheap acting out of performers, the crassness of player interactions that even informs our broader culture. Life, culture, and sports as pro wrestling. His was an overwhelming presence that came at a high price, ultimately to himself and the character of sports. Worse, far beyond Joe Louis, he continues to be guided in a mindless display like a sightless man feeling his way through the empty rooms of his remaining history.

PATHOLOGIES

Only his face remained as I remembered it. Eight years had elapsed since I had seen him spiral through the final, perilous years of his career, and even at age forty-two it still held at bay any admission of destruction. There was no zippered flesh, no blistered or pulpy ears, nor eye ridges that drop into sagging eaves; the nose remained agreeably flat without distended bone or hammered spread. Always the centerpiece of vanity—this face, so instantly transportable into world consciousness—it was betrayed only by his eyes, his words. Where once his eyes publicly spilled with tumbling clowns, they were now a dance hall at daybreak. Where once the words streamed in a fusillade of octaves, they were now sluggish and groping.

Three years removed from the ring at this stage of his steep physical decline, Muhammad Ali was living in L.A. in the gated community of Hancock Park, amid sculpted shrubbery and swishing fronds in high trees. It was said that among his occasional dinner guests were Clint Eastwood and Orson Welles. That would figure: Ali had always loved a good Eastwood picture, drawn with unbridled wonder to showdowns on dusty Old West streets; Welles appealed to him less as a film colossus than as a hammy fat man with a bag of magic tricks. Just a question about Welles and the illusions he performed brought a smile to Ali, who eased himself up on his toes in an effort to levitate. "See it, it's scary, ain't it?" he asked. But he remained earthbound, and soon enough he stopped, short of breath, his left hand afflicted by a spooky tremor—the same hand that he used to whip out in four thousandths of a second.

Ornate Middle Eastern furniture lay in deep pools of shadow, giving the house an uneasy stillness broken only by the whisper movement of his manservant Abdel and the wild squawking of *Ali, Ali, Ali* by a couple of scam-eyed parrots on the veranda. "Can you shut 'em up?" Ali asked Abdel, apparently weary of hearing himself addressed in such ridiculing decibels. Boxing seemed to bore him on this day, and he waved off any allusion to it with a grimace, as if he were Tom Thumb being asked about his pituitary gland. Getting back into boxing at any level would lead people to believe that he was needy for fame. Ali was beyond that at this point, said that he had become a missionary for the Muslims to the poor and irreligious. Headquarters for him these days was a Louis IV desk the size of a jet wing.

Slowly, he stood up from behind it and showed what he had been writing, barely legible copying from a Sufi tract that, in so many words, said: *Forget the past, follow your true nature.* What was his true nature? "To save heathens like you," he said. He smiled, then suggested a tour of the house that began on the top floor. Ali switched on a dim light, revealing a long room of memorabilia. In one dark corner crouched a tiger with yellow eyes peering out, a six-foot-long, hand-carved gift from Deng Xiaoping. "Good little man," he said. "Leader of China. No bigger than my nose. He asked me when I'm gonna quit.

Didn't have an answer. He said, `Mountains can't grow any higher.' He was right."

Dusty fight posters dangled from the walls in the humid air. A stray, cracking boxing glove rested palm up on a packing crate in a thin ray of sunlight, its laces falling limply. Ali stood by a brilliant red and white robe on a hanger, stroking it gently. In a sudden gesture of respect in Las Vegas, Elvis Presley had taken the robe off his back and given it to Ali, saying, "From one king to *the* king." Ali kept his fingers on the robe and said, "He a kind fella. Elvis dead now. Bein' too big killed him, I think." He moved over to a pile of photographs on a crate and picked through them: Elvis, with his own troubles in his eyes; the president of Egypt, Gamal Nasser, in a white suit, a little on the hefty side, yet easily passing for an exotic young contract player at MGM; and John Wayne, against whom Ali always measured his own fame. When he came to a shot of Idi Amin, the butcher of Uganda, he pulled back in horror, then told of a bizarre incident, maybe true.

Amin believed himself adroit in the ring. Ali was the guest of honor in Uganda, and they were having dinner at a long table filled with people: Ali at one end, Amin seated at the other with a dwarf at his side. Ali remembered: "He's feedin' this dwarf soup with a spoon, stops and hollers over the table, bangin' his fist." Guests cowered, the silverware jumped. Amin boomed: "I want to fight the great Muhammad Ali!" "Over and over again," Ali continued. "I get to kiddin', say he must've had a nightmare. Then, he goes under the table, opens a case and dumps all this cash. Must've been a half million. But I wasn't goin' to count. Then, he say, `You a champion or a coward?'" The next thing Ali saw was Amin pointing a gun at him, saying, "Now, what you say, Muhammad Ali?" The dwarf scooted, everyone else dove under the table. "Nobody there now. Just me and him. I'm mad and scared at the same time. I whup this bag of fat, and he gonna kill me for sure. Why not? He already kill everybody in the country.

It just dead quiet now. Like John Wayne goin' into a saloon. I'm just lookin' at that gun, my heart poundin', then suddenly he drop the cannon right in the soup in front of him, and the soup splashes all over his uniform, his face and them medals, and he lets out a laugh that would chase Satan and his helpers away."

Casually flipping the Amin photo back into the crate, Ali discovered another set of pictures, all of fighters who formed big and small pieces of his career. Here was the forever penitential Floyd Patterson; the picaresque Jack Johnson, still defiant with his grin; the champagne smile of Sugar Ray Robinson, whom Ali admired the most; Joe Louis, with his spare grimness; his true mentor Archie Moore, with the silky ease and nonchalance of a horn player; the scuffed face of the doomed Jerry Quarry; the sharply ridged prominences of George Chuvalo, who, with an asphalt jaw and nothing else, first tapped into the attitude necessary to beat Ali. He lingered over George Foreman, back then the dark at the top of the stairs, then passed without comment until he came to the squatting gargoyle Sonny Liston. He pointed an accusatory finger at Sonny, and said with conviction: "He the devil. Not enough fire in hell for him." Contrary to the impression that has come down through the years—that Sonny had caved in psychologically under the hysteria that Ali had whipped up—Ali had feared Liston always as a small child might a strong night wind in the trees.

One jarring absence existed in the gallery of photographs: Joe Frazier. The Ali legend had been galvanized by their personal, spend-it-all fights. Where was Joe? Was it just an oversight, or did it speak to the wariness with which he still held Frazier, the deep division that existed between the two to this day? Ali had always viewed Frazier as if he were an inferior item on a menu, and always said so publicly: "What he do? He showed up. That's all." But deep down Ali always looked upon Frazier as a enveloping presence with a black hood over his head and an ax in his hand.

What Ali said in public was far less revealing than what he said in private. Audiences of more than one person were generally justification for a flashing, highly allusive, and ensnarled rodomontade, depending on the theme of the day; it was the pro wrestler rap long before it arrived, the spin retailer way ahead of his day. You had to get Ali alone to delve beneath the rhetoric, and even then there was just so far that Ali would go when it came to Frazier, of whom he could be starkly dismissive and altogether evasive in giving him his just provenance. Privately, Ali would be spare in his comment, given to long silences and sudden observation: "Boxin' just a short time, my brain is his forever." Or: "People don't want art, they wanna see war. I ain't leavin' my face in that ring." Publicly, he would always stray into long and convoluted sermons of showy redundancy, which had been adapted from Muslim gospel with a disregard for even a speck of originality. His easily most famous line, "I ain't got nothing against them Vietcong," was slyly dropped into his presentation by Sam Saxon, an early Muslim watchdog and headbanger more warmly known as Cap'n Sam. The Cap'n himself told me years later of a conversation he once had with Ali.

"You got nothin' 'gainst them Vietcong, right?" the Cap'n said.

"No, not a thing," said Ali.

"Then say it," said the Cap'n. "We behind you. We ain't fightin' no honkie war."

"Yeah. I ain't got nothin' 'gainst them Vietcong."

"Now, now you're talkin'," said Sam.

Ali led the way to the floor below, by an open door to the bedroom where wife Veronica slept, a space arrayed with expensive white linens and fragile black dolls set up along the windowsills. Acolytes who had run with Ali during the old days were wary of Veronica, a statuesque beauty who seemed to them to be in hot pursuit of celebrity and an acting career rather than providing strength to a husband who needed it badly. They also writhed at her excess of spending; odd this, coming from followers who, on the old Ali tab, went through his money like fire ants. Word was Jimmy Jacobs, the film archivist, became so suspicious of the grabby atmosphere that surrounded Ali at his Hancock Park estate that he stopped sending contractual checks in the mail. Ali stood by the open door to his bare bedroom and glanced inside at a cot with an institutional cover. While Ali always had been frugal when it came to pampering himself with worldly possessions—and had a deeply held commitment to the ascetic—he suddenly found himself obliged to reassure that he had gotten out of boxing in one piece financially. He cupped a trembling hand over his mouth and said, "I got three million in CDs in the bank. Nobody knows. Shhhh!"

With that, the doorbell rang downstairs. "Must be some kids," he said, "wanna see some magic tricks again." Ali eased down the steps, then came upon Abdel standing by the door with an uninvited visitor, a young fighter who announced he had come from New Orleans by bus just to see him. Ali motioned him in, then went back to his desk. The kid stood there twisting his cap in his hand, his eyes turning over the ceiling and around the room, then quickly turned back to Ali, who studied him with the disinterest of a man who has picked up an ordinary shell on the beach and was now wondering why. Maybe eighteen, the kid had a small, shaven head, looked like he could fill out to a solid middleweight if he could survive the ignorance and dispassion found every day in the life of young fighters. Ali was always gracious with the species, but knew better than anyone that merely being good would never be good enough.

Ali saw that the kid was staring at him. "Why you lookin' at me like that?" he asked.

"You look different, I mean . . . ," the kid said, his eyes turning over the room again.

"You keep lookin' around my room. You a robber? You gonna come here at night, steal somethin'." He gave a smile to Abdel.

The kid squirmed, said, "I never do that, champ."

"I ain't no champ anymore," Ali said.

"I seen you fight Spinks in Nawwlins."

"Then you didn't see anything."

"I send you a lotta letters."

"I get nothin' but letters. People wantin' all kinds of things. Even pieces of my nappy hair. What your name?"

"Kid Hershey," he said, "like, ya know, in the candy bar. I'm gonna be a champ, and . . ."

Ali looked on blankly. Was his memory being jogged to how he himself had once been? Never one to give the possibility of rejection an even break, the young Clay revved up early for the marketplace. Unlike the old poet Alexander Pope, he did not believe that those who lacked expectations were blessed. He popped up on the phone to trainer Angelo Dundee, who was in his hotel room with his noted light heavy Willie Pastrano. "Willie," Dundee said, "I got a real case here. Some young kid says he's won the Pan American Games, the Golden Gloves, and he's going to go and win the Olympics. He wants to come up." Willie nodded: "Why not? Bein' with you all day, I could use a laugh."

In the presence of enlightenment, the green Clay showed no reverential silence.

"You eat a lot, Willie? How much you eat? You eat good? Gotta watch the diet, a fighter.

"How much roadwork you do, Willie? I can run forever. Spot a horse five lengths.

"You good with cuts, Mr. Dundee? I bet you are. No matter. I don't let nobody cut me. Sorry, I'm talkin' so much. Just need all the information I can get.

"Tell me about Madison Square Garden. What's the color of them seats? Oooooo . . . I bet they gold. And that ring bell. That ring bell give me goose pimples on the radio. And pretty women all over. You don't fool with women, do you, Willie? Can't fool with women, a fighter. Fighter gotta stay pure.

"Sugar Ray Robinson, nobody like him. Oooooo . . . my idol, he somethin'. No disrespect, Willie. And Marciano, what a killer he was. Floyd Patterson, he quick, ain't he. And Archie Moore, he sooo smart. But he older than my daddy. Fighter oughta know when to quit."

When the young Clay finally left, the two just looked at each other and doubled over in laughter. A few months later, Dundee brought Willie back to Louisville for a main event, and he was doing his sparring in the same gym as Clay. Angelo scanned the gym for somebody to work with Willie. "There's that kid over there . . . what's his name," Angelo said. "Wanna work with him, Willie?" Willie and Clay worked a couple of rounds, and as Angelo often liked to recount, "Willie looked so bad I laid him off. Three days before the fight, I had to lay him up. Real stale. Willie doesn't like it and says, `Ange, it ain't me. You got eyes. This kid's a good-lookin' fighter.' And the fact was that Willie was right. I was so busy watching Willie I didn't watch a thing the kid was doing."

Now, Ali was suddenly back to his visitor, saying: "Hold up there. You don't want a piece of my hair. You don't want my autograph. You just wanna see me in person? What you want?"

"I just wonderin' . . . you know, like, ya know . . . maybe you be my manager?"

"I don't manage," Ali said. "Don't even like to watch fights. Don't want nuthin' to do with fights. People see me in gyms, goin' to fights, people think I miss it. People think I'm just another washed-up fighter. You get my meanin'?"

"You can get a trainer," the kid said.

"How many fights you have?" Ali asked.

"Twenty fights."

"What? What you need me for?"

"I need your learnin'. Your name."

Ali moved in front of the kid, took his hands and examined them. "They ain't twenty-fight hands. Your hands too small, too." Ali then held his own hands up, palms facing. "Show me some- thin'."

The kid flicked several untutored combinations to Ali's palms, and Ali turned, saying, "That's enough. How many fights?"

"Twenty," the kid said with less conviction. Ali just stayed silent. The kid said, looking at the floor, "I don't have any fights. I gotta start somewhere. Even you started somewhere, right? Can you help me?"

"I'm gonna help," Ali said. He reached into his pocket, rummaged through some bills, and stuck them into the kid's hand. "Get the bus back to Nawwlins."

The kid said, "I ain't goin' back. I'm stayin' in L.A. I gotta dig in somewhere. I don't want your money."

"You wanna be diggin' a grave?" Ali asked, then added, "You got eatin' money?"

"For a week. I'm stayin' with a stepbrother."

"You keep my money, then. Eat for another week. But if you smart, you go home to your mama." The kid turned away angrily, and Abdel showed him to the door.

"I know how he feel," Ali said. "He gonna hate me. Tell everybody he meet Ali, and I ain't the champ he thought, that I'm a bad man, with no helpin' hand. One day he'll understand, when he a 'lectri- cian or somethin', doin' good, raisin' kids."

As the January light slipped into evening, Ali drew up to eat in a soft chair by the fire. He had picked up considerable weight, yet still seemed hollowed out, like a big fruit shorn of its ripe interior. He labored with a chicken leg that kept quivering in his hand, and finally dropped it in disgust. "I don't know what's wrong with me," he said, and slipped deep into the chair. To distract him, a hypothetical was put to him. Suppose he were a manager, with all he knew and had done, and that kid from New Orleans was Joe Frazier, much older than the kid, small for a heavyweight, with hands that clunked and deadweight legs. "He be on the bus, too," Ali said. He paused, then added, "I don't know anything about fightin', really. Only about *me* fightin'. I couldn't stand lookin' at that kind of style in a gym every day, no matter what the money. I'd see what I could do to him, wanna jump in and whup the sucker." There was an edge to his voice.

It was suggested that it might be interesting to look at the Thrilla in Manila on tape, only his good rounds if he wished. "What good rounds?" he asked. His eyes became unengaged, as if he'd much prefer to pull the ace of diamonds out of his ear. Even sly persistence could not bring him around. He said he'd show the various agonies of Floyd Patterson, or the ignominy of the overvalued George Foreman in Zaire. "I never think twice about George," he said. "He so slow that I eat dinner between his punches." No Thrilla, though, he added, saying, "It was the greatest fight of my life, and it wasn't about style, it was where I had to go for it, a place where you drop through a trapdoor." Why not, then, look at the Thrilla? "I don't wanna look at hell again."

It was not that he didn't want to cooperate on some contrarian whim. The mention of Frazier and Manila seemed to run into a room in his mind that he wanted to keep bare, a steamy couple of hours that took him to the center of himself as a champion and a man. What did he, eight years later, still dread about that fight? Had it not been a masterpiece, a kind of primitive art? A firestorm of passion, of promises kept and value given, of dramatic passage with an honorable end? But there was no end, and that, it seemed, was what Ali could not bear to see, the blinking exit sign for a wondrous career—through which he could not bring himself to step. He added, "Without me, Joe's nothin'. He should stop usin' me, them fights for his fame. It's all over. Look at me, I'm not right, sick. He should be sick, too, all them punches I lay on his dumb head." He stopped, then said with resignation, "Nothin' lasts. We just flies, ain't we?"

Nearing the end of the century, Muhammad Ali still swam inside of Joe Frazier like a determined bacillus. Despite the advice of a few friends and some of his children, Frazier was still keeping an obsessional hold on Ali, sometimes with a freefall into the void between regret and revenge; at other times his contempt just lay there hissing. Much time had passed since my visit with Ali, and if he had been a sonata of sometimes bewildered withdraw, Frazier was a brass section insistent on sending out a triumphal arch of sound not consonant with his early self. The usually remote Frazier had taken on, ironically, the attitude and coloration of the Ali that had once stuck words on him as if he were a store window dummy.

"Didja bring any money?" were his first words; these were also on the lips of all who worked around him. Did he ask me for money when he had had a half dozen fights and moved over the ring like a confused animal with a trap on its leg? "Well, for old times' sake," he relented. He growled about what he thought to be a lack of exposure, the neglect of the public, how his own greatness was being forgotten and how Ali was being made into a god. "A tin one," he added. "I made him what he is." Including his current state of health? "I made him what he is," Joe said. "Take it any way you want." He threw up his hands and said: "Look at him, can't even talk

and he makin' money hand and fist." Was he, Frazier, secure financially? "I got more money than him," he said.

"Joe is for Joe," said Burt Watson, a former business manager.
"Everyone becomes former around Joe. He's not a bad guy. Getting
past his kids and to him without jingle ain't gonna happen. They look
for a dollar in the fog. He's in the Joe Frazier business. Nobody men-
tions Ali round him. And the only picture of Ali around is Ali on his
ass on the gym wall."

A flattened Ali, caught just at the end of gravity pull, took up
nearly the whole wall of an outer office, and there was more of the
same down in the gym. On a bad ego day, Frazier could not turn few
directions without an instant pick-me-up. Right now, he was getting
a boost of another kind from a jug of rock candy, lemon and brandy;
he was not an attack drinker, but a measured one who saw periodic
belts as an elixir, a protection against bodily invasions. For all those
pictures of a wounded Ali and his own steady assertions of singulari-
ty, Frazier was not a natural or even a self-made egotist. As a fighter,
he had always had a cheerful pride and put high value on proper
behavior; he was a rule-follower and, from the signs plastered on the
gym walls, now a diligent rule-maker of gym etiquette and moral
code. "I'm the boss here," he said, visiting the jug again with a lighter
gulp. "Act right, or you're gone. Act like a real fighter." His standard of
dereliction of conduct was Ali. "He's out there," Joe said, pointing.
"On his tail wonderin' what hit him."

Frazier was fifty-five, and he sat in a dark little room, just off the
main office, a bit frazzled, wearing a black feathered Borsalino hat,
an insistent tie on a purple shirt against a well-worn, pinstripe gray
suit, indicating that he was not getting ready to climb into the ring
down below and demonstrate the virtues and intricacies of the left
hook. He looked like someone who was on his way out the door to
check on his stable of working women, but far from it: he and God

had always been bosom-close, and he always believed that he had been selected by Him to knock the anti-Christ, Ali, down several pegs. Joe saw himself as the special issue of the Almighty; the Muslims were infidels and Ali was their serpent. "A man can't think he's God," Frazier said, "and He put me on earth for one reason, made me a fighter, for when the day come I go and slay a false god." Unlike Ali, Frazier had been a muted religionist; now he was in fervent lockstep with the rage of righteous public witness in sports.

Before 1985, it was rare to hear or see the Deity singled out, or vulgar displays (perhaps a vagrant sign of the cross, warranted if you were risking your brain), let alone attended by pious soliloquies with every fat purse, touchdown, or home run. God has become a good luck charm, a mental amulet, armor against the unforeseen, or foundering talent and the thunderbolt of injury. A divinely ignored soul in India might see it as obscenely self-centered, even amusing if he or she could laugh. God preoccupied Frazier in our chat until the subject of his health came up. "I got sugar diabetes. I got hypertension. I got headaches. Pain just about everywhere. What else you want me to have?" Scattered vials of pills suggested a longer list. It was no secret that a medical specialist friend had made at least four impromptu visits to the gym over the years, and each time personally whisked Frazier off to the hospital for convalescence. "I'll outlive him, count on it," Joe said. By now, *him* needed no further identification.

Frazier, divorced, was more pleased to report that his sexual virility was levels above merely operative. Having had eleven children, all of them grown now, he was (with his son Marvis, his constant shadow) a visible figure on the club circuit—and apparently not a bystander. His financial picture was easier to gauge, if only for the location of his gym, near an ever-expanding university that will need the land. The gym, with his name embossed with a Roman look above the front, was a well-known center in a gunned-out area. His aim was to keep it as a place of work and instruction, not to let it become a pit stop for drugs; he was vigilant for gossip, or any furtive transaction. He lived upstairs in a vast, somber loft, a tidy and favorable place for the chewing of unlimited angst.

French workers have an observation when a coworker shows signs of wear: "The trade is entering his body." With Joe, as with Ali, it was long past entry, it had taken up firm residence. No other sport expresses its cost so starkly as boxing does. Each face and brain is a map of risky travel, revealing the length of the trip and all the bad roads. Frazier had been worn away like an old rock, helped along by a rapidly graying beard. He tried to summon up his old carefree cool, but there was a gauntness around lightless eyes, the effect being of an abstract presence. His vocal cords, commanded by the left frontal lobe of the brain, had been blasted into strands, leaving him with a voice that seemed to struggle for audibility. His words jumped here and there like balls in a lottery machine, its line of emphasis too quickly toppling into dissonance. His motor skills did not seem impaired, though you wondered how he would fare in a rudimentary clinical test of them. No dragging of a leg, either, a large feature in Dr. Harrison Martland's old and classic analysis of the punch-soaked fighter. Physically, he had a few scuffs here and there, but I wondered: How were his eyes?

It was not idle curiosity, for there was much rumor that he was going blind. Most startling, by his own confession, he had said he had fought his whole career, from the Olympics on, blind in his left eye, and it was presumed that the other was fading too. He said that during prefight physicals he had memorized the charts, or used his good eye. His manager, Yank Durham, was the only one who knew, yet it seems hard to imagine his longtime trainer, Eddie Futch, was kept from the secret. How could Futch, an honest man with a subtle antenna for defects and tactics in the game, not know? Was he relieving himself of responsibility, not his usual way, long after the fact, or was he as genuinely baffled as he said? "The claim beats me," he said not long ago. "Hard to believe." The revelation had come in his auto-biography and received no attention whatsover from a media that can spend days reporting and analyzing the dimmest of banana-peel slips.

Yet, if it was true that Frazier had done it all with one eye, what an extraordinary achievement of will and tactical cunning. Close your left eye, and you instantly understand how you would be dangerously at a loss: the left side of the ring suddenly becomes a nether-land, your bearings unbalanced. Working with only half a ring—if that was indeed true—Frazier became the most skillful, devastating inside puncher in boxing history, so effective that he has to be ranked in the lower tier of the top five heavyweights of the century. How did he manage it? It required a true belly for fire, a good chin, a diamond-hard concentration, no panic, and a subtle choreography of feet to keep the opponent from taking him to the dark side where he was open to being destroyed. He could never relax and had to retain his rhythm of attack-manipulation, simultaneous and relentless. Against an Ali, say, he had to keep him flowing to his own right side, away from his bad eye. Only one punch could do this, and it had to be pun-ishing and steady: a left hook, to the body and to the head. "When I looked up to the lights," Frazier said now, "all I ever saw was milky glare. I had to get in on his chest, follow his breath, damn near his heartbeat."

"How is your eye now?" he was asked. "Or eyes?"

"In good shape."

"Show me."

"Put up some fingers," he said. He looked, looked again, then laughed, saying, "Which hand?" When he stopped laughing, he said, "That's four on your left hand . . . one on the right . . . five on the right. See. I got an operation some years ago. See good now."

"Suppose I move across the room?"

"Don't have to do that," he said, quite annoyed. "I can see."

Suspicion still lingered over whether his vision had been totally corrected; he had diabetes. Frazier stood up from his chair, half bent, and bumped into furniture, yelling out for someone to help him find "my pain pills." Otherwise, he walked well enough through the gym. Who knows? Of his claim to a one-eyed career, there is a solid inclination to believe him. Philadelphia fighters and managers knew all the tricks in prefight physicals, and were helped by a supple, if not duplicitous Boxing Commission; out-of-town bodies were no less so. And, too, Philly gyms were notorious rendering plants that left few fighters intact. The wars there, amid shafts of dusty sunlight, were better than most main bouts. "We trim the fat to the heart down here," Yank Durham used to say. "In a serious way."

Like Frazier a showstopper in the gyms, Gypsy Joe Harris was also a star of those exchanges. A stablemate and good friend of Frazier's, Gypsy was a scuffed marble of a welterweight, five five with a shaved head, and close to a title shot. The crowds loved him. No fighter, including Ali, had his speed, agility, and creativity; not a puncher, he was a point-building, skittering electron that released a volume of leather from any angle. Under Durham he, too, had reached the top with only one eye. Trouble was that Gypsy saw life as having no more distance than that from his nose to the end of a pool stick. He carried a knife almost as long as he was, and once asked to describe it he called it "sixty year in jail." Often, Frazier said, it was mighty hard "keepin' Gyp alive." Gypsy was a determined profligate, a gym truant, and not pleased with the close attention that Durham always paid Frazier. He felt he was not getting the respect due a risin' man. When he flirted with better treatment from a millionaire dilettante (while still with Durham), he answered a sudden request for an ophthalmological exam by the Commission. Out of nowhere, the most popular fighter in Philly and his one eye were set down for life.

"I know a secret," Gypsy confided soon after. "Ol' Frazier got a big physical problem. Nobody know, and I ain't sayin' either. He a friend, and I ain't no squealer. But it hurt bad to see how I have to pay."

A couple of years later, 1969, Gypsy recalled the triggering event that caused the bitter rip between Ali and Joe. They were on the way to see the unsuspecting Ali at his home in Cherry Hill, New Jersey, outside of Philly. Frazier was so angry that Gypsy offered to drive, futilely. Joe seemed tired, tight, until he, forever the gospeler, turned toward Gypsy and said, "Trouble with you, Gyp . . . you just never learned to behave. Street ain't givin' you nothin' back." A few years earlier he would never have been so critical of Gypsy. Frazier had once been just a heavy, wide kid whom Gyp would leave lunging for a trace of presence like a hunting dog with a bad nose. Even well into being polished, it still took Frazier three rounds or so to find enough of Gypsy to graze with a glove. Gypsy was vital to the development of Joe, helped him grasp the concept of economical footwork. With Cubist moves that always dazzled the eye, Gypsy taunted Joe into quick punching angles until it became dangerous for anyone to speculate that Frazier could be boxed into confusion. After being banished, Gypsy said: "I weren't his light bag. He act like it sometime. He forget I was a star, too."

So they rode on, and Gypsy said, "Yank sold me out. Just like that, they find my eye. They find nothin' in physicals before."

"You sold yourself out," Frazier said.

"Oh yeah?" Gyp said. "Well don't be worryin' 'bout me. Best you be worryin' 'bout the big man. He be comin' for you down the road. 'Member we go all those rounds. I too fast for you. Big man, he gonna be too fast, too." He added sharply, "And a one-eyed man know a one-eyed man when he see him."

Frazier, caught off balance, slammed the car to a stop and said, "What kinda shit you talkin'? What you signifyin'?"

"I'm just talkin', Joe," Gypsy said. "Why you upset? So, where we goin', Joe?"

Frazier sat behind the wheel in thought for several minutes. "You oughta watch things ya say, Gyp," he said, adding, "We gonna see your big man. See how big he is."

"You gotta be kiddin', right?" Gypsy asked.

"I ain't no joker like you."

Gypsy was wary and excited. Joe could be positively scary in a mood like this. Generally, his pal was a man of small temper and could trade insults with the best in the gym if it was all in the right spirit, but Frazier was not someone who ever tolerated being shown up or embarrassed. Once when Joe was young and shadow boxing, another fighter the same size stood by laughing at his poor coordination. He let him have his fun, then walked over to him, saying, "You finished?" The fighter said, "I'll let you know." Joe grabbed him, lifted him in the air, and sent him bouncing across the floor into a wall. "I think you finished now," Joe said as he stood over the guy, who was clutching a broken arm. Gypsy remembered that encounter as he looked across at Joe from the passenger seat. Gypsy had thought Joe and Ali got along, but it was clear to him that something decidedly nasty was "comin' down." Way too personal. To Gypsy, professionals were impersonal, they moved across nightscapes into big arenas like revenants, gave what they had, left as little blood behind as possible, and picked up the money. But Gypsy was game for any ride, often to areas where coroner vans glided silently through the night.

Yank Durham believed Frazier had an unhealthy respect for Ali. "Don't tell me what the man can't do," Joe was telling Gypsy one day in the gym. "The man does what he want in a ring. He a wonder." Gyp called him Smoke because of the heat of his ring pace, and the name began to stick. Yank heard the talk and grumbled, "You betta get that shit outta your head, Smoke. Ali goes to the bank with that kinda thinkin'. He's just a man." Frazier met Ali the night following the Zora Folley bout in the Garden, his last before he exiled for evading the draft. Durham recalled, "Somebody takes Joe over, 'Champ, this is Joe Frazier,' and I'm sayin' I don't want this happening. I want Ali remaining a face, a name, nobody important now. I'm training a dog, you see, to eat a dog." Ali sized Frazier up and said, "I know who he is. Stay healthy, Joe. I'll be back. We gonna do some business." He then snapped Joe's suspenders, saying, "These won't keep you standin'. You not big enough for me. But we'll make some money anyway." Joe gave him a big smile and said, "Could be." Sensing too much softness in Joe, Durham broke in, saying, "Clay, you ever need some money, we'll always have some sparring work for you." Ali just looked at Yank, then turned away, with his aide saying to him, "Can you believe that country nigger?" Yank pulled Joe aside and said, "You best get some sense in your head, boy. You too impressed by him. You're *somebody*. Got a big future. Get them stars outta your eyes, else he'll pick the gold right outta your pocket."

Unknown to Durham—and not much was—Frazier and Ali remained close during the early days of the exile. Ali was a lonesome king, as all kings soon are without treasure to dispense. It had come down, so the inside word was, that the champ was even short on grocery money, and that certain members of his entourage often turned up with bags of food at his door. To his annoyed wife, Belinda, a proud and resourceful woman, that inside word was merely a line floated to extract sympathy for Ali. Joe gave him a couple of hundred here and there, but denied a report that he personally took $2,000 to Ali so he could pay his hotel bill in New York. "Wasn't much I give him," Frazier told me, quelling rumors Ali over time was into Joe for anywhere between $20,000 and $200,000. Even with the entire

Milky Way filling his eyes when it came to Ali, Frazier was so attentive to money that those sums are ludicrous. But Joe was willing to do almost anything else, and always said: "Not right to take a man's pick and shovel." While he did not approve of Ali's military position, he disagreed with his license being lifted.

Until Ali went on the college lecture circuit he was cut off from making money but also from what he most needed, the energy source of a constant audience. According to Belinda, he feared that he was shrinking, that he would become smaller by the day until there would be nothing left. Frazier tried to allay his dread, "You'll be back. Better than ever." Ali said, "Joe, you the big man now. You gotta keep my name out there. Don't let 'em forget." To that end, Frazier lobbied the press, Commission people, and rallied some old champs like Joe Louis, who was unsympathetic to Ali, largely because of his black nationalism, his loud presentation of self, and his evasion of the military. Infuriated by how agreeable Joe was when it came to Ali, Yank Durham exploded one day, "You better start keeping your mouth shut about him. We don't need *him*. *He* needs us! Don't you understand anything, boy? He using you. Wake up, for chrissake!" Durham would not hear of the philanthropic bargain Joe would strike with Ali. Gypsy told me of a day he once drove to New York with Joe and Ali, how the two worked up plans for one day meeting for the title.

"An even split, okay, Joe?" Ali asked. "Right down the middle. I don't have much. I gotta come back big. I'd do the same for you."

"No trouble there," Joe said.

"Your people, they ain't gonna like it."

"Don't worry. I'll get you well."

"Promise."

"I promise," said Frazier, whose character would never permit him to retreat from his word.

"I'll give you a return," Ali said.

"A return!" Frazier shouted. "What make you think *I* gonna *need* a return?"

"Joe, you a good fighter," Ali said. "But no disrespect, you not big enough for me, not fast enough. I'll tell you what. You beat me, I'll crawl across the ring and kiss your feet."

"You promise," Joe said.

"You got my word."

"Maybe I'm gonna knock you so cold you can't crawl."

They both laughed, and Ali said, "What you gonna do when I whup you?"

"If," Joe said. "There ain't no *when* in a ring. Not with me. Besides, I already give you an even split."

"Yeah," Ali said, "and I thank you. But I'll be puttin' them asses in the seats."

Joe shook his head and said, "You're somethin'. I got the name too. You ain't gonna be much without me. Maybe I be givin' the return. I ain't studyin' on losin' a bit, and damn sure I never crawl across a ring to you."

"Well, I will," Ali said. "That's how sure I am."

"I'll be waitin'," Joe said.

Frazier never forgot that exchange. "Yank was right the whole time," he said now, with regret as he took another small pull on the brandy jug. Nor would he ever forget what took place some time later, in 1969 in Philly, the abrupt severing of what Joe thought to be a bond between them. The pair arranged a meeting, designed to attract press attention and heat up the perception of them as inseparable rivals. Ali was on WHAT-Radio, and Joe and Gypsy had the interview on in the gym. "He somethin', ain't he?" Joe said to Gyp with a laugh. Ali was into his usual government rant, then suddenly shifted targets and began calling Joe clumsy, a fighter without

class, an Uncle Tom. Ali called Frazier a coward, and said if he was-
n't, he should show up at the PAL gym in an hour and they'd settle
the matter. Gypsy recalled: "Joe crush the radio with his foot. He
say, 'He makin' a fool of me in my backyard.'" When Joe reached
the gym, it was packed, the ring posts bent by the surge of people
inside. With Ali screaming, Joe hurriedly stripped off his shirt. A
police sergeant, Vince Furlong, jumped between them, saying:
"None of that here. Take it to the park." Ali said to Joe, "You follow,
or you a coward."

Joe declined as Ali led a big crowd through the black ghetto to
Fairmount Park. But Durham hopped into his car and joined in the
parade behind Ali. Durham got up, raced up to Ali, and jabbed a finger in his face. "I'll fight you when you get a license," Yank said, using
the personal pronoun that always bemused Frazier. "What the hell
you tryin' to do here? You want work, come to our gym, and you can
work with my kids. I'll pay you good. Joe's no chump." By not joining
Ali in the park, Joe felt silly, used, an object of ridicule and diminished
in stature. After Joe and Ali appeared on *The Mike Douglas Show* the
next day, Ali waited for him outside across the street. He then ran
across to Frazier, and threw a punch, a soft right, that caught Joe on
the shoulder. They grappled. Ali sent out another right, missing Joe
and zinging Durham, who held his eye. "You crazy mothafucka,"
Durham shouted. He then motioned to some in the crowd to help
pull Joe away. On the way home, Frazier kept saying over and over to
Gypsy, "I can't believe I trusted him."

And so that same evening they drove over to see Ali at his Cherry
Hill house. Gypsy was saying, "Smoke, this ain't right. Let it pass. He
wanna see you like this. He ain't right in the head. You playin' his
game." Joe said: "It ain't no game to me." He then said, "You tell Yank
about this, and you be no friend of mine. Ever." Two Muslims with
shoulder arms answered the door. One went back to fetch Ali, and he

came to the door with a big smile. He looked down at little Gypsy. According to Gypsy years later, here is what took place.

"Who's the shrimp?" Ali asked.

Gypsy shot back, "Yeah, gimme five inches, and I whup your faggot ass good."

Ali ignored him, saying to Joe, "Come on in. My, my, we have some fun today."

"Right here'll do," Joe said. "And it weren't no fun for me. Showin' me up like that. Right here in my hometown. Callin' me names."

The Muslims drew in closer to Ali. Joe said to them: "Them guns don't mean shit to me."

Ali said: "Just fun, Joe. That's all. Gotta keep my name out there. Don't mean nuthin' by it."

"Coward? Uncle Tom? Only one I've been Tommin' for is *you!* Names like that ain't just fun. Those sorry-ass Muslims leadin' you on me. It gonna stop right here."

"Don't talk about my religion," Ali said. "I can't let ya do that. Go home and cool down."

"Ain't ever gonna be coolin' down now. Fuck your religion. We're talkin' about me. Who *I* am." Joe extended his hand, saying, "This is black. You can't take who I am. You turn on a friend for what? So you impress them Muslim fools, so you be the big man."

Ali said, "We finished talkin'." He turned back into the house.

Frazier snapped, "That's it, get the fuck outta here. Hide behind your shooters. You and me, it's comin'. But I'll die before ya get an even split."

On the way back to the car, Gypsy asked, "You feelin' better?"

"Yeah," Joe said. "For now."

*   *   *

True contempt is seldom visible in sports. While greed, envy, and smallness run through games like congealed blood, they are commonly concealed, if for no other reason than they are disruptive to the supposedly idyllic code of sportsmanship that athletics promotes; such contempt is far too personal. Although true contempt is viewed by and large bad for business, Oakland Raiders owner Al Davis always has been a lone exception as a career-long sustainer of uncomely passions.

Of the various levels of contempt, two are of interest in relation to Ali-Frazier. The contempt that Ali held for Frazier during the final third of his career and in retirement was at the level of "Hobbesian indifference," which William Ian Miller, author of *The Anatomy of Disgust*, points out, is designed to render the target invisible or nonexistent. But Ali was not always Hobbesian. Early on, as Cassius Clay, he had an insolent contempt, a promiscuous spray of disrespect that indicates someone trying to secure rank by mere display; a rather mean fool. When he became champ, he accelerated the contempt that shames and humiliates, especially against those he saw as threats to his superiority and rank among blacks, particularly the much-loved Floyd Patterson and later the implacable challenge of Frazier. Joe's contempt, ceaseless and unsparing, was a different sort from the outset. His was that of the "blood-feuder," and remains so today. Besides responding to the pain and humiliation Ali caused him, he wanted and wants to reduce his rank, to show him that he failed, that he never measured up, that he claimed much more for himself than he was. Ali has sat in Frazier's gut like a broken bottle.

That psychic unrest erupted when Ali lit the Olympic flame in Atlanta, when a sentimentality so often seen in sports poured down on him. Frazier could barely control his rage, saying, "I hope he falls in the flame." In the low church theocracy of sports, this was seen as poor form. Contrary to opinion, the sports press likes to fling incense, be part of the show, create stars, and to that end prints and televises a fraction of what it knows. Heroes fuel circulation and ratings: ride the star, retain access. Unless, of course, his image is corrupted by too many trips to the police blotter; he is caught in a sexual fumble, or he beats his wife. Prime examples are Dennis Rodman and the over-rated Mike Tyson, both of whose talent has been overshadowed by their determination to be behavorial retards. While he did not have the tattoos or the dyed hair that Rodman adopted, Ali was easily in his league when it came to brainless exhibitionism.

By the time Frazier wished for Ali's incineration, it had long been fashionable to beatify Ali. How could Frazier nurse such a grudge for so long, dispense such violent talk and personal malice? *Give it up, Joe, it's embarrassing* went the general view. Joe later was even more inflammatory in his autobiography: "If we were twins in the belly of our mama, I'd reach over and strangle him." To Frazier, a justifiable attitude considering how Ali stomped on his identity, turned him into a point of race scorn that he contends still follows him today; Ali gets a boulevard named after him, Frazier is passed over as an inaugural inductee for the Wall of Fame in Philly.

Didn't Joe once say while recuperating on a bed after Manila, "Lawdy, lawdy he's great"? He replied that he had said no such thing, and if he had he must have been out of his head with dehydration, or saying what he was taught. "Like bein' a good sport," he said. "For the public, that's why I say that. I never felt them words inside." He suddenly wanted to know who I thought were the top five heavyweights in history; I did not have enough insensitivity to tell him that his old trainer, Eddie Futch, had left him off his list. I told him: Ali, Joe Louis, Marciano, Jersey Joe Walcott, and Frazier—with Sonny Liston a very close sixth. "Well," Joe said, "right from the top you got that all wrong." Where would he place Ali? "Not in the top five, for certain. I beat him three times." He waved away the public record, saying, "I don't care about that. I know in my heart! He do, too." Of the latter, it is a lock bet that such an admission by Ali would never be forthcoming—even in a delirium.

Having dismissed Ali as a man and a fighter, indeed tossed him into a pile of subalterns, Frazier did not seem to have any place farther to go with him—yet held on to him as if he was there and would disappear in a second, and in doing so would take him along. "When a man gets in your blood like that," Frazier said, "you can't never let go. No matter. Yesterday is today for me. He never die for me." Ali in mist, Frazier in shadow walled in by heavier shadow. So unmoored from what they were and did, the ghosts of Manila.

PASSAGES

On March 22, 1967, Sugar Ray Robinson drove to Loew's Midtown Motor Inn, across from the old Madison Square Garden. It was 2 A.M., cold with piles of dirty snow on the street, and nothing could have got him out of bed, not even the throaty summons of a woman. Those days were behind him as well as his career, twenty years of casting the longest shadow it was possible to do then in a sport. Because he always needed money to sustain a glamorous social life, he fought frequently against names that still bring a shudder: LaMotta, Turpin, Fullmer, and so on. There were few breathers, even the journeymen were tough then and required serious intent. The middleweight division of this period, postwar on through some of the sixties, was the preeminent in all of boxing history, and with aristocratic bearing and the style of Fred Astaire and Duke Ellington, Sugar was its master. No one admired Robinson more than Clay-Ali, who set out to be just like him.

Except in the ring, Ali would never fit his model. Ray was a prince of the night, lighting down wherever the champagne flowed and girls whispered in his ear, a smooth boulevardier in Saville Row suits with a small entourage in his wake and a manner that lit up London and Paris. He once said after a lengthy stay in the latter: "I left my legs in Paris." Until the second half of his career, Ali never left his legs anywhere. Early on, he saw women as temptation, was uneasy in their presence, to the point that many of the old hustlers in boxing thought he was homosexual. He was generous to family and friends, frugal with his own spending, dressed usually like a timekeeper on a construction job, black shirt and pants and heavy boots. He would far surpass Sugar's entourage; he ended up with one the size of those old unemployment lines.

The two first met in 1960 prior to Clay's trip to the Olympics in Rome. He had been waiting outside of Sugar's Harlem nightclub for hours. When Ray finally stepped out of a flamingo pink Cadillac, such was the maestro's glitter that the young Clay thought of beating it down the street. But he suddenly pounced, picking Sugar up at the curb and ringing his ears with a nonstop petition. He was going to be the heavyweight champion, and he wanted Sugar to manage him. "I can't manage you," he told the teenager. "I'm a fighter." Clay wasn't hearing too well. "I want you to teach me all your tricks," he said. "You the best ever, Mr. Robinson." Sugar kept walking, and said, "Good luck, a . . . a . . . a . . ." Clay blurted: "Cassius. Cassius Marcellus Clay. Got a nice sound, don't it?" Sugar opened the door, saying, "Cassius, right. Good luck in Rome, Cassius." A few minutes later, Sugar turned and saw Clay's face up against the window, looking in wistfully.

Over the next ten years, they saw each other on occasion, mainly because Ali kept seeking him out. Ali grew on Robinson, though Sugar didn't like his loud "line of bullshit," his tendency toward the manic, almost a berserk attitude in a ring. If the ring was art to Sugar, he also knew it to be a very sober matter, and was fond of relating what Jean

Cocteau, his friend and fight enthusiast, once told him in Paris when talking of artists. Cocteau looked upon Ray as an artist and said the real artist was always conscious of what was at stake, if only to himself. "The Muses," he said, "open the door and silently point to the tightrope." The young Clay didn't see any of that. Sugar tried to explain it to him once in so many words. "Where? A tightrope?" he asked. "I don't see any tightrope." Sugar wanted him to develop a sense of craft, an imperturbable ring presence; Ray himself strode into a ring as if he were going to buy the building, hair pomaded, no sweat, all cool Italian marble. As Ali rose in the ranks, Ray became concerned for him, suspected that he wasn't emotionally arranged yet for living or his work. He was childlike, easily led, with an innocence that pulled you to him and also made you fear for him. "That boy's going to get hurt one day," Sugar told his manager George Gainford.

Despite Clay's exterior, Sugar sensed that he was often unhappy. He sent Drew Bundini Brown, from his own entourage, to cheer him up. Bundini would stay on with Ali to the end and was the father of "float like a butterfly, sting like a bee," and almost all the rhyming doggerel that TV loved and made dogs run. Prior to the Liston fight, Clay persuaded Sugar to come to Miami, saying he needed him there to beat Liston, he didn't know how to take Sonny. Robinson found a camp in chaos, too many people, too much noise, a fighter not paying attention; he'd run two blocks, turn, and come back. Ray didn't tell him what to do, said only that for big fights he himself never felt secure without running five miles a day. Thereafter, Clay did his five miles, too, with urgency.

Clay wanted Sugar to quit the ring, to stay with him. He said: "Elijah Muhammad will give you seven hundred thousand, collect a dollar from each member, if you become a Muslim." Ray brushed off the fantasy offer; he didn't trust Muslims. And there were only twenty thousand of them even with tampered roll keeping. "When are you going to wake up?" he asked Clay. "You can't be a country boy all your life. Be your own man." How to beat Liston? With a lot of cape, and then the sword. The matador and the bull, just the way he had done it with Jake LaMotta. "I couldn't match the strength of LaMotta. I had to outsmart him. Wear him down for the kill. He was a tough bull. Like Liston." The two watched a film of the LaMotta fight night after night. Bundini took Ray aside one day and said: "Sugar, you right, he just a country boy. I love him. But he's got a fistful of mean in him the Muslims give him, and he's gonna be a lot of trouble down the road."

Ironic, though: Clay had rushed toward the Muslims like an orphan, while the sect saw no utility in him, no gain, despite Malcolm X's interest. Clay was a Muslim in his own mind, that's all. Elijah Muhammad had forbade Malcolm to talk to Clay, though he had been cultivated by Muslim underlings working on their own long before Malcolm's arrival. The Muslim hierarchy barely knew who Clay was, while the troops in Miami filled his head with dogma and privately laughed at the idea of Clay beating Liston. His name was also a minor point of derision at the Chicago headquarters. The focus there remained on Malcolm's disobedience; he was meddling again and would bring ridicule to Elijah with his "association with a fool fighter." *Muhammad Speaks* did not even send a reporter to cover the Liston fight. Besides, old Elijah hated boxing, fighters were "slaves run by fat men with cigars who stole their money." No black man should perform in any capacity for a white man; had Clay lost he would have been dropped, or drifted away, without a single Muslim hand reaching for him.

When Sugar showed up at Loew's, he was met by a young Clay who was gathering tread, if not much wisdom. He had been married and divorced from Sonji Roi, a petite woman with the slink and cat-like knowing of an Eartha Kitt. Herbert Muhammad, son of Elijah, had introduced them and was amazed when Ali married her almost instantly. Sonji didn't care about the Muslims; they were whacked-out robots to her. She saw Ali as a tender, confused man who didn't know much. She tried to adapt to being a Muslim woman, no short skirts, no smoking, no painted face, yet he wanted her to reek sex when they were alone. Her sexual electricity overwhelmed him as well as the status of his own Muslim face. To Herbert, she was a bad influence. She was planting doubt. She wanted a house and family. Ali said the Muslim Mother Ship was going to bomb all the whites, pick up all the Muslims, no need of a house. Why then, she asked, was Elijah padding around in a mansion in Chicago?

Ali began to see her as a temptress, a betrayer. She had too much to say. The Muslims began to cast her as a mistake for Ali, a slick bar girl, a woman after his money, and circulated false rumors that she had been a hooker. She tried with Ali, but she wasn't about to spend the rest of her life in long dresses and looking up to the sky for the Mother of Planes; it was insane, demeaning. They fought often, once so loud and physical that Sugar Ray raced into their room to inter-vene, and Ali warned him to go away or he was going to cut him up the way Jake LaMotta never did. Herbert, through Ali, forced her out. A member of Ali's entourage years later capsulized his dilemma of spiritual loftiness and lust. "Aren't we all hypocrites?" he said. "Ali wouldn't think twice about that now."

Malcolm X was gone, too, assassinated by the Muslims who feared his worldly new direction and his steady inquisition of Elijah's financial practices and his diddling of young Muslim women. Malcolm saw Ali as a new kind of Muslim, wanted to protect him. They passed each other in Ghana airport, with Malcolm in a white robe and carrying a prophet's staff. Ali turned to Herbert, laughing: "He's so far out he's out completely. Elijah is the most powerful. Nobody listens to Malcolm anymore." It was Elijah, the prophet's teachings, that had turned Malcolm from a drug pusher and a thief into a leader; that's what Ali saw. Malcolm's power belonged to the old man. His murder would jolt

Ali, drive home a point that he had given no thought; the Muslims played for keeps.

In Africa to broaden his world appeal, Ali stayed long enough to insult the looks of Nigerian women and, saying it was just a little place, he beat it to Egypt, the fortress of mighty Islam and home to the women he had remembered from Cecil B. DeMille epics. Gamal Nasser, the leader of Egypt and irritant to U.S. policy, was the kind of messianic strongman Ali found hard to resist. He reacted to power, the real kind that could hurt people or save them. Power was impenetrable, spooky. Nasser was a basilisk of control. They sat in his office, and Ali was mesmerized when a single fly landed on Nasser's prodigious nose and the great man made no unmessianic effort to disturb it until Ali wanted to swat it himself; power was about control. They drifted down the Nile together, Nasser in a shimmering white suit, being fanned, and later Ali in native dress rode a camel to the pyramids. Squinting up to the sun, he said: "No white devil make anything like this, could they?"

With the arrival of the Black Panthers and their street sweepers, the Black Muslims by 1968 had become a revolutionary antique. Worse, the Muslims' businesses, shops, newspapers, bakeries, were failing through systematic self-looting and bad management. Membership began to wane; they had always looked for confused kids, small-time thieves and whores; they were strong in prison, where inmates took a correspondence course from Chicago. There were rigid rules: Never eat pig, dress right, and pull your own weight; never forget the devil white man. They wanted contribution of man-hours and money. If you sold their paper, *Muhammad Speaks*, on the streets and didn't make your quota, or if you were a backslider, they took you back to the temple and worked you over. Women were reduced to chattel. The Muslim goals were self-love and separatism; they wanted the United States to cede them a state.

"Ali is the Muslims," Bundini Brown said, weary of the cadre of

Muslims in black suits and little bow ties acting self-important. Were it not for Ali's name the Muslims would be looked upon as a social club of dozing members. Whether he liked it or not, Elijah had a big cigar in his mouth, was the manager, overseer of a mere fighter, a long way from the day a strange man, W.D. Fard, tugged his arm on a Detroit street, said he was an emissary of Yacub, or God, said he wanted the white man destroyed, wanted Elijah to free the black race. Elijah became a prophet on the spot and, with a dash of science fiction, put up the Mothership, a mile wide, in the sky. Black men were at the controls, and they never smiled. There was no up or down, heaven or hell; that was a Christian concept. Just that plane up there, circling, watching, and waiting for the old man's orders. Elijah was a wisp of a man, his face mottled by age spots, and he favored a hat with half- moons and stars. He was seldom in public view, had no flair for oratory. Did Ali and Elijah ever sit down much and talk?

"He too busy to talk," he said. "He makes plans. He so wise."

"Does he play cards? To pass time, maybe?"

"Prophets don't play anything. Next thing you wanna know what he eats."

"Does he?"

"Just soup and gruel." He paused. "Hey, we're not talkin' 'bout an ordinary man. Do he eat? That's not funny."

Ali was sitting on the bed, eyes downcast, when Robinson entered his Loew's room. Sugar said: "You got a fight tonight. You need sleep." Ali got up and handed him a thousand dollars in cash. "What's this for?" Sugar asked. "I told you I can't be in your corner. I don't have a second's license." Ali said: "Keep it. You're a good friend."

"What's the trouble, champ?" Sugar asked.

"The army. They're gonna want me soon. But I can't go."

"But you have to go. What's this 'can't'?"

"Elijah Muhammad told me," Ali said, "that I can't go."

Ray said: "You won't see a gun. Box some exhibitions. It'll be a snap. If you don't, they'll send you to jail, pick up your license. You want to blow up your career, all you have, for nothing."

"Well," Ali said, "Elijah Muhammad told me."

"Forget the old man," Ray said, annoyed now. "Is Elijah going to go to jail, and all those other Muslims?"

"But I'm afraid, Ray, I'm really afraid."

"Afraid of what? Of the Muslims if you don't do what they told you?"

Sugar pressed for an answer; he never got one. Years later he recalled: "He never answered. The kid was terrified. I left him with tears in his eyes. If you ask me, he wasn't afraid of jail. He was scared of being killed by the Muslims. But I don't know for sure."

Malcolm had told Clay long before: "Nobody leaves the Muslims without trouble." Hardly a comment easily forgotten. Now that Malcolm was pointing at the Muslims as a criminal organization, with extensive ties to the American Nazi Party and the Ku Klux Klan, his every move was being tracked. The Muslims, who owned his house in Queens, evicted him—with a firebomb. Betty Shabazz, Malcolm's wife, went to Clay for help, saying: "You see it. You know. Stop it if you have any feeling at all." Clay shrugged: "I ain't doin' nothin' to him." After Malcolm's killing, if his name came up and a remark was made about what a loss it was to black people, Ali would mumble: "What people? Malcolm was a leader of one. Himself." Sunni Khalid, a print and broadcast journalist and a student of Ali and the Nation of Islam, says: "Ali threw Malcolm away like a pork chop. Even today, those who really know can never forgive him."

But Clay had no import in Muslim decision-making; he was merely a follower, a useful idiot with a name to them. Yet his lack of empathy stung followers of Malcolm. Clay had been far more than just nurtured by Malcolm. He had listened to his every word and wanted desperately to be like him, even to the point of taking on his mannerisms. Clay, like Malcolm, would turn away from the camera while a question was posed, then look directly and challengingly into it while answering; like Malcolm, he would also poke the index finger of his right hand into his cheek while listening. When Malcoln was on the ropes with the Muslims, Clay asked him if he should stay in the movement. Fearing for his own life, Malcolm told him to stay in line—for the moment.

At the time, the police were wary of a black civil war. Only hours after Malcolm was killed, a fire broke out in Clay's second floor apartment at Seventy-first and Cregir on the Chicago South Side. Conveniently, Clay was having dinner with his wife, Sonji, at the Arabian Sands Hotel in Chicago when John Ali, the Muslims' executive secretary, called him with the news. Firemen later called the blaze an accident, but it looked suspicious; the neighboring apartments were hardly damaged. Insiders believed the fire was an attempt by the Muslims to remind Clay to stay in line. Much more worldly and observant than Clay, Sonji suspected that her husband was being watched and tracked closely by the Muslims, and hinted to him that the Muslims had set the fire. "Nobody knew where we were having dinner," she said. "The night of the day Malcolm X was murdered! It was too coincidental." Retaliation by followers of the fallen Malcolm would come later, not against Ali but Elijah. While the bomb squad was summoned to his Chicago mansion, only to spend a long time opening a delivery that contained a ticking grand-father clock, the real thing later exploded in his Harlem mosque. Elijah was cordoned off, and Clay relied on a small group of guards, called the Fruit of Islam (Fruit of the Loon to detractors), who walked about with ears laid back and dead eyes. They would always be at Clay's side. Tex Maule, of *Sports Illustrated*, who could forgive Clay almost anything, showed up at Clay's quarters prior to the

Folley fight, and he was amazed how easily the Muslims pushed him around.

Maule was trying to console Ali about the military draft, saying, "The way they'll treat you, it will be like you're on vacation." Ali was clearly agitated, like a man who was seriously divided about a decision he must make, and time was running out. He asked Tex if he had ever been in jail. "Tex!" one of the Muslims intruded. "Man with that name never been to jail. He *put* people in jail." He was referring to the fact that Maule was from Texas. Another Muslim added: "He say no problem. Why, that white trash out there send your ass to Nam in a second. And they'll lynch you way up in a banana tree." Tex tried to dispute their fantastic analysis of Ali's situation. A Muslim waved him off, saying: "Some bullneck cracker corporal put a blade in him before he even get to Nam." Another quickly added: "You be doin' the stockade shuffle. Jist 'cause you don't wanna wash dishes." Tex urged Ali not to believe "this bullshit." Ali said: "I don't know what to believe." A Muslim walked over to Ali: "Champ, go take a walk." Ali said, "I don't feel like it." The Muslim said: "Listen to me! Jist get out, okay?" When Ali left, the three Muslims moved close to Maule, one of them pointing his finger and saying, "You best stay outta our business. Now haul your white ass outta here. You got nothin' to say here."

Current hagiographers have tied themselves in knots trying to elevate Ali into a heroic, defiant catalyst of the antiwar movement, a beacon of black independence. It's a legacy that evolves from the intellectually loose sixties, from those who were in school then and now write romance history. The sad truth was that Ali was played like a harp by the Muslims, a daft cult with a long record of draft dodging from Elijah (who went to prison) on down. His posture was not about unjust war, it was mainly a stratagem by the Muslims to keep themselves on the revolutionary scoreboard, to flex their power and image. Everyone who knew anything about racial politics then knew the press exposure given them was extravagant. They were into profit and running things like Papa Doc ran Haiti. They were, in fact, anti–civil rights, despised Martin Luther King, and nowhere near as serious as the Panthers, who *were* anarchic, helpful to the poor, and "ready to die on the spot." Malcolm X had wanted Ali to be a man of the world, to be a leader; Ali, mindlessly or fearfully, settled for being attached to a string on an old man's hand in Chicago.

The press coverage of Ali (seldom called by that name) and his troubles was as misguided and excessive as the throwing of flowers in his path today. Being on the same page of empirical right, the press followed the nation and was too eager to finger a symbolic villain to stand next to a growing number of body bags being sent home and the hated anti-war movement on campuses. Why should this clown-black militant stay home to burn down your city and home? World War II and Korea were still fresh emotional wounds for Americans and newspapermen, many of whom served as war correspondents. To Jimmy Cannon, the *New York Journal-American* columnist and favorite of Ernest Hemingway, Clay was an affront to all the young boys he had seen die. A traditionalist, he also saw him as the embodiment of a disintegrating culture. But to say—as some liberal columnists have ventured—that Cannon was a racist who liked only good blacks like Joe Louis is absurd and politically correct to the point of being addled.

It could hardly be said that Milton Gross, of the *New York Post*, was a racist. He was a rigorous liberal on a paper often hit for being a cut above Communist. He detested Ali, mainly for his shameful treatment of Floyd Patterson, and measured Ali's courage against the grunts in Vietnam. What about the usually well-modulated Red Smith, the kindly fly fisherman, who noted the screech of Clay "who makes himself as sorry a spectacle as those unwashed punks who object to the war"? These men were simply conditioned by another time. Their peers were Joe DiMaggio, Willie Mays, Rocky Marciano, and Joe Louis, whose character was in their work—not their rhetoric and politics. They were sharp drama critics, with no interest in statistics and the endless hype that dominate today, but in performance and backstage. They tried to bring performers to life, sometimes without interrogation and with a bit too much sentimentality. They didn't prattle about role models. Hardly saintly themselves, their private sins were ignored. If they had a central complaint against Clay, it was they believed him to be a phony and, sin of all sins, unheroic.

Not all of the perspective on Ali was a mountain slide. Jerry Izenberg, of the *Newark Star-Ledger,* was one of the first to rally to Clay's side, along with *Sports Illustrated.* Missing was Howard Cosell at ABC, who would eventually never lose a chance to characterize himself as a tower of journalistic boldness on the subject of Ali. Early on George Plimpton had gone to see Cosell to enlist his support. Cosell said his life would be snuffed out in a second if he said over the air that Ali should be allowed to fight. "I'd be *shot!*" he said. "Right through that window!" How could Cosell bear the drama of his life? He added: "There's a time and a place for everything, and this is not it." He would ultimately join himself to Ali's hip, use him as a prop to promote himself as a man of intrepid, compassionate wisdom.

Clay was certainly not winning any PR wars across the country. He had been under steady heat from politicians and from those within boxing, beginning with Harry Markson, a staunch liberal and head of Madison Square Garden boxing. He viewed him as a dangerous force, and when Clay showed up for the Patterson-Chuvala fight at the Garden, Markson refused to let him be introduced as Muhammad Ali. Clay walked out. Arthur Daley, of the *New York Times,* urged a boycott of the fighter and his hate group. Congressmen like L. Mendel Rivers (South Carolina) and Frank Clark (Pennsylvania) came down hard on him. Said

Clark: "The heavyweight champion turns my stomach . . . a complete and total disgrace." He wanted to see empty movie houses (the venue then for closed-circuit fights), "and that would be the finest tribute to that boy whose hearse may pass by the open doors of the theater on Main Street, U.S.A."

If we are to believe a Louisville friend who grew up with him, knew him like a brother, Clay was far removed from the depiction by the press and politicians. The prospect of being drafted paralyzed him with fear. The white world was a threatening environment, what more the military. "He finds it safer to be with Negroes," the friend said. "It allays his fears of all those things his father used to tell him the whites do to him. He's scared to death to venture away from it. The idea of going into the army with all those strangers, to put himself into that strange environment, with *white* people at that—man, that really hit him where he lived! He was scared to death. That was the *real* Cassius Clay!"

Clay's lawyers made a final effort in Houston on April 25, 1967. Their contention was that there were no blacks on the Louisville draft board that had called him up. They were after an injunction to prevent any arrest of Clay if he refused induction. Clay took the stand and delivered his standard speech. He said he had given up a pretty wife for his religion, given up a "fortune of business offers," and wrapped it up by saying: "War is against the teachings of the Holy Qur'an. I'm not trying to dodge the draft. We are supposed to take part in no wars unless declared by Allah or The Messenger (Elijah). We don't take part in Christian wars or wars of any unbelievers." Ali was at ease on the stand, and he looked like he might find being a martyr a nice fit to the grand estimation of himself.

The next day Clay reported to the induction center without a traveling bag. He went through the physical, joked with the other twenty-six recruits. According to one, he said: "The Vietcong don't scare me. If they didn't get me, some guy from Loosiana or Texas would. I'd have to watch for them slant eyes and the guys behind me, too." He was given sandwiches for lunch and threw away the one with ham. There were protests of young blacks outside, some shouting Muslim refrains while others tore up their draft cards; nothing like the riot Clay had predicted. Clay refused three times to step forward for induction. He was warned of "felonious action," then he signed a statement. Clay's legal argument had four points; no war except for Elijah; no blacks on the draft board; exemption as a working minister; and as a black he couldn't kill other people of color. Of the last it could be said by his critics: Who killed Malcolm X? Larry, Moe, and Curly?

The legal and illegal pace against Clay shifted into high gear. First, almost simultaneously with the induction procedure, he was stripped of his title by the New York State Athletic Commission, an action by political flunkies that, in the "best interest of boxing," deprived him of the right to work. Forty-nine states followed the New York lead, and Clay was in a limbo that he and the Muslims hadn't calculated. A violation of civil rights? Without question, it was an obscene example of vigilante moral vengeance in cold and blunt opposition to due process. On May 8, he was indicted by a federal grand jury in Houston and pled not guilty. The man who signed off on the indictment was Ramsey Clark, LBJ's attorney general, later the gushing conscience of the left and the rest of the universe.

Clay was in poor financial shape. The Louisville syndicate that had his contract could never contain his spending. He'd buy tickets for hundreds of Muslims and just about let anybody use his hotel tab. A pair of "virginal" Egyptian women at the Patterson fight once worked his bill like they were using play money, buying two-hundred-dollar evening bags and having their hair done every day. At his previous divorce hearing, he was asked where the money had gone; he had been close to jail for missing payments to Sonji. "Seventy percent," he said, "goes to the government. Then, I support my mother and father some. I owe my wife one thousand, thirteen hundred. I got eight hundred in a Chicago bank." He pointed around the room, saying: "I owe him. I owe you. I owe everybody in this room." His final divorce settlement was for $15,000, and $22,000 for her legal fees. Ali sent Sonji a note: "You give up heaven for hell."

Sonji might not have agreed after seeing how her husband handled money. He drifted between being a miser (as Ali, this phase would disappear entirely) and a welfare office. When someone would come by to put the touch on him, he would play a record called "Your Friends." The two would just listen, and the borrower would say, "You tryin' to tell me somethin'." "Oh, no, brother," Clay would say. "It's just a pretty tune. But some truth in those words, don't you think?" He and his father, Cash, fought the Louisville Syndicate fiercely over a $50,000 pension fund. Wisely invested by smart heads —which they were—the pension deductions surely would grow into a minor, maybe handy fortune. "It was always a battle with them," a member of the Syndicate said. "They didn't understand money." Clay mainly liked the feel of cash. He'd carry $40,000 around Louisville in a satchel, and when he went to Chicago, he would put thousands on display. "I've seen him do it," a close friend said. "He likes to feel it, run it through his fingers."

After earning $800,000 for the two Liston fights, his box office draw began to descend coincident with his throwing in with the Black Muslims. He got $300,000 for Floyd Patterson, another fight that caused public disgust, and then he had to beat it up to Canada for $66,332 and a long night with George Chuvalo. The U.S. market was tight, and might get worse. With trouble in the wings—jail or the army—he took on a torrid pace, six title defenses in eleven months, two in England, one in Germany. He saw Europe as a source of treasure, ignoring the more serious problem that he was fast running out of credible opponents. By the Ernie Terrell fight, another ugly affair, Herbert Muhammad, son of Elijah, had become his manager, placed there, as Elijah said, "to protect his money." What did Herbert know about boxing, Angelo Dundee was asked. "He knows they use gloves," he said. Clay's father, Cash, chipped in: "Elijah meant to say protect *our* money."

When he was called up for induction and the Commission's retaliation came, he had earned $2.3 million over his seven-year career, with not a great deal left. He outlined his predicament to Tex Maule, after first asserting that he would work for Elijah as a minister for $150 a week and be happy the rest of his life. It was a comment that instantly incited psalmodic flight. "People ask me," he sang, "how you gonna eat. I say, look out there at that little robin peckin' and eatin'. Look up at all the stars, planets in the heavens. They are not held up there on the end of long, steel poles. Allah holds them up there. If he has this power, will he let his servant starve, let a man doin' his work go hungry?" Wasn't the Lord's caseload a bit heavy, what with all the death in Vietnam, the babies all over the world with big bellies and sunken eyes? Why would the Lord think Ali was so special? Not batting an eye, he said: "Well, Allah always gotta have his favorites."

He then pulled out a little notebook. "My wife," he said, "she cost a hundred twenty-five thousand. Spent forty-five thousand on my mother and father. Gave her a Cadillac and a house. Give my brother twenty-five thousand for a little house. I paid Covington (Hayden, his draft lawyer) sixty-eight thousand, and he say I owe him another two hundred thousand. My home cost sixty-one thousand. My own personal expenses, say thirty thousand, not much. The government took roughly ninety percent in taxes. Not much left," he said. He calculated $463,000. Maule's calculations, assuming the tax bite, showed that Ali was $233,000 in the hole, not counting the $200,000 Covington was claiming. And if he stayed out of jail he was looking at a lot of money for appeals. Ali shook his head at Maule's figures, saying: "I don't know what I'm gonna do."

Ali went to trial on June 19, 1967. Up to the last second, even during the trial, government lawyers believed he would accept a deal with the Army's Special Services. Trouble was that the Muslims insisted he never be in uniform and never be given a rank. "The Muslims," a lawyer said, "seem to want him smack up against the wall. They want him to go down for the cause. I don't know. We don't want this. They want it." *Generous* and *fair* or *sympathetic* are not words that come to mind about prosecutors. They are often ruthless, spiteful, and undiscriminating in pursuit of wins for themselves and departments. But the motor for the Justice Department's chase after Clay came from J. Edgar Hoover, the petty, abusive FBI chief, a specialist in creating wild dogs his whole career, and he saw them and rebellion around every corner. An obsessive-compulsive snoop in all sorts of corners, he loved to crush wayward groups and their symbols. Clay was not a lone, crusading, principled obstruction as is commonly believed, and had he not become a Muslim chances are he would have remained "unfit" for duty, 1-Y, after failing two previous tests that put him near the moronic level.

Throughout the trial the next day, Ali sketched absently at his defense table. The jury soon retired, then returned in twenty minutes with a guilty verdict. Ali wanted his sentence immediately. The lead prosecutor, Morton Susman, asked Judge Ingraham for a reduced sentence, calling the outcome "a tragedy," blaming it on the Muslims, who "could not hide behind religion" but were political up to their bow ties. Ingraham gave him the maximum five years and a $10,000 fine; his passport was turned over. He left the courtroom like a man who had heard the will and got the expected safe-deposit box and the waterfront. No bravado, no spleen or sorrow, no riffs or burlesque repartee. The drawings left on his table said more: first, a plane high up in the sky, a child's depiction of puffy clouds and bright sun, then on the next sheet, rain and fog, and the aimed descent of the plane straight toward the top of a mountain.

Twigs and cold fires are too often all that's left of the trail from the kid to the life. Desperate to see the child in the man, and to reach for connecting psychological tissue, it is easy to land on a pointed head. Usually, what is strikingly apparent is all there is. Fighters, by and large, have been colorful translators of what they did and felt, that is until the intrusion of the mass press conference with its numbing etiquette, prefabricated and surface inquiry. There used to be a direct path to fighters, and lazy days could be spent in productive talk until you left with a bit of confidence as to who they were. Not so with how they were formed or grew up; they became reticent or they didn't know how to answer, perhaps because to some of them their origins were so hideous that they looked upon it as another lifetime. There had been no other time, this was it, the closet full of clothes, the identifying car and a woman or women to match. They were contenders.

For a good period, Joe Frazier seemed as if he had been born at the age of twenty-one. No one knew much about him. In many conversations he was agreeable enough, but there was a strained cheerfulness, and just below a restrained hostility. Or was it? Perhaps it was just a matter of confusion within that was behind his vague remoteness, a distrust of white people, a frustration with his ability to articulate or know how to act confidently, or that he hadn't come to accept himself as a contender. He never looked you in the eyes, never seemed to want to be there. Gypsy Joe was asked about his pal's demeanor and said: "He just a warrior. He afraid to say much." Most likely, all of the above was true about Frazier then; he left the personality of himself up to his manager, Yank Durham, who gladly obliged. He was seldom without Durham by his side, and over the years it become discomfiting and eerie how the manager seemed to think he was the fighter, how he even ended sentences for him, like: "I don't think this fight will go long. You won't see any lumps on my face after this one. I wanna do some dancin' with the girls tonight."

A big man of large gestures, Durham had a deep, magisterial voice and an easy personality. When he and his sidekick Willie Reddish walked into a ring in satin smoking jackets, you half expected someone to give them a brandy and a cigar. Yank, without being overbearing, relished attention. He had never been in the big time before, just a respected presence at the PAL gym in Philly. He had been an amateur boxer, then in the war a Jeep hit him, broke both his legs and put him in a hospital for over a year. He was a welder when he found Joe—and an ace hustler like Joe's father, Rubin. He made corn liquor at his house (just like Rubin), and used Frazier in the early days to deliver it. He promoted card games and all-night craps games. "Gimme a smoky room and lots of suckers," he used to say, "and I'm a happy man." When he cut deals for Joe's fights, he made backroom deals for himself, but he always gave Joe the details of them. Joe loved him like he did Rubin. "As long as I'm alive, no matter what happens," Yank said, "this kid'll never want for a buck."

It wasn't until Ali began to humiliate Frazier about his blackness, tried to turn him into a white pawn, that he started to respond about his youth and bleak times. The last of eleven children, Joe was raised in Laurel Bay, not far from Beaufort, South Carolina, the otherworldly low country that was the oldest and most historical settlement of the slave culture in the nation. The people there were perjoratively called Geechee, but they were actually Gullah and they spoke a language of their own. They had their own way of living, had a silent contempt for whites, and were suspicious of other blacks, who viewed them in turn as backward and dangerous, a people who had not moved beyond slavery. They were in fact a proud, independent people who clung to African ways (to assimilate was to lose their souls) with small adjustments for reality. Once there, you could never forget the people or the land, filled with large trees weeping Spanish moss, thousands of whispering, steaming waterways that easily concealed bootleg stills and smuggling. "I remember the nights," says Burt Watson, who grew up there. "You couldn't see your hand."

So did J. E. McTeer, for decades the High Sheriff of the low country; no power was larger there. He was a diligent man, benign, and ultrasensitive to the culture. He was convincing once when he said that the "Geechee threw a bone on Ali before their first fight." What kind of bone? "The most awful," he said, "a black, catfish bone." If Frazier knew a bone was in play, he said, he didn't have to know much else, such was the enabling power of the belief in it. In order to deal with the Gullah and earn their respect, McTeer became a scholar of their thinking to the point that he became a feared purveyor of "white magic." He wrote a book about the Sea Islands, remarking how the blackness of night was a heavy weight, how the people "rushed inside at dusk, saying nothing aloud inside of what they believed and feared." It had an extra blackness, he wrote, "carried here by their forefathers, sensed rather than seen." Drums beat across the swamps, "root doctors" knelt on their knees in graveyards at night and dug for the juju that would cure illness and bring good times to their patrons or evil to their enemies; the black art of "Root" pervaded. Its master and McTeer's adversary was the legendary Dr. Buzzard, a tall man whose eyes stayed behind green-tinted glasses and who was celebrated as an "ender" of vendetta in a place where memory was long. "I don't think Frazier knew the term Uncle Tom," says Ricki Lights, a poet and medical doctor in Philly who was raised there. "You never heard it. To call a Gullah an Uncle Tom would be asking to die. I mean it."

Slave history of the low country supports that view. Class distinction based on skin color was drawn almost from the beginning of the settlement. Mulattoes, the fair-skinned progeny of white slavers and African women, were the emerging group and favored by owners. They got the better jobs and a big share of the largess (such as it was) that was handed down on the whim of their masters. Purebloods from Africa, seen as nonadaptive, resented sharply the superior airs of the mulattoes, who were too eager to conform to white culture. In various rebellions that were often chronic, the mulattoes were rarely included in conspiratorial plans; the blooded didn't trust them.

While Frazier would later call Ali a "half-breed" in Manila, the phrase was not just a passing comment of frustration; it leaped out from a tribal flash of racial memory. Always able to feel the lancing invective with which Ali assaulted him, Frazier began to see it as an orchestrated campaign to crush any respect he had in the black community. Blacks who understood the mulatto and pureblood equation winced. On display every day in the streets, it was now being played out in a large public way.

The Muslims, it should be pointed out, mirrored the age-old divide of color. Their leader, Elijah Muhammad, was "color struck." He taught his followers that they were descended from "Asiatic blacks," meaning that they were from Arab stock, not from the sub-Saharan Africa. Elijah was a light man, and so were a large part of the Muslim hierarchy; the so-called sub-Saharans in the movement had subordinate roles. When Malcolm X established contacts with newly independent African nations, he was admonished for associating with "these people." Unlike Malcolm, Elijah would avoid travel to sub-Saharan Africa during his pilgrimage to Mecca in 1959. During at least two later visits to Africa, Ali himself would remark that African women would be more attractive if they had a little white blood in them.

The young Frazier and his family were on the rim of the culture, the father Rubin being too much of a pragmatist and survivalist to become lost in the world of the black art. But his mother, Dolly, was never far from it, often telling the kids stories of the always looming Dr. Buzzard. She smoked a corncob pipe and was sensitive to spirits. A swarm of crows meant death, a strange noise in a walk by a graveyard meant that "the people were buried alive." She worked in fields, tomato canneries, and picked crabs by hand on a small assembly line, with endless hours that rarely yielded more than five dollars a day. They lived on a ten-acre farm that Joe and his father tried to work with two mules; the earth didn't give up much except watermelon; no vegetables for the table. Hard sun and flooding rain ran easily through the wood-tin roof of the six-room house that had no phone or plumbing, only an outhouse nearly a hundred yards away.

Rubin was a one-armed man, having lost his left wing over a woman. Her full-time lover was jealous, suspected Rubin, and shredded his arm with a pistol. He was lucky, he could have been hit by what they called a "ten-cent" pistol composed of lye, human urine and honey that disfigured, a prospect not to the liking of a ladies' man such as Rubin. He once told Joe that, in all, he had fathered twenty-six children, an attainment of high order that Joe hoped to duplicate, such was his admiration for his father. When Joe was born, his father named him Billy, after his rugged old Ford that never let him down on the dark back roads he raced through. "He gonna be my left arm," Rubin said of the baby. By day, Rubin was an overseer on the Bellamy farm, at night he cooked up "white lightning" that he sold for seven dollars a gallon. Turned age seven, Joe began helping him with late-night liquor deliveries. "I was never little, or played little," he would say. "I ran with my father."

In the early fifties, Rubin bought a small television, and the high point of Joe's week was watching the weekly fights with his father and uncles. No matter who was fighting, the talk always ended up with the name Joe Louis. His father respected Louis so much that the name blazed in Joe's head. To show his father that he could be Louis, too, he put a bag on a tree limb filled with bricks at the center, rags, and corncobs, and he pounded the bag day after day with an audience of his two mules, Buck and Jenny, until his hands were bloody, the hand-wrapping with his father's ties being little protection. The stern Dolly didn't like it much, and allowed him only an hour with the bag. She tried to curb his father's influence by taking him to church, where his main function was to hold on to his mother's hysterical friend who would be so in rapture that she might shake herself into injury. A dedicated truant in school, Joe was soon working with his father on the Bellamy land, and he lay awake plotting how he could make his way elsewhere, away from a place where doctors treated whites first, where a white store had a parrot that sang: "Niggers teefing, niggers teefing." Teefing meaning stealing.

It was at the Bellamy farm where the kid came to the aid of a smaller black boy who was being beaten by one of the Bellamys out in the field. He told the other workers that "it wasn't right to strap the kid," and the word got back. The man approached Joe in a rage, saying: "Tell you what, nigger, I want you off this place before I take this belt off again." Joe told him to keep the belt for his pants, "'cause you're not usin' no belt on me!" He saw the future clearly, he had to get out, and Dolly, worried, told him: "Son, if you can't get along with white folks, then leave home' cause I don't want you gettin' hurt." Not even "the dog" (the Greyhound bus) stopped in Beaufort. Soon after, the Greyhound started making stops there, and in 1959 he took "the first dog North." He was only 15, with not one asset to recommend a decent continuity of life.

He went to live with brother Tommy in Brooklyn, where for two years he looked for any kind of work, lay around, and then desperate that he couldn't pay his own way he began to steal old cars with a friend and sell them for fifty dollars to a junkyard. Besides, there was his girl, Florence, by now pregnant. He decided to go and live with relatives in Philadelphia. He had blown up to 220 pounds, felt disgusted; what had happened to the kid who had attacked the bag of corncobs? He talked his way into a job at Cross Brothers slaughterhouse. He swept the floor, hosed blood down, threw the waste down a chute. Sometimes, he'd cart huge slabs of beef into the freezer, where he practiced combinations, his mouth streaming vapor. Sylvester Stallone lifted that from him for *Rocky*, and took some more, Joe's later habit of doing roadwork up the famous museum steps, only there wasn't any victorious soundtrack then.

Fed up with the size of his thighs, he went to the PAL gym to lose weight. "The more I got whipped on," he said, "and it was often, the more I wanted it." Duke Dugent, head of the gym, saw a serious kid who could whack if ever taught, and he told Durham about him. "Does he have any balls?" he asked. "More than I've seen," Dugent told him. Under Durham, Joe became a top amateur, but he was robbed of a decision in an Olympic trial against Buster Mathis, a three-hundred-pound ballroom dancer in the ring. Joe was down, wanted to quit. "You a baby, that it," Durham said. "Go on, then, butcher them cows the rest of your life." He was still at Cross, often slicing his fingers with knives; his hands were showing more stitches than a baseball glove. Durham talked him into being a sparring partner for Mathis. Buster was lazy, unmotivated, and the coaches saw it. Stick around, they told Joe. If this guy catches a cold, "you're in." Buster came up with an injured knuckle. Joe went on to win the gold medal at the Tokyo Olympics in 1964.

Frazier was in bad shape economically when he returned. He was now married to Florence and had two children. Local sportswriter Stan Hochman heard of his problem, and soon gifts and money began showing up, one of them a golf bag filled to the top with five- and one-dollar bills from a collection that had been made on the street. How now to make his big move as a pro? Durham went to black business leaders. They turned him down cold, saying that Joe was too small, his arms too short for a heavyweight. "Fuck 'em," Yank said, "we'll do it alone." Back to Cross and more stitches; one day a bull escaped inside and headed right for Joe; it was shot dead. With all the blood, the smell, the long hours, cut off from the gym in a full-time way, he began to feel like one of those steers, shackled and hoisted, just before the rabbi slit its throat. He told Florence: "Man, I gotta get outta there."

It has been said that every generation gets—as with presidents—the heavyweight champion it deserves. It's an interesting observation, and handy transport for character and failures. But is it accurate, or just a claim by boxing religionists to impute to the ring more than its naked animalism should carry? On inspection, there have been some reflective conformations of champions and their times. As far back as 1805, William Cobbett, Tory reformer and journalist, brooded over Britain's spiritual decline driven by what he perceived to be an outbreak of foppish manners, and he predicted that "when champions like Jem Belcher no longer have respect be assured that national cowardice is at no great distance." No such stirring attachments attended the early American ring of outlawry and crudeness, a period of migratory punch-ups on gaslit barges and small islands illuminated by torches supported by the upper and lower classes and largely an expression against the moral intrusion and social airs of the middle class.

John L. Sullivan was the first to shoulder national identity, and he mirrored the Gilded Age in many ways. Loud and obnoxious, predatory by instinct, by every trait a bullhorn in tune with the national mood of expansiveness and acquisition; Teddy Roosevelt tagged him as a national treasure, convinced that American blood ran highest in his veins—not to mention usually enough whiskey to drop an elephant.

After Sullivan, some champions became inseparable from their times. Jack Johnson, with his restless eyes for white women after the turn of the century, his presence and skill in the ring being like a night terror to white supremacists like Jack London, who begged the challenger Jim Jeffries to wipe that smile from that face and "restore our national place." Joe Louis, with an exterior as silent as cathedral stone, a thirties profile of racial memory in repose so he could survive professionally while blacks dangled from trees in the South, and he was regarded as a human replica of the quaint black jockey on the lawn in the North. Until World War II approached, when he was raised to a bright symbol of patriotism and American might against Max Schmeling, Hitler's claim to racial superiority. Rocky Marciano, with his immigrant's desire to please and respect authority, the follower of orders for the sake of the tract home and lawn; but the sharp reminder that whites still could brawl despite his manifestation of corporate sensibility in the so-called embalmed fifties.

For the purists, the dignity of the world title, of "the office," had been devalued by Ali. Dignity might seem here a romantic pastel as a word. How could it be assigned to a sport that produced the I.B.C., had been dragged before more Washington hearings than the Teamsters, and whose history was a film festival from a crime studio like the old Warner Brothers? But before and during many of Ali's years, the man who wore the title belt was viewed as someone who had attained high office, and his residence was in the mythic and tribal part of us. The champ held the chair of "manhood and courage," quaint notions now, but then heavily valued. What man, warmed by a few drinks, didn't think he had those qualities in spades; it's not insignificant that fighters have always been confronted loudly in public, or that John L. Sullivan had to fight his way out of saloons. And the tribalism was palpable, the way a showdown pulsed with generational memory, old tales handed down, and forced millions across a vast and impersonal land mass into a single, compressed attention and expectancy. A champion—and what he did with and to the title—was tracked as closely as the presidents and, indeed, the pictures of Joe Louis and Marciano often hung next to Franklin Roosevelt and JFK in bars and urban living rooms. When JFK called Patterson to the White House, he wanted the unworthy Sonny Liston eliminated and alliance with the constituency of the heavyweight title.

A champion also lived in the eye of hate. After a modest interlude, say a couple of defenses, loathing was soon the dominant emotion. A dethroned champion was much more likeable, defeat was more human, unless he was defending against a foreigner. By losing, he faced what the rabble felt every day, the quixotic nature of life. If he had character, he would come back—just like they would—and he would soar far beyond his original appeal. Of all the champions, only Louis and Marciano would sustain the public's admiration. Both lacked complexity, a taste for assertion or notoriety. Rocky approached his work like a trade unionist, and if you told him it was snowing in Haiti he would agree. How, then, did a champion become virally unpopular? It took some doing; personal morals were not eyed closely by the press; scandal could impede—only to a point. Usually, it took a jolt to the tribal illusion, something that was in direct conflict to the heart of the real-man qualities expected. A good example was the mauling of Jack Dempsey (1919–1926).

Just before he won the title, Dempsey was accused of avoiding the draft in World War I. The public was pacified when he was formally acquitted and took a "war essential" job in a shipyard. The trouble was a photographer showed up for a couple of shots. There he was in his overalls, with his rivet gun—and in patent leather shoes. He was vilified as a "draft dodger" on the front page. The promoter Tex Rickard seized the chance to match him against Georges Carpentier, a handsome

French war hero, who got beaten badly. The public was satisfied only when Gene Tunney beat him. Even so, his rehabilitation took time and was much helped by his opening of a Broadway restaurant where for years he would sit near the big window like a pugilistic artifact, or stand at the door and greet so many tourists and members of the press that he eventually entered the kingdom of the sanctified, patent leather shoes and all.

Romance, idealism, nationalism, it all seems trivial against what was down in the dark boiler works of the ring. "There is so much hate," Patterson said after the Vegas fight with Ali, "so much contempt inside people . . . that they hire prizefighters to do their hating for them." He wasn't talking about catharsis for people who've had too many bad days at work, or resented rising prices. He was talking about the snake of race hatred, race pride, and dominance that had been the engine of boxing since Jack Johnson. When critics were aghast at Ali's racial thrust, they were being either disingenuous or stupid, at the very least inattentive to history. The ring had always been a test tube for race politics and amateur eugenics (go to the belly of a black man, "they don't feel nothin' in the head"; and it was said the black was lazy, unreliable, and would run like a scalded hound in the late rounds).

But it was the champion Jack Johnson who was the bold preface to racial lash. He was an unshuffling, confronting giant, a picaro whose go-to-hell presence and "armfuls of white women" incited white America to fear and a sense of inferiority. Jim Jeffries, just about threatened out of retirement, was selected to remove the "bad nigger." Calling him Master Jeff, Jack whipped Jeffries on July 4, 1910. Afterward, there was social chaos. Blacks took over a town in West Virginia for hours. In Georgia, three blacks were killed in a gun battle. Two more were attacked in Oklahoma by a man with a knife who claimed he was the second cousin of John L. Sullivan. Marines were sent to Norfolk, Virginia, and anger combusted in Arkansas,

Missouri, Ohio, Maryland, and other places. The toll was 19 dead, 249 injured, and nearly 5,000 arrested. Big Jack was then pursued "legally." Accused of everything but incest, he was later arrested under the Mann Act, a "white slaving" law so obscurely written to include any man who motored a woman across a state line (wives excluded) and had sex with her. He was never caught in the act; sex was presumed since he had made countless trips with a woman named Belle Sheiber. An all-white jury convicted, and he drew a year in prison. Johnson jumped to Europe, where he dissipated his body and money. In 1915, he agreed to meet a new white hope, Jess Willard, in Cuba, where he was counted out in the twenty-sixth round—one hand shielding his eyes from the sun, a hint for experts years later that Jack had come up with his own plea bargain and that, rather than true defeat, he had wearily resigned from office.

Imagination had been vital to the ring's popularity; look at the old newsreels and study the eyes by the radio bringing a big fight. A man could go out and hit a ball, catch a pass; he could relate physically to these things. To hit or be hit in the face, to have your masculinity so nakedly tested, that was something else; visualized, yes, but still incomprehensible, a mystery. The great fighter was distant, a man to be invented and shaped by the fan's imagination. The less you knew about him the better; it added immensely to the suspense, their expectations, to a ritual of instant reckoning, made important and deadly by the nonverbal hostility that ran through it; words only diluted that starkness and aloneness of the ritual that most men felt and few wanted to enter.

As a radio fighter, Ali would have been far less inciting. Words were not ready for his act, could never have fixed him in the public mind or accurately brought his talent to life. Seeing him as a radio fighter, though, is time-machine fantasy. Given the racial climate of the radio days, Ali as we know him could never have been—not even as the pre-Muslim Clay. Imagine the young Clay listening to instructions the way Joe Louis did in his early days; his handlers tutored him often with regard to public table manners and inoffensive commentary. But with TV, Ali had the good fortune to have a medium that seemed to be invented for him. He didn't pervade it, he invaded, demanding that you become a participant in his career, a rapt listener to his egoistic mantra. If your mind was still on Louis or Marciano, the old matrix for the hero, get it off there and start moving; this, *he* was the new age. He seemed to know instinctively what it was about, the shameless selling of self, breakfast cereal and audience. "Be pretty, be loud," he'd say, "and keep their black hatin' asses in the livin' room." Going into exile, Clay had defamed "the office" for white Americans; he might be "the new man" as he claimed, but not one with manhood or courage and, worse, with no mind of his own.

In the forties, Louisville, which thrived on blooded horses, bourbon, and tobacco, had the feel of a plantation big house, was seen to have a sensibility about race not like the rest of the South. Space and humanity for all; the reality was just don't get near the corn bread cooling on the porch. The Clays lived on the crowded West Side, and as in all ghetto cultures, distinctions were made about the quality of blackness, sometimes expressed aloud in street verse: *White, you're right/ Light, you can fight/ Brown, stand around/ Black, stand back.* The theme of lightness and blackness is in a lot of black literature. Wallace Thurman's heroine is still in the cradle and being scorned for her blackness by relatives. "Try some lye," they joke, "it may eat it out, 'cause she can't look any worse." Saunders Redding writes of the girl who overcomes her color only to dissolve as a human being. The poet Amiri Baraka sees in color steady conflict, hue against hue. Light is plastic, middle class, cursed by the aching malaise of wanting to be white. The young Clay was light, and as his father said: "He faced tauntin' many times on the street for it."

The Clays were strivers, ambitious and makers of plans—without destination or a ladder. They lived in a one-floor, four-room clapboard house on Grand Avenue. Odessa was a cleaning lady in white mansions, while Cassius Sr. was a sign painter, occasionally doing murals in churches for twenty-five dollars and a chicken dinner. The son watched from a distance in the church darkness, better to see the assorted seraphim gaining shape on the clouds. "His crucifixions," Clay would say later, "like to make me cry." He once asked Odessa: "Mama, is you white lady, or is you colored lady?" and to Cash: "Why Jesus always white?" A rhetorical stone he would skip across many future Muslim rants. "Because," his father said, "we supposed not to know who we are, and the white man *thinks* he knows who he is, so he the only one can tell what Jesus is or isn't. So he *thinks*."

Neither parent saw himself or herself as poor. Clay didn't either until he nearly hit bedrock trying to align himself to a desolate, more suitable reality for his Muslim autobiography. He insisted he was a child of the slums, how he was left to roam the streets in tatters, how he was so hungry. His father had to put cardboard in his secondhand shoes. His clothes came from Goodwill. The house was nearly falling down; the roof leaked, the toilet didn't flush. He and his brother, Rudy, seldom had bus fare for school. I asked his parents one night over drinks in New York about his son's claim of early poverty. Odessa just smiled placidly, shook her head with resignation; his father said, "Sheeeeeit."

Odessa was full of laughter, gracious, with an infectious gentleness that often could be seen in Ali. He got his flair, his paradoxes, his quickness to invent new exteriors and much more of a darker nature from his father. Cash was a shape-shifter, a puzzle on the wind. Grab a piece, and you'd have the neglected artist who saw a small facility as a major talent denied. "I think I'll paint the Mona Lisa," he'd say, "and jazz her up some." He once looked at the tomato cans of Andy Warhol and said: "Ain't them white folks got some scams, my, my." He then seemed visibly depressed over some lost opportunity that only he seemed to understand. "This joker can't hold a candle to me," he said. Grab several other pieces, and you'd have a thwarted dancer, a singer, and a true romantic who was certain he resembled Rudolph Valentino, screen idol of the twenties.

Cash slipped into many shapes. If he was in a Hindu mood, he'd take a rug, stretch it out under the sign he was working, kneel on it, and begin to chant. As a Mexican he'd sport a sombrero and pretend he was taking a siesta. His longest-running part was that of the Sheik (Valentino's character), and he strode around with a tasseled hat and a shawl slung over his shoulder. The quick-change roles seemed to provide an exotic, safe haven from frustrations that sapped his spirit. He was a few shades darker than his son, a fact that he would lament or boast about depending on his mood. "Old Cash," a friend of his said once, "knows a lot 'bout color in a painting, but he sure don't know what color he is." When Clay became known and the press came around the house, he was fond of saying: "I'm Arab. Don't I look like an Arab? Damn sure."

"Looville ain't no prize," the father said. "They just sneakier here about race." He once put his sons in line at the Kentucky State Fair, saying, "You all are first now. Stand right there. Don't let nobody get in front of you." A white lady heard him, and she yelled: "Lookee here, you're still in the South." Cash didn't spare the kids dark tales of rape, the white man's mendacity, how the whites go to church on Sunday and "hang a black man on Monday." The stories struck fear into the boy Clay. Like: the Pope's war against the Ethiopians (Italy in World War II), where "he trapped the Africans. Burned 'em up!" What did the Pope have to do with it? "The Pope! The Pope is the leader of Rome. He's the head of the Holy City, man! Got a lot to do with it." The old man was stuck between hate for the whites and going along; resolution in anything was elusive.

Tension and sudden anger threatened the family at all times. In the presence of his father over the years, Ali was seldom at ease, and not only because he had to stand between his father and the Muslims. He never stopped listening for intonation of behavior that might signal combustion. A family friend explained to Jack Olsen: "There's more apt to be a violent strain in a smart Negro family than in a dumb one. Dumb ones go their way like animals . . . just like dumb white ones. But the smart black could feel the pain of what was happenin' around him, and at the same time there wasn't a thing he can do about it, 'cept make it worse. Sometimes this passed down to the kids. And every once in a while somebody shakes the whole soda bottle, and it explodes." Cash's brother, a top mathematician, committed suicide. Odessa was of Irish descent, and said: "Ain't a thing I can do about it."

Police would sometimes show up at Grand Street. One night they found Odessa in a rage. Nothing had been done to her, but Cassius had a bleeding gash on his thigh; he told the cops he had fallen on a milk bottle. They let the incident slide after telling her that she "could take out a malicious cutting warrant." On another occasion, Rudy flew at the father when he tried to tee off on Odessa, and he had to be sent to live with friends. But Cash was not really a violent man. It was just the gin that sometimes touched him off and heightened the futility caught by the poet Langston Hughes . . . "liable to be confusion . . . when a dream gets kicked around."

Ali liked to recount dreams he had as a young kid, some that left numbing fear, beckoning death, escape, suspense, and the spectacular. In one he was on top of the Empire State Building. "Everybody lookin' at me. Thinkin' I'm gonna kill myself. Firemen and police tryin' to talk me out of it on a loudspeaker. 'Don't jump!' And I say, 'I'm gettin' ready.' So I jump and stop right in the air. Flap my wings like one of those little birds in Disney movies. Everybody's faintin' and screamin' . . . Oooooooh! Then, I just float down and land on my feet. Then, I wake up."

His first contact with boxing came when he nearly knocked Joe Martin over after his bike was stolen. He was crying, his body trembling. Martin was a cop and head of the Louisville Recreation Center, one of those anonymous people who often show up early in great careers, who grapple with raw material and point the way. He also had a periodic TV show called *Tomorrow's Champions* in which he would showcase boxing talent. "No, I can't fight a lick," the kid told Martin. "He was all of eighty-nine pounds," Martin would recall, "and his hands shook as I laced the gloves on him, but when he walked out of that ring he was all smiles." Three months of training, and he was on his first TV card.

Boxing brought a change in Cassius. No longer did he brood around the house, and adolescent games seemed beneath him; he expected people on the streets to know who he was. "I'd never seen a kid so taken by boxing like him," Martin said. His education took a step down. He had no interest, he would say, "because there was no future in schoolin', 'cause I knew too many who had it and were layin' 'round on corners." Martin had him for 106 amateur fights and until age eighteen. He noticed much about him. His mind was a jungle of fears. Of ghosts, violence, blood, "you name it," Martin said. He was emotionally wild before a fight. "He'd build himself up into a regular frenzy," Martin said, "letting that fear out by tormenting his opponent." If he saw blood, he'd go in for a clean end; messiness made him queasy. He couldn't bear air travel. Odessa would fly with him, and she had to stop. He'd say: "Mama, you 'fraid yet?" Odessa recalled. "I couldn't bear to see him so frightened, his eyes so big and red."

A light heavy, the young Clay went to the Rome Olympics in

1960. He worked the athletes' village like a cardinal dispensing to the poor. When he beat the Pole Ziggy Pietrzykowski in the finals, a Russian reporter caught him afterward, found not a revolutionary but a robber-baron capitalist. The Russian wanted to know if he would return to the United States and eat with whites. The young Clay snapped: "Tell your people we got qualified people workin' on them problems, and if I'm not worried why should you? To me, the U.S.A. is the best country in the world. It may be hard gettin' some- thin' to eat sometimes, but I ain't fightin' alligators and livin' in a mud hut exactly." The exchange hit all the wire services, and Clay later said, "Poor old Commie, he went draggin' off with nothin' to write the Russians."

Back in New York, Williams Reynolds, heir to a tobacco fortune, booked him into a suite at the Waldorf, right next door to the Prince of Wales, it turned out. He never heard of him, but he was famous, which was what mattered. He knocked on the door and a butler answered, saying: "We have not requested room service." Reynolds was trying to get the jump on several other groups of gold-leaf sportsmen back in Louisville. The kid, through Martin, had worked on his estate, where he would claim in the future that he had to eat on the porch with the dogs and work like a slave. Martin kept a close eye on him out there, saying: "He raked a few leaves and mostly pulled the spigot on the milk machine." Reynolds lost out on the con- tract to a wealthy group called the Louisville Syndicate. Martin had been trainer in the Reynolds deal. The whole package was check- mated by the father: "I don't like cops," Cash said.

Louisville greeted Clay back with a large celebration, and arriving at his house he found the steps had been painted red, white, and blue by his father. His contract with the Syndicate called for a $10,000 signing bonus, a guarantee of $4,000 for two years, generous training expenses, a house at the location he chose to train, and 50 percent of all earnings. From each purse, 15 percent of his end would go into a pension fund, untouchable until the age of thirty-five. This was new ground for boxing; a young fighter was being treated as more than a side of mutton. A ferret-eyed old manager named Honest Bill Daly observed the changing times and noted: "All Rocky Marciano got from his manager Al Weill was a cup of coffee and a kick in the ass." The kid gave his parents some money and then bought a pink Cadillac just like Sugar Ray's.

The Syndicate said they were in no hurry. Clay needed direction and protection, "would not be sacrificed." They submitted him to the light of Archie Moore, still a fighter, and known as a sharp mind; Alexander the Great meets Socrates. Ali always credited the wrestler Gorgeous George "for my actin' skill" and approach in the ring. No use telling him that George was a preening semi-idiot, a farcical homosexual in his role. For he'd reason, "They watch him, pay attention, don't they, and he pretty like me." But it was Archie who truly shaped him whether he knew it or not. In the future as Ali, he'd often allude to secrets he knew—and never described—about the ring. Archie was never withholding, he brimmed with glorious, verbal monographs of craft.

Moore had a diet passed to him by the Aborigines; really progressive fasting, but that was too commonplace for him. He chewed meat, retained the juices, got rid of the bulk, a "distasteful etiquette but it works." Floating forever between the light-heavy and heavyweight ranks, he lived with constant weight loss. There were also aspects to his ring technique. *Relaxism*, he said, required slipping into impregnable defense until danger passed against heavy punchers. He called it the "turtle shell," and Clay used it (naming it Rope-a-Dope) against George Foreman in Zaire. *Escapology* was backpedaling; *Breathology* was conservation of breath. And *Applied Muscular Tension* was the use of feinting and moving to defuse the other man's tension, a grouping of striking force. His every move was calculated, a patient search for one moment, where he would drop an eight-inch right hand from a ninety-degree angle. "With five hundred pounds of pressure per square inch," he would add. Ever the scientist with examining monocle, Archie.

Archie was a man of many parts. His diction was precise, his manner effortless and worldly. He played piano, was an expert pistol shot, a splendid cook who needed three wardrobe sizes as he chased the money well over twenty-six hard, hard years in something like four-hundred fights. He was the first to look different as a fighter, stepping into the ring in blazing colors or looking like a Moorish king. He was the first to make predictions (usually wrong) and to create rhyme. In London he walked the streets in a top hat, striped pants, and tapping a cane. Clay would later make all the papers and the cover of *S.I.* doing the same. On Fifth Avenue he could often be seen wearing a white dinner jacket and white Bermuda shorts. The Syndicate thought Archie would give the kid some maturity, cultivate discipline and presence.

Clay turned up on the Moore grounds outside San Diego in 1960. Archie joked that the place was more suitable for indigent managers. He'd supply them with cheap cigars, get them out of bed "with a black snake whip," and give them an hour to lie and boast after five miles of roadwork. He'd have a common name for them—bum; that's what they called the "kids they lived off of." It was a hot, desolate camp, suitable for Archie, who thought deprivation and isolation cleansing; the place was called the Salt Mine, and the gym was the Bucket of Blood, all of it on a rocky ridge of hills, up which Clay would have to run daily. "The place was hell," he'd say. He had expected a retreat, perhaps a shaded oasis where he and Archie would sit around eating grapes and contemplating the kid's infinite future. He instead saw an Archie Moore, divested of his plumery, who looked like a tenant farmer. Archie handed him some blue overalls. Sometimes, during a break, they sprawled on the rocks, and the old campaigner would discuss ring craft as if he were probing quasars. They talked about comportment, the need to have character, bowing to no man. They didn't talk about race except when Archie told him about his role in the movie *Huckleberry Finn*, how he resented the word "nigger" in the script and quietly went around the director to get it excised.

He told Clay: "Remember this. People don't *see*. They hear what others tell them to hear, others shape their opinion. It's called public relations." Clay pondered: "You mean I ain't got nothin' to say 'bout it!" Sure, Archie said, "with your character. Listen. Ever see a big-name fighter take a beating and the public goes around talking like they didn't see any beating? You or somebody gets the public on your side. They only see their good idea of you that's been driven into their minds."

"I wanna stand straight and high as a champ," Clay said.

"So does an oak tree," Archie said. "But you have to bend and sway. Oak makes good coffins, too."

Once an ex-fighter, not too old, came by, and Archie slipped him some money and gave him a meal. "He lives out in the desert here," Moore told Clay, "like a prairie gopher. You can see he's not well mentally. The trick, son, is not to end up in any kind of desert, to be smart, *know* the road out."

"Took too many punches, huh?" Clay said. "Well, I don't take punches. That's for sure."

"The ring isn't play," Archie said.

"Don't be worryin' 'bout me."

"Well, with that attitude, I'll tell you where you're going to end up. With people laughing at you in the gym, or people feeling sorry for you. People dropping a buck on you, and if they remember, and you were good enough, maybe a benefit to help you, and then they'll forget. There are no pensions for boxers, no old-age homes."

"That's not me," Clay said. "Do I look dumb?"

"Listen. Look at me. What do you see?"

"You got some years on ya, not much else."

"Do I talk like I got a mouthful of mush? You see a man behind these eyes, a working brain?"

"Come on, Mr. Archie," Clay said. "I don't like starin' at people."

"Just get out like me," Archie said. "That's all I want. You're a good kid."

Friction soon broke out in the camp. All the young trainees had steady chores, and Archie insisted they be carried out; just as vital as good gym habits. Clay began to object to the meniality. It disfigured his idea of his own rank. "I ain't washin' dishes no more," he told Archie. "I ain't no pearl diver." Eventually, Archie called Bill Faversham, head of the Louisville Syndicate, saying: "I have to ask you to bring the boy home. My wife is crazy about him, my kids are crazy about him, and so am I. But he just won't do what I tell him to do. He thinks I'm trying to change him in some way, but all I want is for him to grow." Faversham said that, maybe, he needed a good spanking. "He sure does," Archie said, "but I don't know who's going to give him one, including me."

Archie summed up his view of Clay years later. "Underneath," he said, "he's a fine human being. But his ego and fears are always in battle, and sometimes it leaves him empty inside. He's always going to be that, a lonely and hollow man. He's scared of life, never learned to live it right. He wanted to listen. But his ego wouldn't hear. I'm not so sure the Muslims are using him. It may be the other way around."

Two years later Archie got a spanking from Clay. He must have been flattered even to get the bout, for he had begun his career in 1936, and here he was in 1962 being taken seriously. Well, not that much. Clay advertised what he thought of Archie by hiring a sixty-three year-old sparring partner and another named One-Round Andrews. He put Archie away in the predicted four rounds, and the crowd booed as he stomped around Archie, shouting: "Where's the dishes? Where's the laundry? Gimme the laundry!" After the fight he visited Clay. "I'm tired," he said. "I'm done. Never show up other fighters, son. You may be coming down yourself one day." Clay shrugged him off, laughed; to him, Archie was just a busted-out swami.

Clay soon moved to Miami to be under the eyes of Angelo Dundee at the Fifth Street Gym, a specialist in Cuban fighters with a large influence among the national press. He immediately saw in Clay a heavyweight with a welterweight's speed, as rare as finding a jaguar on the streets of Kansas City. He was a shrewd matchmaker, crucial for a young pro. Overmatch him, put him in against the wrong style, and his will can dissipate. Dundee guided him smartly when he looked desultory. He kept the atmosphere light, never indicating in any way he wanted any part of Clay's stage. Instruction by indirection worked best with Clay; make him think that all was his discovery alone, that a change in technique was something he had on his mind all along.

After the Archie Moore fight Clay got his first close glimpse of Sonny Liston, the champion. Sonny drew up to him as he was rouging parts of his face with a red powder from a disc, and Clay said, "I keep lookin' like an angel 'stead of a punched-up fighter." Sonny was almost avuncular in approach, putting a hand on Clay's shoulder and saying: "Take care, kid. I'm gonna need you. But I'm gonna have to beat you like I'm your daddy." Clay was speechless, which alone impressed a veteran manager who was there. "The kid looked at Sonny," Ketchum said, "like Sonny had a gun to his head. Don't let anybody tell ya that Clay wasn't scared to death of Liston." Sonny was in no hurry; prison does that to a man. Though he insisted otherwise much to the annoyance of the Syndicate, Clay wasn't ready to trade leather or blinks with the inglorious, aspiring sociopath.

Much doubt followed Clay's progress. The public and the old heads in boxing were used to seeing big, coiled men with the skimpy moves like Joe Louis, or windmill brawlers like Marciano and Jack Dempsey. Why did Clay fight with his hands down by his sides? His punch was not good enough to keep a resolute big man at bay. He had an aversion to working in the pit, inside to the belly where fights were set up to be won. And what would happen if he ever got tagged? Classicists viewed his predictions as carnival; incompatible to serious work or intent. Marciano was unmoved by him, Dempsey thought he was laughable, and Louis labeled him fundamentally unsound. The last stung Clay. Louis was in personal decline. His retort was withering to his early goal of being well liked. "I never want to end up like Joe Louis," Clay said. "He broke and everybody feel sorry for him."

There really was no reason to believe that Clay couldn't handle a big punch. Early in 1962, Sonny Banks had burned him with a left hook, dropping him early in a Garden fight, and he got up to knock Banks out in the fourth. Dundee sighed with relief; he had seen what you can never foresee, a positive response to a direct, crumpling hit. Clay returned to the Garden some time later to meet Doug Jones. The newspaper strike at the time did not please him. But he found an outlet before the New York legislature, where a hearing was being held on boxing. One legislator asked if all his seventeen victories (fourteen by knockout), being suspicious of his predictions, were on the level. "They say it take a crook to know a crook," Clay said. He missed his prediction against Jones. Trying to win over the crowd, he entered the ring with tape slashed across his mouth. They howled injustice when he was given the decision.

Despite hectoring the Syndicate for a shot at Liston, who didn't want him anywhere near him, Clay showed up in London for more controversy against Henry Cooper, a chivalrous and proud left hooker. British heavyweights were not respected in the United States, but Cooper was of solid mettle and was cherished, with one big negative—

a butter face. But he was a serious man, not a straight line for Clay's comedy. The Brits weren't too enamored of Clay, though Noël Coward pronounced him a man of "grand style." He had emulated Archie Moore with his dress, and having gone to a hatter to be measured for a bowler, the man told him his head was lopsided. "You mean I'm not perfect!" Clay shouted. "Can't be." One other beauty observation was made during the physical exam when the doctor said: "My God, man, you do have an extraordinary arse!"

The fight found Angelo Dundee in the middle of an incident that is still misapprehended. With blurring combinations, Clay dug a deep cut on Cooper's eye. In the third round, Cooper banged a high-grade left charge off Clay's jaw, dropping him to the count of two as the bell rang. Unaided, Clay moved back to his corner, where Dundee motioned to the ref to examine a split in Clay's glove. The story came down through the press and British public that extra time was bought by the request for a new glove. No new glove was produced, no time was lost, yet many at ringside believed that Dundee had slit the glove with a razor to give Clay's groggy head time to clear. "Never happened," Dundee told the press. It didn't help matters that Clay then carved Cooper into a filet. Accusations of tampering with the outcome spread through the crowd, and that part of the press that disliked Clay later embellished the harmless incident. Clay said afterward he got tagged because he had looked down and was distracted by Richard Burton and Elizabeth Taylor. Having worn a royal red robe into the ring, he was now being hatted with a crown by his brother, Rudy. Dundee stopped the coronation, saying: "Get out of here quick. This crowd's going to kill us."

Clay had been in with some genuine bangers, did not for the most part have the usual dreamy skate through the ranks. His narcissism had deceived; he could take a real shot to the mouth. But the problem that would detonate, be one for many years, was still embryonic, known by only a few. "The Louisville people," Odessa said, "should never have sent him to Miami. They let the Muslims steal my boy." "No," Cash told her, "it was that idiot Rudy who did it. 'Member they call collect from out of town and say, 'This is Rudy X with Cassius X,' and I say I'm not 'ceptin' any calls from X's." Early on Rudy had been at war with the white press, and Cassius had to tell him to "hush, this is my press." Dietary preference was also telltale.

Refusing to fly once more just into his career, Clay was on a train with magazine writer Myron Cope, who was digging into a roast loin of pork. "Poke give me a headache," he said to Cope. "Doctors tell me poke 90 percent cell parasites. Poke ninety percent maggots." Cope gulped and said: "Very enlightening." Clay continued: "You let the poke lay two day, and it gets up and crawls. The hawg is an unclean animal." Cell parasites? Far from his frame of reference. No doctor told him this; it was verbatim from the Black Muslim tract on pork. Who cared about his distaste for pig? What the press and public would come to deplore was one of the linchpins of his future mythology, his repudiation of the Olympic gold medal.

Just back from the Games, barely dropped off by the mayor's police escort to his home and planning to purchase half the earth, the kid was suffering spiritual occlusion. The colonially shackled were shouting to him from all parts of the globe. That's Clay, the budding revolutionist at the time, according to the Muslims. Not the kid who walked around town wearing the medal, who slept with it, already a self-promoter to the bone who went glum if not recognized. The medal was not an object, it was his calling card. Here also was a kid that avoided confrontation on the streets, rock throwing and such, and did not, his father said, even like for a long time "to sleep alone in a dark bedroom." But suddenly he was deep into an incident that threatened his life, an evolving narcissist who could not stand seeing his face marked in the ring.

With the Hell's Angels, of all people. After a racial incident, Clay and a friend, Ronnie, got into it with a pair of them. The action shifted to the highway to dueling bikes, then crashes, knives, guns, whizzing chains, and more Hell's Angels. When the Angels, mind you, fled, and with blood flecking his gold medal, Clay went to the side of the Jefferson County Bridge, tore the medal from his neck, and, with rain whipping his face, threw his prize into the dark Ohio River. Trouble was that the thrown medal is only divulged *after* he became a Muslim, a nice propaganda touch to show that Clay had been turned long before their arrival by the natural evil of the white race. "The medal," his father said, "was lost or stolen. Plain and simple." Bundini Brown said, "Honkies sure bought into that one." It was wonderful material for the press who liked him, and for those who didn't. I asked Ali about the medal during a trip to Korea years later. He shrugged it off, his eyes suggesting that it had become a decayed ornament of his myth, or that he was bored with such trivia. "Who remembers?" he said; so much for a scenario that once seemed to make smoke rise from ears.

Frazier and Yank Durham did not have to go it alone. They were soon directed to Bruce Baldwin, who ran a large dairy. "I don't know," he told them. "I just sell milk." Even so, the civic-minded Baldwin said he'd see what he could do. He eventually came up with a plan to sell stock in Joe to anyone who would buy it. Businessmen as well as average people jumped on, the price being $250 a share, and 8,000 shares were sold. The group was called Cloverlay, and when Frazier left them each share would be worth $14,250. Among the partners was Jack Kelly, brother of Princess Grace. The deal called for a job, a draw of a hundred dollars a week against 50 percent of purses, and a loan on a house. Like Clay, he was now a walking corporation, and one that never had holidays.

Under the whip of Durham there was no respite, seven days a week in the gym soaking his head in brine and with the cannon voice of Durham banging at his every move. *Cocksucker, get that left hand out of your ass and throw it!* Or, *Water, you want water! I got no water! Gimme a big round, then I got water!*

For certain, Joe wasn't ready for bronze. His left hook looped, and his feet did not talk to each other. "You're fuckin' hopeless," Durham shouted. "I'm losing my voice with you. Go home, get some rest, come back and show me why anybody should be backin' you with their money." Slowly, Joe began to gain some definition as a puncher. And he could handle severe punishment. The best workmen in Philly drilled him with shot after shot, and he absorbed them like a heavy bag. Yank never had to tell him to stay in on a guy; the ring was a phone booth to him. "That's it!" Yank would yell. "Stick to him like chewin' gum. But, hey, cocksucker, throw punches. This is your life. You're gonna live or die on his chest. You wanna be a catcher, join a baseball team!" So it went, day after day, in the early days in the gym and through his first tentative fights; ten knockouts, one TKO. "We're gonna step you up," Yank said.

It was a risky step, given that the opponent was Oscar Bonavena, who fancied himself the next Luis Firpo of the Argentine, the Wild Bull of the Pampas. All agreed that Oscar was wild, certainly a bull. Where they split was whether or not he was a fighter, or even human. His punches were an abomination, slung out as if attached to barbells. He didn't move, burdened by an ample belly and ankles as big as softballs; his specialty was, with jaw sticking out, the collision rush. In street clothes, though, he could pass for a frayed Italian tenor. In and out of the ring, he was a bane to owners, an untutored oaf whose only desire was to leave the United States with 14 million pesos and enough left over for five *estancias* just like Firpo. After a fight, Oscar liked to scratch figures on an envelope, rather than talk about the fight he had just made. What was that about? "He's a banker," Charlie Goldman, the little man who had trained Marciano, said. "He doesn't care about sense, just cents."

But Bonavena had unlimited stamina and never quit. He was twenty pounds heavier than Joe, and he used it. This was Joe's first big fight, a Garden affair that was supposed to be an escalator to the marquee. Bonavena dropped him twice in the second round, and shareholders back in Philly were ready to call their brokers. The two early knockdowns prefigured what would be a problem for Joe through his career, extreme vulnerability to punches early on until he could segue into a pulsating rhythm; he needed time, sweat. For a while, it looked as if Oscar were just one big horn flipping, then playing with an object. Joe steadily regained his composure, built up volleys through the fight and dug home the hardest shots, causing Oscar to wince and brake his rushes. Joe survived—that's all you ever did against Oscar—to take a split decision.

"You did fine," Yank told him.

"Is that all?" Joe asked.

"What? You want a bonus."

"I thought I was pretty good."

"You did good to stay off your ass," Yank said.

Durham was tickled by his resilience; now the sculpture had a face, a big puncher with a chin. Joe knocked out Doug Jones, retired him, then went on to the Canadian-Croatian George Chuvalo, with a jutting rock of a jaw, a face with heavy bones and a nose that told you what he had been doing too long. Before a larger Garden crowd, George came away with a face split like a cantaloupe that had been too long in the sun. Joe burrowed in and took George apart piece by piece, and what was left of him was stretched on his dressing room table, his chest heaving while blood flowed from the sponge going over him. The doctor worked on a cut, shaped like a scimitar, below his right eye, just a slit ready to burst; later the cheekbone was found to be fractured and needed surgery. A gash was slashed on his scalp, and another cut was outside his other eye.

"He didn't take all that much punishment," his manager Irv Ungerman, said, looking down on him.

"What the hell you call this?" George mumbled.

"George's gonna be rich," he said. "A trail horse. Every kid on his way up is gonna want a piece of Georgie boy."

"Please don't say that," George said hoarsely. "I'm not a trail horse. Not for anyone."

One of the best people in boxing with too much heart and no dimension, Chuvalo had been stopped for the first time in his career. That night, George sat in a darkened hotel room on Eighth Avenue, the shadows of cars from below riding around the walls. "Felt like I was being hit by four hands," George said. "He looks easy to hit, but he isn't easy. Everything moves, his head, shoulders, his body and legs, and he keeps punching and putting pressure. He fights six minutes every round. He doesn't let you live. Whoever get him from here on will catch hell." Durham had come by the dressing room to see how George was, and returned to Frazier, saying, "What a mess. Go look at him. If you ever stop bringing that smoke, you'll look like that. A catcher. Damn."

Why were catchers like Chuvalo such open, gracious men? The glovemen, the dancers who moved like a clarinet glissando, were strung tight, the megaton punchers moody and secretive like big cats. "Maybe catchers ain't got no sense," Ali joked once. Balling his fist, he said, "You sayin' I ain't gracious." The old trainer, Freddy Brown, Chuvalo's this time out, dwelt upon the subject. His face looked like crushed, old peanut shell. "'Cause catchers," he said, pausing to disclaim being gracious himself, "they get all that hooman meanness punched out of 'em. 'Cause catchers sit in automats over old coffee all alone waitin' for someone to say hello, 'cause the only people understand 'em are cut men and their doctors and drunks who know what it is to get worked over and not know it. The one thing a catcher hates is a mirror. Who needs a catcher . . . they're a lotta work and messy with all that blood."

"I want Clay," Joe said to Yank.

"Clay. What Clay? I don't see a Clay."

"Come on, Yank . . . you know."

"Clay's gone. He don't exist." He paused and said: "Think he's gonna be Chuvalo, do ya? Clay *moves*. And your feet don't. Not the way I want. Fuck Clay. I hope he's out there and gets the clap."

But Yank was certain he had the best heavyweight in the business now. To match his optimism, he made a bold move. He stayed out of the WBA heavyweight elimination tournament, an effort to crown its own champion. He threw his lot in with the powerful Madison Square Garden, which wanted its own king. On March 4, 1968, Frazier won the New York heavyweight title by knocking out an old rival, an elusive and timid Buster Mathis, in the eleventh. Jimmy Ellis, Ali's favorite sparring partner, won the WBA title. He was a natural middleweight, quick and wise, and he had had some wars in that division. But the climb in weight was too much for him, and when it came time to unify the title few thought he could handle Joe, who was now out once more against Bonavena.

Oscar bothered Joe, first because of the first outcome with him, rather ragged, and second because he was certain the Argentine was a racist. Whenever Joe was in the same room with him, Oscar sniffed, acted like he smelled bad air, made a face as if to say, "You niggers all stink." Frazier controlled him this time in defense of his title, taking a decision in fifteen rounds. "Jesus," Joe said. "It was like bumpin' into a refrigerator all night. I was tryin' to bust that sniffin' nose of his, it was like poundin' into concrete." By February 1970, two months later,

Ellis felt like a feather, and Joe floored him in five; he was the heavy-weight champion. Or was he? The press tried to goad him about Ali, his claim to the real title. "Clay ain't got no title," Yank cut in. "You talkin' to the title right here."

Frazier bought a new house for $125,000, had six cars in the garage and a Harley-Davidson bike that infuriated Durham. He had had it for a while, and twice took bad spills on it, injuring his feet and scraping his arms another time. Durham said to him: "Man, look. You got a Chevy, and you wrecked that, then you knocked a Cadillac to pieces. Now it's a motorcycle. You'll get killed. What do I have? Stupid fighters. You as bad as Gypsy. He empties all the distilleries in the state. After the Emile Griffith fight, I go lookin' for him to give him his money breakdown. I found him. He can't see. He looked at the sheet and fell asleep. I got stupid fighters."

"Get me Clay," Joe said.

"You deaf? Clay can't get a license."

"Just this then," Joe said. "No even split on the money when he does. No way."

"What's this now?" Yank asked. "Before, you wanna give him your house."

"I don't care. That's it."

"No, it ain't. You got stockholders. You fight, they count." Yank eyed him closely. "What's goin' on?"

"Nothin'," Joe said. "He's a bad man."

"Maybe somebody'll kill him before he's back," Yank cracked. "Save us the trouble."

"I hope not," Joe said.

Shortly after being stripped of the opportunity to fight, Ali made one of the smartest moves of his career by marrying Belinda Boyd on August

17, 1967. The event immediately decreased his exposure to sexual trouble, curbed desires that would have led him into contact with unsavory women, for since Sonji he had become a determined hunter of sexual favor. Sex was never far from his thoughts. The official Muslim doctrine had an austere view of sexual behavior. Through sex, men lost control of their lives; answer to physical needs frequently, and you were answering to the lower beast of self; discipline was elevation. Adultery brought inquisitional techniques like flogging back at the temples.

Abstinence would "mark me as a great man in history," Ali said in an interview with Alex Haley. He said he had always had two big, pretty women beside him after each fight. The Muslims had saved him from reprobation. Plucking the words right from Elijah's mouth, he said: "The downfall of so many great men is that they haven't been able to control their appetite for women." Of course, Elijah and most of his top lieutenants were energetic seducers of young women for many years preceding this.

"Oh, and you have?" asked Haley.

"We Muslims don't touch a woman unless we're married to her," Ali said curtly.

With a straight face, Haley continued: "Are you saying that you don't have affairs with women?"

"I don't even kiss none," he said, "because you get too close, it's almost impossible to stop. I'm a young man, you know, in the prime of life." There was a mildly plaintive tone to his recitation of sexual trials: women—white and black—forever dogging him, knocking at his door in the early morning; others sending him pictures and phone numbers, begging for a call or secretarial work. "I've even had girls," he said, "come up here wearing scarves on their heads, with no makeup and all that, trying to act like young Muslim sisters. But the only catch was that a Muslim sister wouldn't do that." It was reverse psychology; he invariably melted at the sight of a smart, wriggling figure. Sonji had released the satyr that he would come to be. By 1967, there was little left of his comic and innocent rectitude; he was an indiscriminate sexual marksman.

Even though he didn't drink or keep late hours, a big name like Ali, footloose and adrift from his center, was perfect for victimization, whether through sexual traps or flash violence from being in the wrong place at the wrong time. There were no more Muslim bodyguards. With the prospect of jail and being all alone—a condition he could never bear with any poise—he needed ballast. By agreeing to marry him, Belinda gave him domestic grounding. He was heavy duty for any woman, let alone a seventeen-year-old, herself in the daily turbulence of change, suddenly thrust in with a wild libido and an atomic ego.

But Belinda was not an ordinary young girl. For one thing, it was hard to imagine her ever having yanked the string on a Barbie doll, black or white, and hearing: "What should I wear to the prom tonight?" Where she went to school there were no such dances, and such a doll, hardly permitted, would not have matched her exterior—tall, attractively handsome, and distant, silent eyes that measured and probed. She was the acme of Ali's then perfect woman: a sturdy Muslim sister of lineage, a pureblood in Ali's eyes, one who knew her place, would fetch for him and bear his children steadily with robotic precision; in sum, a woman without temperament or complaint. But Belinda had a tone of demand, a flicker of independence to her voice. Seeing his autograph, she told him to "learn to write and read properly."

Belinda recounted how Ali pressed her hard for premarital sex, even bringing the equal of Vatican authority to the problem. The son of Elijah, his own manager, Herbert Muhammad himself, "said it was okay." He'd have done better introducing the name of someone who ran an escort service. Herbert! Never mind whether or not old Elijah fiddled in the mansion, and Herbert wafted through the streets like an unchained sexual melody, Belinda Boyd would not defy her

Muslim teachings; besides, her parents would turn her into one of whitey's Boston cream pies if they ever found out. Ali would have to take a cold shower. If she had been suspicious of Herbert, an old family friend, she would now not trust him at all.

The couple settled in a small South Chicago house. Belinda was real bunker material. She was not afraid of hardship. She sewed her own clothes, cooked, and each morning Ali drove her to school. Later she would become proficient in karate—regrettably, for Ali—and study photography. Right now, she was learning to type so she could answer his letters. In ankle-length Muslim dress around the house, she was of impenetrable visage, polite and careful to his each stage mark for a Muslim wife when around reporters. "Belinda doesn't talk much," it was pointed out to him. He answered rather proudly: "That's 'cause she ain't got nothin' to say. I do the talkin'." What was his view of women—outside of a four-poster bed? "Our women," he said, "should be honored, but they should understand their inferiority. Man gotta look down on women, and women up to men whether they standin' up or layin' down. I don't take any sass." He called out for his food: "Belinda! What you doin' with that meal?" Soon eating, he called out again.

"Belinda, bring me a diet Coke!"

"Belinda, bring the steak!"

"Belinda, bring the brown sugar!"

Requests granted, he said: "The okra's too runny. The steak's too tough. Bring me the chicken."

"It's cold," she said.

"Bring it anyway."

In company, she never sat at the table, and when he drove her to school, if there was a visitor, he ordered her into the backseat; forget about opening the door for her as she left. By every action, she seemed intent on showing the Muslim husband as disciplinarian, as the center of unrelieved attention. In the sixties, her kind of marital comportment attracted a blizzard of thrown bras. But a Muslim marriage, for a wife, was a delicate transaction: public servitude for private rule. Behind closed doors, he listened, she talked, much more as she got older, and her influence would not go unnoticed by Herbert Muhammad.

Belinda was the easy part of the show, sincere and natural in her role. The trouble was that Ali could never find his character, or kept blurring the lines. What did he want the world to believe during this period of stress and trial, for he always wanted it to believe something. Like when he used to take a limo and chauffeur up to Harlem, stop it suddenly, go into a small joint and order a $1.50 hamburger, and then leave behind the desired effect: *Yeah, brother, you got the machine, you got the steam, but you know where you come from.* Politicians and evangelists have been working this corn forever. Anyway, for now, what he wanted to illustrate were a number of things: his true Muslim marriage; his self-reliance; the wall of Muslim caring and protectiveness around him; his supreme indifference to money and boxing, "a white European sport invented by lowdown animals."

And the press, he figured, would corroborate all of the above. If he held an impromptu press conference, he'd count heads: "Is the AP here? I see. The UPI? Good. Anybody from *Time?* No. *Newsweek?* No again. Guess they can't make any money since I'm gone. Television? Where you from? Local or network?" The fare was standard—jokes, Muslim harangue—but sometimes he seemed to be trying out new material for maybe some college-speaking work. Intermarriage: "You want a kid with kinky hair? No, you don't. And I don't want any green-eyed blond kid, either. That's why I got a wife looks like me, so I have a kid looks like me." Hate: "I ain't got no hate. People that take my title, they the only ones got hate. People been lynchin' us for a hundred years, they got the hate." Hardship: "You see me starvin'? They ain't gonna starve me out. Allah will provide. I give my wife money for us to eat that you all spend just for snacks in a week. We can eat on three dollars a day, she such a good cook."

By 1968 he was ready for the colleges, lined up for him by the Dick Fulton Speakers Bureau. He had worked hard on the little cards that contained his subject matter, gleaned from the Bible, the Qur'an, and Elijah's messages. Belinda helped him with his writing and spelling. The lectures made him feel significant in a different way, that he was tossing nets into the sea for Elijah, that he was an inside player in some large conspiracy for right. "I loved it," he remembered later, "meetin' students, the black power groups, the white hippies, and we'd all have sessions and dinner was then planned in the hall, and we'd go to the Student Union buildin' and I'd give my talk and then they'd ask me questions, all the boys and girls, black and white. Like what should we do, or what do you think is gonna happen, you know—just like I was one of those sleepy-lookin' senators at the Capitol."

The audiences were not all so convivial or supportive. Some middle-class schools greeted him as a rather quaint figure, the Ivies examined him the way they would iridescent flora, while others saw him as the leading act of a touring revue. In the main, though, he was being heard, and he seldom lost the crowds. There were often snickers and loud hecklers, whom he fumbled with at first, then learned to handle with the ease of a nightclub comic. His rap was the usual that had appeared in one form or another over the years, now much smoother and elongated, delivered with the cadence of a ring-wise preacher. At a white college in Buffalo, he looked at the many signs behind his platform, reading: LBJ, HOW MANY KIDS DID YOU KILL TODAY? He wouldn't speak until they were removed. He sniffed the air for the smell of pot.

Seldom has a public figure of such superficial depth been more wrongly perceived—by the right and the left; he was reminiscent of the simple Chauncey Gardener in *Being There* by Jerzy Kosinski; for his every utterance, heavy breathing from the know-nothings to the trendy tasters of faux revolution. In the mangle of cross-purposes of the sixties, Ali looked down a clear sight. He was not about the anti-war movement; that was peripheral, a college-kid issue that he tolerated and used. "You see," he'd say, going into his wallet, "I ain't burned *my* draft card." He was not about the counterculture, and certainly not women's rights; in his view both were avenues of disintegration, if he ever thought about them at all. Ali *was* about Ali—for his right to work and the teachings of Elijah that nourished him.

The "briefcase of truth" that he took on the road was given other resonance. Each group would attach their own values to him, just as Chauncey's talk of topsoil and the life cycle of the rhododendron was inflated into comic wisdom. *Being There* could be seen as a remark on the sixties, the willingness, the desperation to believe *anybody* in the face of intellectually destitute leaders, searching, confused, perhaps evil in blind resolution. Ali could not have picked a better time for campus exposure. The social and political climate finally matched him stride for stride. An old America had abused his rights and isolated him, now a new one was suddenly by his side. It was a sky lit with the celebration of chaos. The atmosphere was caught perfectly by Saul Bellow in his novel *Mr. Sammler's Planet*, when old Sammler, eternal student of the mind and friend of H. G. Wells, was pressed into talking about the British scene of the thirties at Columbia University.

He hardly begins when a voice starts to attack him, shouting: "Orwell was a fink. He was a sick counter-revolutionary." The young man turns to the crowd, shouts again: "Why do you listen to this effete old shit? What has he got to tell you? His balls are dry. He's dead. He can't come." Sammler was struck by the will to offend. Bellow writes: "What a passion to be *real*. But *real* was also brutal. And the acceptance of excrement as a standard? How extraordinary! Youth? Together with the idea of sexual potency. All this confused sex-excrement-militancy, explosiveness, abusiveness, tooth-showing. Barbary ape howling. Or like the spider monkeys in the trees, as Sammler had once read, defecating into their hands, and shrieking, pelting the explorers below." Days later Sammler, having twice spotted a black pickpocket in his act on a bus, is followed into the empty lobby of his apartment house. The black pickpocket hurls him against the wall, grabs him by the neck. He does not intend to kill the old man. He simply pulls out his large penis and makes Sammler look down at it; the thing is shown with a "mystifying certitude"; black power is irrefutable, old America.

Ali drifted back into the news in December when he was picked up for driving without a valid license. He spent seven days in a Miami jail where, according to a fellow inmate eager to sell information, he wrinkled his nose at the food and spent much time looking wistfully out of a window. A taste of jail sobered him—privately. "It's a baaaad place," he said. "You get lousy food. You think of home, you think of people walkin' around free." But Washington insiders precluded any jail time down the road for him, so charged was the public atmosphere; he wasn't just a Muslim anymore; he had become incorporated into the whole fabric of civil and uncivil disobedience. Tex Maule told Ali of a discussion he had had with a key figure in the Justice Department. After Martin Luther King's death and the riots, Tex related to him, "Putting you in jail would be politically stupid, though you'll have to play it through the courts." He looked at Tex with wonder. "Why should I believe they got smart just like that?" he replied. "They been so stupid so long." To Tex, he appeared agitated over being reduced to a minor role when told of the government's disinterest in jail time "when I got more of a followin' than Stokely Carmichael and Huey Newton put together." No, being a bit player with major legal bills, and facing more, was too bizarre even for Ali's mind. "Ohhhhh no," Ali said, "I'm still beeeeg trouble in their minds.

If I wasn't, they'd give me back my passport." The usual fate of saints did not elude him. "I could get killed any minute," he told Maule, almost too agreeably. "All eyes are on me," he said. "Ain't it somethin' to see. I don't miss the ring."

He did miss the money, though his financial condition was hardly that of a robin pecking at the ground. Herbert, his manager, was hardly a financial guardian angel at this time. While Ali said he could be put on railroad tracks with a hobo's stick and Allah would lead him to "gold on the train," Herbert was less than convinced. Once he went to Herbert and said: "I am looking for Allah to do something. I am his servant. Allah, they're punishing your servant!" Herbert had no answer. If he missed the big money, it was because it pinched his style; a contemporary, blossoming prophet needed to be munificent, money dispensed added a glow to the prophet's robes. He was not being trampled over by mendicants, and was hardly suffocated by so-called friends who had long since fled. But he repeatedly stressed the importance of the $500 to $1,000 college talks. Yet it was hard to gauge how marginal he was. He would show up and tell a reporter that he just bought a new silver limousine for $10,000, "I mean cash, baby." Then, he would express shock over a cleaning bill. "Got to be a place cheaper," he'd say, then take the writer to a bakery and ask him for "thirty-five cents for a bean pie."

Ali knew the Muslim directive: he was to give no indication at all that he needed the white man's fame or money or media. For all of his career, Ali thought most reporters were groupies content to be in his presence and fill notebooks with his gibberish, or if he thought they were clever they were no match for his own cleverness. He was suspicious of those who didn't take down his every word. He was not concerned about accuracy; the note-taking process assured him that he was in command. Domination of content, the neutralization of hard questions by swarming nonsense, was what he was after. "Why aren't you taking this down?" he'd often ask. A pencil and a notebook, worst of all, a tape recorder made him think that he was talking to millions.

"People ain't supposed to see I care anymore," he said. He began to throw punches in front of a mirror, started to bob and weave around a glass coffee table, and put an opponent in with him; already he was looking down the road at Joe Frazier. He supplied narration, even the sound of the bell. Belinda came out and kept a steady eye on the coffee table. Before winning, Ali let Frazier knock him down in the second round, and he dropped with a thud to the floor, his legs twitching dramatically. He then disposed of Joe quickly and collapsed back onto the couch, puffing and laughing. "He's always doing that," said Belinda. "He's crazy."

So, it was clear, he was still much more the fighter than the preacher; in a tenuous self, boxing was still irreducible. Later, I spent a few days with him in South Chicago. In these days he seemed unstrung, on an aimless search for the briefest reinforcement, from people in barber shops, bakeries, and the La Tease beauty shop filled with giggling women. One evening he ended up looking at his boxing gear. He said nothing about a past life, simply wrote with his finger *M. Ali* on the patina of dust on a boxing glove. He looked at it absently, then said abruptly: "Let's take a ride. I got some business."

The tawny Cadillac Eldorado moved on the highway toward Milwaukee. He was eerily silent (for him) and kept looking at the speedometer. "Cops'll put me in jail for anything." He continued on, then finally said, "You don't ever ask questions?"

"'Cause I know the answers, maybe."

"You don't know any answers. What color is God?"

"Which is why I don't ask you questions."

"You're poor company," he said.

"All right, how's your money situation?"

"I got more money than you."

"That's not hard."

"What else you got?"

"All right, they're going to the moon soon. That's amazing, don't you think? Kind of makes you feel tiny. How 'bout you?"

"Not me, it don't," he said. "Black men put the moon up sixty trillion years ago, and . . ."

"Oooops, wrong question."

"And there weren't no white trash on the planet then. Whites just learnin' 'bout gravity. The Honorable Elijah Muhammad says that black men drilled a hole in the earth, and with high explosives caused a piece to go into space. That piece is now the moon. Can't nobody live on it. No water. When the white man goes up there, his eyes'll pop out or sumpin." He paused, adding with finality: "God is a black man!"

"Okay."

"You don't care?"

"He could be a porpoise."

"A what?"

"A porpoise. It's said they're smart."

"God's a porpoise!" he said. "You gonna go straight to hell sayin' that."

Did he give $135,000 to the Chicago mosque?

"There you go. Changin' the subject. You always do it. We're talkin' 'bout a *porpoise*, and now you're in my wallet." He thought for a second, then said, "If I did, just like you puttin' money in your church collection."

"I don't go to church."

He said: "You not goin' straight to hell. You already there."

"If eyes will pop on the moon," he was asked, "there must be a lot of eyes you'd like to see pop here."

"I'd fill the moon ship with white women," he said. "They *dangerous*. They lure you in with them smiles. But they'll never get me.

Then, on the second trip, I'd load it up with all those kinky-headed half-black niggers from mixed marriages."

"You're not so dark yourself."

"Never mind that. My soul . . . it's as black as night."

"You got business in Milwaukee?"

He laughed. "Yeah, the only business I got now." He added: "Just think, we get in a bad accident in the city. To die in Milwaukee. When I've been 'round the world. You . . . they not even goin' to know you're dead. It just be Ali this, Ali that. What was he doin' in Milwaukee? Always a mystery, Ali." He paused: "Nobody gonna remember you ever. Not even a church, 'cause you got a porpoise for a God."

We drove along in silence for about five miles, and he said: "Tell the truth, I shook you up. You're thinkin', 'Suppose he wraps me round a phone pole, who gonna care 'bout me?' What you need to do is get you a God like me. Life is a scary place, even when you the king of the world like me."

"The king of the barbershops."

He folded his upper teeth over his lower lip as he always liked to do to show humor, cocked his left fist, while keeping his right hand on the wheel. "You talk like that," he said, "we *are* gonna have an accident."

"No, I was just thinking of your immortality. I figure for ten years. After you're dead."

"Ain't that the truth," he said. "We just flies, aren't we? Just a whooooosh from God, and we're dead all over the place, and soon all them flies that knew you, they all gone, too. Ain't the world strange."

We arrived in Milwaukee, and I kept waiting for him to park and go into a hotel or someplace to conduct his business. Instead, he kept cruising up and down the main street, around and around, the car now like some traveler lost in a fog bank. He'd pull up to a red light, turn full face to the car idling next to him, and wait for recognition, and there never was any, and he'd go around again, lingering at the lights, his eyes silent and almost intense as if he were searching for witnesses to his existence, then after a while his silence turning into rapid speech and sound as he reproduced the thwack of gloves tracking toward his face; the feel of first sweat snaking down his back; the comradeship of the gym; the feel of a punch shivering up his arm. For a moment, it was as if he wanted to get out and stand in the middle of the traffic, so confounded was he that not one pair of eyes had met his and said, "Yes, you can't fool me, I know who you are." A cold, ineffable sadness billowed the curtains of the mind as he finally headed back toward the highway and Chicago, and there was no need to point out what he had done because he was now saying that he had made the trip several times in the past, going nowhere, around and around, and if there was a larger meaning he kept it concealed in what seemed a migratory soul—as the midnight car lights streaked across a quiet face, and he said only one sentence the entire trip back: "I know I'll never fight again."

It was now almost two years into his exile. He was handling it with grace. The crucial point was to stay out of trouble; being picked up in Miami with an invalid license was more a reflection of FBI–local police targeting, an effort to make something happen, and they must have been badly disappointed when they didn't find a gun or drugs that could be used to discredit him. It was rumored that he had once carried a gun for a few hours, then threw it in a river. If so, that would follow; real violence had always spooked him, and the sight of a gun in his hand or pocket would have rattled his consciousness to unbearable distraction; likewise with drugs, for even an aspirin was foreign to him. So, with the help of Belinda, he was doing more than holding his own, he was surviving with dignity. And the college lectures were keeping him afloat financially, though the money hardly supported the new limos that he said he had just purchased. Nor did the college money give him any relief from his legal bills. There was no aid from the Muslims. In Elijah's mind—not Herbert's, the son-manager—Ali's life as a fighter was history, and good riddance. He did not have to worry about his food or domicile, the Muslims would provide. Elijah was going to make good Ali's wish to be a $150-a-week minister. Ali would subsist for life at the Muslim table. "We'll take care of you," Elijah said, offering a fork at the Muslim table.

As the months wore on, it became more difficult for Ali to disguise a growing anxiety. When someone like Ali could make one comment on a 70-mile trip back from Milwaukee, it was clear that a terrible frustration, if not depression, was beginning to overwhelm him. By now, his future as a fighter, his right to the title, began to dominate his conversations with Belinda during long drives to the colleges. "We were sure," she said, "that he'd never fight again. It got to him in a bad way." Early in 1969, he finally gave mild release to his frustration on a national TV talk show. He had appeared on these shows often before, full of japery and vows of never wanting to fight again. Now, asked once more if he would ever return to the ring, he answered: "Why not? If they come up with enough money."

The comment just about blew in the windows of the House of Elijah. To Elijah, it was more than doctrinal affront, it was a repudiation of *his* humble fork, it was an eager acceptance to the white man's banquet. He summoned Ali to the mansion and, with Ali looking like a grave prelate, he defrocked him of whatever he was supposed to be. Ali was stripped of his Muslim name, suspended for a year, and generally denounced as a helpless fool, slithering on the floor in front of the feet of white power and money.

In the Muslim newspaper *Muhammad Speaks,* Elijah elaborated in a statement: "We tell the world we're not with Muhammad Ali," he began, then went on to say that Ali could not "speak to, visit with, or be seen with any Muslim, or take part in any Muslim religious activity." He described his actions as those of a fool, of someone who did not want his survival to come from Allah, but from his enemy, the white man. "Mr. Muhammad Ali," he said, "has sporting blood. Mr. Muhammad Ali wants a place in this sport world. He loves it. We will call him Cassius Clay."

The inconsistency of Elijah's edict shouted for illumination. He had allowed Ali to fight as a minister. He had even let his son manage him. Muslim laws, that is Elijah's, were in pieces already. Now, by his condemnation, he was fortifying the government's case that Ali was not sincere in his beliefs. One of Ali's lawyers was as befogged as everyone else: "It doesn't make sense. No use in trying to figure it out, because we are not dealing with reasonable people." Nor did it make much sense to Muslims close to Ali, who had done everything asked of him.

His conviction appeal to the Fifth Circuit Court was at this point also pending, and Elijah's casting Ali as an unworthy Muslim was bad timing. It probably had no impact on the denial of the appeal, but it compromised him badly to his detractors and doubters; there, you see, even Elijah was branding him as a phony. The appeal denial did not shake Ali; the old man's excommunication did. He was contrite, puzzled, and now vowed to silence, for "talking too much has got me into this trouble."

He hadn't talked too much. After all the frustration, Ali had only started to share Herbert's optimism, suddenly fired by what he thought would happen legally. If Elijah was harsh and erratic with Ali, he didn't glance at the culpability of Herbert, who should have been bounced, too. Prior to the appeal, Herbert seemed certain they would get a *nolle prosequi* (a refusal of the government to prosecute further), and three days before Elijah's purging of Ali he was trying to arrange a fight. With that view on his mind, Ali took seriously to roadwork in the morning, and he understandably felt that his return was imminent, hence his response on TV. Herbert would ultimately misread the government and be caught off-guard by his father's new slant on Muslim veracity. Ali said he was now going "to pray hard and study hard, no runnin' 'round on television." He was asked by a friend soon after, if he was still running in the morning. "Sure enough," he said.

Physically, he was trim, a man who looked like he was ready to fight with four to five weeks' notice. Inwardly, he felt more bewildered and alone than ever. He was a laughingstock to his political enemies, a heretic to his own Muslims, many of whom ducked him in the shops he liked to frequent. Even Herbert publicly renounced any association with Ali. To his critics, a main revenue source for the Muslims (when he was active) had been used and dropped on the first pretense, more shabbily than by any traditional manager.

Herbert was going to make sure that his father would never hear the words *debt* and *money* emanate from Ali again. In the meantime, he was allowed to forage for paydays. The college lectures were fewer in number, his novelty either having faded or the kids having become wise to his narrow platform. When the boxing film archivist Jimmy Jacobs approached him about appearing in a documentary, Ali nearly kissed his hand. There were five days of shooting, and at the end of each Ali was given a thousand dollars in cash. By carrier pigeon, perhaps, Herbert notified Ali that he was going to relocate him in Philadelphia, in the shadow of the most violent Muslim mosque in the country and under the watchful eye of a diligent "minder" named Jeremiah Shabazz.

As bleak as the picture was, especially with Richard Nixon now president and exercising his own brand of dementia on Vietnam, the bandwagon was definitely heading Ali's way. The national consensus for the war was fragmenting rapidly, with mainstream families whose sons were exposed to the draft, who were only thirteen when it had begun in earnest, now leaning heavily on their politicians. The atmosphere was fast becoming perfect. The government wouldn't risk a loss of face by giving him his passport back, but it couldn't interfere with commerce. So thought Harold Conrad, to whom the opposition out there was now just "a few big-mouth congressmen." Conrad was the reigning authority on the campaign to reinstate Ali. "I've been to more states than rain," he said. "Reagan stopped me in California. I was close in Montana. They wanted a hundred grand or so for pocket money. I think we're getting close again; the hysteria is over."

What Conrad needed was the perfect juxtaposition of motive and power. "Politicians did in Ali," Conrad said, "and they'll let him back." And well into 1970, he found a triad of influence that disputed reason and proved how anemic imagination is when it comes to politics. He had a black state senator, a Jewish mayor in, of all places, Atlanta, an Old South town in a state run by a governor who told his troopers during Martin Luther King's funeral that if marchers got out of hand at his capitol they were to "shoot 'em down and stack 'em up." On the narrow plus side, it was true that Atlanta was heavily black and the base camp of civil rights leaders. It was also evident that Atlanta had grown bored with its *Gone with the Wind* reference in the national mind and eager to replace magnolia and rustling crinoline with the high-rise office buildings, job markets and culture that identified the classic cities of the world. Where was the common ground for such a spectacular event as Ali's return? While state senator Leroy Johnson and Mayor Sam Massell of Atlanta supported the fight, Governor Lester Maddox opposed it.

Though he had a lot of company at the time, Maddox would prove to be the last practitioner of what Robert Sherrill called the "gothic politics of the South." He was from the lineage of Earl Long, Herman Talmadge, Leander Perez, Orville Faubus, and George Wallace, his Alabama peer, who seemed to wonder why critics wasted column inches on Lester when he could do away with him in one line: "Y'know, Lester ain't got much character." Wallace always treated him as if he were Boo Radley in *To Kill a Mockingbird*, the harmless simpleton, his

political actions dictated by moon phases. Civil rights leader Hosea
Williams didn't think he was harmless, calling him a "living crime, an
offense to God Almighty, a cancer that must be rooted out." In another
life, he ran a chicken shack called Pickrick and chased blacks away while
waving an ax handle and a pistol. He didn't improve as governor. He
had a cure for hippie anarchists: "Make 'em drink a Molotov cocktail
and give 'em a cigarette real quick." He wailed against any government
intervention in poverty; such programs kept "whorin' nigra wenches in
food while they turned out more bastards" to help the "Commonists."
He said that he would dearly love to conduct an "African hunt" in
Atlanta. If you believed that Lester Maddox would step aside for Ali,
then you had to accept Elijah Muhammad, mother ships and all; in a
way, they weren't dissimilar in the size of their furies.

Maddox also had a big thing in common with Ali's credo, his race
fundamentalism. Desegregation, "race-mixin'," was "ungodly." Citing
Deuteronomy 22:10 he would bellow, "Thou shalt not plow with an ox
and an ass together." Ali often used wildlife to make Elijah's point of race
isolation. But they parted company when it came to geography, allowing
blacks their own nation. Such an idea could only have come from "a rotten Suvit Commonist, 'cause the races must learn to live together." No, it
was not likely that Maddox would do a Lazarus for Ali. How would he
ever again be able to share a chicken wing with his Klansmen and red-
necks? Except: Lester Maddox, near the end of his term, was now in a
sort of political life review. There was the matter of a second term, and he
was casting his "baby duck" eyes toward the presidency, one of many
textbook self-delusions that Wallace thought made him psychiatrically
committable. Lester had taken office in 1966 by a legal technicality that
left the Georgia legislature, with a heavy Democratic majority, with the
task of naming their governor; Lester was put in through the machinery
of the courts. He was an hallucination to blacks, a fool and outcast to the
monied Georgia aristocracy. Now, suddenly, Lester was dead-game on

being viewed as a sensible bigot. Lacking a State Athletic Commission—the principal tool used nationally for denying Ali a license—through which he could kill the fight, he counted on Washington, where Ali by now had the attention of only a few demagogues. The most-sung name in racial politics was cornered, between having no constituency to back him up and his newfound pragmatism, and all Lester Maddox would ever do was proclaim a day of mourning in Georgia when Ali signed to fight Jerry Quarry in Atlanta.

Quietly, Ali said, "My, my, right under the nose of Lester Maddox himself. Ain't the world strange. The Lord must have a lot of fun, don't he?" He was belly-down on a table in a little dressing room in the back of the Fifth Street Gym in Miami Beach. A gospel song floated thinly from a radio, "Yes, Jesus loves me . . . I know he does." The bony fingers of Luis Sarria, his ancient, black masseur, worked through his muscles. These were the early days of his return, and it was all off-center to him, and he looked out from the table, eyes dead, as if he were wandering about in some labyrinthine daydream that maybe could help make sense of it all. This was the gym where he had begun ten years before, and now he was trying to make it a launching site again for a trip from the claustrophobic recent years into a ring hyperspace. "Who knows what I got left?" he brooded. "That ain't just talk, either. For a fighter, I'm goin' way out there now." Bundini entered and referred to him as the "Blessing of the Planet." Ali waved him away with a curt hand. He was in no mood for the arabesque curve of Bundini's phraseology. He sat up on the end of the table and began to prepare for a workout.

The dressing room door soon opened, and out came Ali, with Angelo Dundee smiling and Bundini yelling: "Look out, give him room. Here he come now, the king of allll he see!" Ali swatted him on the head with a taped hand, then seemed to squint as his eyes met the sun-swept, white-washed walls that always made the gym look like a Sicilian hill dwelling.

His first stride was toward a full-length mirror, where for a long moment he studied his visual progress and what centimeters of excess fat he would cleave off today. As he began to move, he got a big hand. Movements for a fighter are as important as the scales are to a pianist: jab, jab, dance, quick shuffle, several trunk twists, then coming out of the twists, the jabs exploded again, and then three rights almost as imperceptible as the flutter of a dragon wing. Inside the ring now, he worked a number of rounds with two sparring partners, steadily grouping his concentration, patiently searching for the spaces and geometry that were central to his composition, and then he'd spin toward the ropes like a billiard ball, let himself be whomped to the body, then fire off with a flurry that moved the other man backward and was notable for its ferocious suddenness. "Like lightning," Dundee said. "Big man . . . he moves like silk, hits like a ton."

He was now in temporary residence at a small retreat on the ocean, a frayed place for elderly Jewish people on fixed incomes. The lobby smelled of immigrant cuisine to Ali, "recipes they must've brought over on the boat." Outside, on the porch, the old people rocked back and forth, talking in Yiddish. Often, Ali would join them, get in rhythm to their rocking, and sit mutely looking out over the ocean. It was a surreal frieze, broken only when he would joke with the old women, saying, "You all come down here from New York to get away from us people. Now, here I am right next to you. Ain't you scared? I know you're scared."

The women just laughed and kept rocking. "I'm crazy with loneliness," he said. He lived in a small apartment upstairs. Belinda was not on the scene. Bundini, sleeping on a sofa, woke him each morning for his roadwork. "But I got to get myself ready," he added, "and I can't have any distractions, for this is goin' to be the biggest night in ring history, every eye in the world's gonna be on me to see if the government beat me." He looked at a picture of himself taped to a long mirror, one taken around the second Liston fight. He measured his sides with his hands, pinched the extra flesh on his belly, checked his jowls. "See how narrow and trim I was," he said. "My weight's not much different, but everything else is broader, fuller, my face, my arms, my legs." In the gym, and now alone here in this Gregorian chant of a room, he seemed retracted, with no appetite at all for the imbecile proclamation, content to let his body, and what he could make it do, speak firmly of what he himself dared not sing prematurely.

Muhammad Ali returned to the ring for the first time in over three years at a former opera house in Atlanta against Jerry Quarry, a pale Irishman from California, transplanted from East Texas. It was the place to be, and every con man, pimp, ragged hippie, and boxing fan in the world seemed to be there, including press from around the world, just an ocean of bodies in flamboyant thread on Peachtree Street and in the lobby of a hotel, tricked up architecturally into a vision by Arthur Clarke of a new world. Revolution was snoozing, its props of berets, field jackets, and the fixed scowl were nowhere to be seen. Capitalism reigned, with big rolls of green flashing, with mink jumpsuits and even a long convertible with an alligator-skin roof. "Where did they all come from?" a grizzled old bellhop asked. "I thought the circus was the greatest show on earth."

Ali was staying at LeRoy Johnson's house, watching old fight films projected on a torn sheet. He was quiet about Quarry, didn't try to heap race on a presence that shrunk by the day and nearly faded to black on the screen by fight time. Quarry had been a top contender for a long time until Frazier a year before had trimmed him like a bony shad in a vicious seven rounds. He might have been a champ had he not been so star-crossed as to have been in the same era as Ali, Frazier, and George Foreman. His problem was that he could never properly assemble himself, never knew precisely what to be: boxer, brawler, or counterpuncher. His instinct was to brawl, but his true skill was as a counterpuncher; he was quick and stinging when he was thinking right. He came from a tribal, Steinbeckian family, Okies who moved west, the father of which was meddlesome and never satisfied with Jerry.

Enrico Caruso, the great tenor who once worked in this same building, surely never heard such a roar as that which greeted Ali as he entered the ring. Practically before the crowd sat down it was on its feet. Ali dazzled, and it was clear that he was beyond any optimistic reach that Quarry had entertained. Ali cut him in the third, the fight was stopped, making it inconclusive whether it had been the true reemergence of the most lurid comet in sports; for now, the sputtering tail of it was enough. As for Quarry, after so many self-deceptions in so many fights, the essayist William Hazlitt had him pegged: "He has lost nothing by the late fight but his presumption."

For Ali, it was on to Oscar Bonavena in December at the Garden; at this rate Oscar might get to buy all of Argentina. Ali had his hands full with Oscar; he seemed weary, punched out as Bonavena kept dropping on him like a falling safe; Ali mocked his style. Bundini Brown yelled from the corner: "Stop it! Stop that! Box like Sugar Ray. Get vicious!" Ali came back to the corner and said to Brown: "Here, take my gloves. I don't know what to do with this clumsy fool."

Frazier was sitting next to Durham, his nails up to his mouth, his eyes fixed for calamity. "If he keeps foolin' with that bowlin' ball," he said to Durham, "we could lose millions." As the fight wore on, Durham said, "Joe damn near jumped in the ring himself." By the fifteenth, with both fighters exhausted, Ali ripped a left home. Oscar went down.

"Now he's mine," Joe said, sighing.

"Go up and shake his hand," Yank teased.

"I got nothin' to say to that clown," Joe replied.

THRILLA

Miles above the Pacific, on the last leg of a twenty-one-hour trip that began in Allentown, Pennsylvania, and a few hours into the ten-hour slog from Honolulu to Manila, was no place for a phobic flyer. Every grumble and wheeze of the plane became a fatal signal, every nerve was a gymnast whirring through a high triple flip with uncertain outcome. Not wanting to think of the vastness below, dark water with limitless species of hungry sharks, I riffed with a vague recall of island specks where a jet in trouble could land. Micronesia? The Marshalls? Tonga? What was the mathematical probability of surviving a splash? Bundini wasn't calculating a few rows ahead; he was deep into a Chivas Regal dream with his mouth open. The cabin was quiet, dimmed to a reassuring calm, the propitious moment (wasn't it always?) for the plunge to disaster. Ali's presence, somewhere in the back, comforted some; as a psychological talisman he was worth at least the presence of a dozen cardinals.

Just as I began to flirt with the surface of sleep from nervous exhaustion, there was a loud bang to the back of the seat, then a steady vibration. The senses went into full alert, girding for a turbulent, terminal dip of the plane; the bang was a familiar sound now, since I'd heard an engine blow out once on takeoff from London. Would the contour of Saipan or Tarawa, any blessed, jungle-rot strip, be below? Breath came in gulps, brain and body honed in for the rattle of the plane. But there was none, just Ali's sizable army scattered and as restful as clams. The source of the disturbance was soon evident—Ali, eyes popped wide, standing over the seat back. It was a relief to see him; better an untimely prank than some bungled little screws torn free somewhere.

"You're scared," Ali said, "and I got you more scared." He slipped into the seat, muffling his laughter. "I love to scare people."

"You torture rabbits, too?"

"Man, this plane goes down, we don't have a chance," he said. "All them octopuses and man-eaters down there. Gotta be able to swim."

"Like you? You can't swim."

"Even if I could save you," he said, "you'd be last in line. What you call me recently? A . . . a . . . a . . . I can't remember."

"A simpleton."

"That's it! A simpleton. That's not right to do."

"You missed the second part of that. A simpleton and a genius of the primitive."

"I don't read," he said. "My people tell me what's said. All the bad things." He paused, then said: "This plane ain't gonna go down. Not with me on it. Besides, those pilots don't wanna die, either."

"Never overestimate humanity."

"I used to be more scared than you," he said. "I don't care anymore." He held up his hand. "See how steady. No nerves at all. I ever tell ya about the time I was going to the Olympics? They had to talk to me for days in New York. When I finally said okay, I went down to the surplus store and bought me a parachute. I sat on that plane the whole way to Rome with a parachute on. It was rough, a rough trip, too. Without that chute, I'd've turned white for sure."

"What good was it? It was worthless."

"How you know? Maybe I got lessons." He laughed: "Nah, I probably didn't even have it on right. But it felt better. Just having it with me. It's all in the head, fear."

"No kidding."

"You got no faith in nothing," he said. "All you gotta do is keep sayin': Ali won't let the plane crash. Over and over. Say it. You have to beat fear with a whip. Hard."

"Mind if I think about it?"

"Crash if you want to," he said. He paused. "Know any jokes?"

His oblique effort to calm and distract was telling. It showed Odessa's side of him, as well as someone who intimately knew this fear in particular, and fear in general; that side was gaining on him. Gone, for the most part, except for lame filler material in public, was the insufferable drone of self-love; it had become by now, to the press and himself, the shrill whir of a mosquito drilling into a dead horse. Gone, too, except when Frazier was in his sights, was the dog-bite ugliness of the first half of his career, when he seemed to be trying to match an official attitude of the Muslims. Walk into a room, and there was the icy hostility of, say, Ali in bed, covers up to his chin, his face crusted with determined, silent rudeness. "They've changed my boy," his father, Cash, would lament until it became a mantra.

Friction ground on a long time between father and son. Besides meddling, Ali saw him as too proprietary, too critical, too eager for bows, and the son fired at him once, saying: "Lot of people say they made me. Who made me is *me!*" Ali often grabbed the front of his shirt and supposedly whopped him with an open hand one time. "Nooooo way," Cash said. "For damn sure. He got me by the shirt sometimes. But I told him outright, you do that again and I'm gonna pop you real good." To Cash, denied and misadventurous all his life, his son meant proof of his own genetic greatness, what he should have been, perhaps, as a painter. His son's accomplishments were his own. He'd look at the Muslims lounging around the house like beached sea lions and lose it. He saw each having yachts one day supplied with Dom Perignon, or Herbert with an armful of women throwing bacchanal feasts while his punched-out son was busing tables at a resort hotel. "This Herbert," he yelled, "he and the old man gonna steal you dumb. Where's your money? You care? Where's your money?" Now, in these days, Cash just drifted with the perks, content with the ceremonial role of the father, always to be found, with a drink in his hand, singing "My Way" at hotel piano bars.

Angelo Dundee wasn't immune, either, to Ali's pique. He walked a narrow line with Ali throughout his career. There was an unspoken understanding between them, sharply felt and never abridged. Often, he seemed to serve merely as a statue in the camp and fight corner, a handy and much respected conduit for the press, a producer of excuses and chatter that filled notebooks. Given that exterior, it was not hard for his few doubters to exclude him from the company of Ray Arcel, Eddie Futch, Freddie Brown, and Charlie Goldman, the latter having been the sculptor of the once ragged Marciano. Dundee simply never had any material to shape. Ali never listened to anyone in the ring, he trained himself, and Dundee was never able, for all his pleading, to get Ali to stop engaging in masochism during gym sessions, hanging on the ropes where he took much punishment. And if Angelo announced that Ali was going to work six rounds, the champ would just shadowbox, knowing that it would annoy the press and also show who was boss.

In one sparring session, Dundee shouted instructions, and Ali turned and yelled: "Shut up!" Among the press near the ring apron was Dick Young, columnist for the *New York Daily News.* "Can you imagine?" Young said, loud enough for Ali to hear. "Here's the guy that saved his ass against Liston, stole the fight for him against Cooper, and he tells him to shut up. What a jerk!" Ali moved toward the ropes, looked down and said: "I can treat you even worse." Young asked him if he was going to fire Angelo. "How can I fire him?" Ali shot back. "He's blacker than me."

Nothing, though, caught his crudity at the time more than his steady treatment of the giant Mel Turnbow, a gentle sparring partner, a man of slow gait and even slower speech. Ali was usually good with his gym men. He paid well, bought them clothes when they seemed in need, and he never worked them over in the sessions. "I feel sorry for Turnbow," Dundee said. Turnbow seemed to bring out a cruel streak in Ali. Was it because he was a non-Muslim? Not likely; there were others like Jimmy Ellis, though harassed by the Muslims, who never felt the champ's sting. Or, was it because he despised being around a backward black who disturbed his vision of his race? Ali once went down under a Turnbow barrage. He wobbled to his feet, went down again, this time with his eyes shut and his mouth open. Turnbow stood there, confused and embarrassed. Having been faking, Ali reached out and grabbed Turnbow and spilled him to the canvas while the crowd laughed. From then on, day by day, Ali would torment and batter the giant. A camp member explained: "Mel lives back there with the rest of us. But he doesn't take part in anything. He doesn't look at the television with Ali. He doesn't laugh at Ali's jokes or tell him how great he is. He just sits and eats, and never talks. And this is the one thing that bugs the champ. Being ignored. He'll dislike anybody he thinks is ignoring him."

The plane still cruised above the clouds. If air travel didn't scare him anymore, what did?

He thought for a moment and said: "Dead people. I touched one once. So cold. Besides, they become ghosts. They don't know where they are, see. So if you see them and they like you, then they're with you forever. Gives me the creeps. Don't it scare you? I know it does."

"Some talk right now. Dead people. Wouldn't take much to join them."

"You're right there," he said. "The pilot could have a hangover." He couldn't resist the needle. "Somebody didn't do a job on the engine. Bye-bye."

"I wish I knew some jokes."

"Just like fighting," he said. "Don't take much. Those little veins snake in ya head go pop, and that's all she wrote, ain't it? Scary. This is goin' to be my last fight. I'm tired of it all, worn out. Too much danger, ain't it? It's always been there in my head." He pondered, then said: "I got sixteen million in fights lined up after this one. Can you imagine?"

This instant contradiction, quitting in one breath, looking toward the money in the other, drove some reporters wild: it made him seem transparently false, and a challenge to their own sustained interest in him. Ali's last real critic left was Dick Young, for most of the veterans had given up trying to explain him, and the majority of new ones were deep into hero worship. Young was a tough conservative, a conscientious reporter who was not timid with opinion. The Muslims believed he was racist; Ali never thought so, sort of liked him as the last contrarian in the midst of all the treacle ladled on him, and he treated him convivially throughout. Ali liked writers and reporters who dueled with him, they snapped him out of a chronic boredom that could reveal itself in a flash. Young kept him awake; there was so much he disliked about Ali, let alone the growing idea that he was transcendental and a social martyr.

"He insults the little intelligence I have," Young said. He saw him as a panhandler, a liar, and a moral cheat. The first was because Ali used to like to put the touch on reporters for five and ten dollars when they made rounds with him, especially during exile. It was viewed as Ali's exercise in "getting over." Whites were to be tricked, to be misled, and a few bucks were part of some pallid, snickering little game played by him and the Muslims. Yet Ali seldom carried a wallet. Money as a concept never fastened unless it was in orbital sums: it was ephemeral, uncelestial, just paper. A moral cheat? To Young, Ali broke every tenet of real Muslim law, from whoring to being a truant at Temple service; he was a religious fake who abdicated his personal worth to the Black Muslims for their expediency and draft evasion, therefore counterfeit down to his socks. Was he sincere in faith? Who knows; in retirement he would prove to be a zealot.

As for being a liar, that has too much of a clinical whiff to it. Young just couldn't bear his flashing change of mind on almost everything, it made him untrustworthy, his quotes useless unless you were a lazy slave to his dumb speechifying, and there were many reporters of that type. In defense, it should be said that clarity of word or theme was as foreign to Ali as the understanding of ultra-slow light pulse. He liked intrigue, mystery, to keep the mist-blowing machine functioning on the set. No true liar could have been so indifferent to technique. He was simply a spin doctor without an examining room. Any idea or thought heard from others, if it seized his attention, was put in service without the slightest rumination. It was not insignificant that Elijah had told Herbert: "Take care of him. Never leave Ali's side. He'll follow the last person to have his ear." And, too, Ali had a show to keep going, often with a threadbare script through which he staggered to hit his stage marks. With a high fever, Norman Mailer judged him to be America's greatest wit, an observation that—after the first time around—could have only been produced by a deranged funny bone or an avidity for comic cant.

He was a vamp who needed deep vats of energy to locate his muse, and he sucked it up from wherever it flowed, sometimes from the criticism of writers like Young, sometimes from within his own camp, where he would create stick-figure opposition in people like Turnbow for a while, more often in Bundini Brown, whom he would slap on any pretext or thinly perceived slight. Though others close to him liked to deny its presence as if it would compromise his stature and natural talents, fear or insecurity, we know from Joe Martin and Archie Moore, was never far from him. Even Bundini once said: "That meanness is just fear, that's all, just another tool for him." It helped him acquire a cutting edge that was not naturally there.

To that end, he also was merciless with opponents, whom he humiliated, personalized into caricatures. Ali's first reaction to any fighter was an instant, Holmsian visual once-over. The shape of a nose, a jawline, a tic or a mannerism, a way of speaking were amplified by him, the way many children do in a schoolyard. He created full figures, plopping on physical or mental defects, and he'd try to occupy their minds, tried to relate to them viscerally. The invasion of the other man gave him bolts of vitality from the attention it provoked, shifted the fear to another, helped him to care about the dulling repetition of training, and allowed him to jack up his low-watt attention for the hunt. In the first period of his work, it all rushed out with transparent malice, though he tried to deflect it by saying it was for the box office. In the second half, the compulsion to denigrate, except again for Joe Frazier, made him sound like a drunk who knew only one song; the habit had diluted into a weak tactic that drove smart pencils to stop taking notes. But TV cameras kept grinding; the image on the screen was all they wanted, the one-groove recording, long in the tooth, was presented as arresting news.

"Why do you pick on black fighters?" he was asked as the jet slogged on to Manila.

"I pick on everybody," he said.

"No you don't. You didn't have much to say about George Chuvalo, Jerry Quarry."

"They behaved themselves," he said.

"All right, I'll give you Sonny Liston. He was open season. But Patterson, Ernie Terrell, what did they do for you to go nuts? You're brutal with Frazier."

"They called me by my slave name, Clay," he said. "That's why I mussed them up so bad."

"Only after you disrespected them so much." There was silence. "Maybe you had to show them you were the Muslim superman, the cream of the race, not just another get-along black like the rest."

"We're stronger, for sure," he said. "We let you honkies know where you stand, and the blacks with you."

"Why's Frazier so personal to you? Give him a break. He's just out there earning a buck. Never said he was the greatest anything."

"I don't hate Frazier," he said. "But I don't like him, either. He's got an idea he's my equal." Did Frazier scare him? "Not fear fear. Only 'cause he ain't normal. *That* bothers me. Man takes punches to the head like him can't be normal. Too stupid to be normal. Look at my face. I'm not stupid. I look *normal*. I'm way too smart for an animal like him. Nobody wants a champ like him."

"So why fight him again? For the money?"

"Yeah," he said. "But mostly 'cause I got to."

"Herbert?"

"No. Just me, it's personal," he said, sliding out of the seat and saying with a smile: "Say your prayers the rest of the way. Listen, ya hear that knock in the engine?" He stayed quiet, eyes open, then said: "Don't worry. You're gonna be all right."

To his credit, the show was always secondary to his personal evolution as a fighter. Without being really tested, pushed to the brink, a champion could never be true or great. He was in the ring with history, measuring himself against Louis, Marciano, and Sugar Ray. What he wanted were masterpieces so effulgent that relativity could not exist. The heavyweight ranks had been barren of such offerings. A champion could consider himself lucky if he ever found one opponent who could make him soar to a new, dramatic level; up to Frazier 1, Ali had been sorely lacking in authentic challenge. Louis had had his Schmeling, Marciano had had Ezzard Charles and Jersey Joe Walcott, Jack Dempsey had had Gene Tunney, and even Patterson was taken to the edge several times by Ingemar Johanssen, all dramatic successes that defined the champion. Louis and Marciano had, too, an added appeal that reinforced their pedigrees. They were extremely vulnerable, risk was palpable. Louis's weakness was an early-round proneness to a right hand by even journeymen punchers. The open-faced Rocky was always in jeopardy; next to seeing a knockdown, the fight crowd thrills at nothing more than seeing a man get up. Rocky's face was also irresistible, it was cinematic, meaning it was usually a mess. In many fights, he had to contend with bad cuts. Against Charles, he took the worst cut in ring history, a deep excavation in the middle of his nose, the probable work of a chain saw.

Part of Ali's problem, aside from his defaming rhetoric and scorn of other fighters, was the lack of appreciation for his style; it hadn't been seen before. He insolently used his head with micrometer precision to confound and dissemble the other man's poise and confidence. Getting to it was hard labor, for you had to wade through three kinds of jabs, and if you got to the head it wasn't there. The three jabs, as quick as light, were the probe, the irritant and point-builder on scorecards, and the trip-hammer straight left, which, seen close up, snapped a head nearly off and sent waves of shock down through the spinal column. Zora Folley had it right: "That big jab goes right to your feet, makes 'em just about cry." Legs seldom planted, his head in constant orbit, it was a wonder how he could produce such hand speed, such complex and never awkward punching designs. The most striking part of his game was his flawless sense of ring geometry, of time and space; for each space he knew the required move and tiny fractions of time needed to move in and out of a punching window. He reminded of what drummers call a "far-apart" roll that started on time, disintegrated, then would be there at the end. Or better yet, picture Jimi Hendrix working on his sound alone in a men's room, as he often did, those notes bouncing off the tiles, the electric storm of echo; Ali in the ring was the sound of Jimi Hendrix.

In the gym once, the ballet master Balanchine marveled at the use of his legs, his speed. Fans didn't; he was not what big men should be about. Legs nullified drama, hence vulnerability. He was not a dangerous fighter who portended a kind of higher malevolence that gives a rush to the standard voyeurs. His style was resisted. Art was for the lower weights, the classy little guys who never seemed to be delivering hurt on TV. Americans were a big people, they wanted considerable bang for their dollar or time. Ali at the time was too far ahead of ring consciousness—and available talent. Once, while doing a piece on the Roman Colosseum, I had occasion to talk to Italian novelist Alberto Moravia, and while commenting about theater the subject somehow landed on Ali.

Moravia said he knew nothing about boxing, but he did know a bit about theater. He looked upon Ali as he would a Picasso. "He forces you to see in a new way," he said. "That is one way how I see him. The other is the art of theater. Here, I have a problem. I see in him *una falta de genio* (fault of genius)." Which I took to mean a lack of temper, that it was too easy for Ali. "A fight should have tension, no," he continued. "He is an action writer in his own theater. But he clowns, he fools with your patience. I want to leave the theater. He won't let you have tension, struggle. He makes the funny faces, lounges in the ring. He baffles. Perhaps, he is bored with his own text. Or his characters, the other fighters, bore him." He needed a hard, serious man to put him in relief, to put him at risk; without it, a fight is pantomime, drama buckles.

Ali certainly understood the value of tension and suspense. His head was full of plot lines, from predictions to constant foreshadowing before a fight. He needed one to be a clear movie in his mind, the kind where people were taken to the edge, held there, and released by his immense command. So far he had not been able to get it right; people were talking in the seats and throwing popcorn at the screen. The outcomes were often muddled, his work too eccentric with an emotional immaturity that cost him credibility, and there was too much disfiguring afterburn of too many bouts. Five fights before the halfway mark of his career lit up his problem.

For the press, Charles Sonny Liston was a total abyss. Fall into it, and you would not hit one solid feeling on the way down. Having been in his shadow many times, once having been rocketed by him into a Denver snowbank for questioning his age, I grew to like him, not because he was misunderstood, but because he was like an anthropological treasure. His rap sheet stopped short of homicide. It covered muggings, stickups, muscling for St. Louis crime bosses, and suspicion of dragging beat cops into alleys and working them over. "They never liked me in that town," Sonny once said; what a card. One black cop, a Detective Sergeant Reddick, wanted to take him downstairs and make him "fit only for Decoration Day." Sonny said: "Yeah, Cap'n, a good idea."

One of twenty-five children of a sharecropper who knocked him around like a volleyball, Sonny ended up being given ten years in Jeff City. "He didn't mind it," said Lou Anonimo, a fellow inmate. "An awful place. But Sonny almost liked it. He liked his bath. He learned to box. He couldn't read or write. He was just a suspicious human bein' with an alligator voice." One group he despised and avoided were the Black Muslims. Crime packs were not to his liking, groups were "crazy-crazy," unpredictable, and jailhouse Muslims were quick, psychotic killers to him; they spooked him. When he rose in boxing, mobbed up to his sullen eyes, Sonny scoped the young Clay as just a big-mouthed, spoiled kid, the kind they "motha whip every day in prison." His only interests in life were money and his sweet wife Geraldine, who treated him like a naughty child, or a recuperating, blanketed English soldier back from the front, taking the air on a sea-coast. "Now, Charles," she'd say, "don't catch a chill today."

What a singular character Sonny was. When he lived in Denver, a priest named Father Murphy befriended and counseled him. He drew this conclusion: "I don't know about Clay. Floyd Patterson wants to be reborn. Sonny just wants to be born. Period." Before he was kicked out of Philly, he went to his manager, George Katz (behind him the goniff Blinky Palermo), for advice. The optimist told him: "Be nice, Sonny. It's nice to be nice." His lawyer Morton Witkin once wanted to see how long Sonny could sit without speaking. Witkin threw his hands up after forty-five minutes and said: "All right, what's on your mind?" Sonny walked out.

An incident that is still vivid is when Joe Flaherty, doing a piece for *Life*, and I were with him in Los Angeles. A young hippie approached his Cadillac, gave Sonny a medal with Jesus, Mary, and Joseph scratched on it. "Those cats are right," Sonny said. "Don't worry about a fuckin' thing in the world." We glided past the presi-dential campaign headquarters of Robert Kennedy. What did he want to be president for, Sonny wondered, with all that money? What would Sonny do with such a fortune? He leaned back and dwelt upon the question, Rodin's thinker. "I'd buy me the finest pussy in the United States of America." He cut short his reverie, by now with a dreamy look, and Charles Sonny absently thumb-flicked Jesus, Mary, and Joseph into flight formation on Wilshire Boulevard.

No point in lingering on Liston 2 with Clay, unless you have a facility with Egyptian glyphs. Clay scratched a right hand to Sonny's head, a light cuff if anything, not a punch that would cause him to drop like a bale of cotton almost instantly in the first round. Clay stood over him, angrily motioning for him to get up. Why not? This was the second time his play had closed in the bushes, and it brought shouts from eager reformers in Washington. People have gone cross-eyed looking for that punch on film; there is none unless you, in the interest of Ali's legend, desperately want to see one. Liston 1 is the fight for the magnifier. It should have been the frontispiece to his greatness, the first unimpeachable challenge to his throne; it wasn't.

No one gave Clay a shot against Liston in Miami on February 25, 1964; he was a 7–1 dog. Overnight, Sonny became America's cop, an idea that didn't sit too well with him. "Sheeee-it," he said. "I'm nobody's good guy." Even the fight establishment wanted Sonny to win. Clay and the Muslims would be impossible in deals. So what if Sonny was a blight? Horror plays well at the box office, too. What does Clay know about Sonny? He knew he had a crack-of-doom right hand and was no sloth on his feet. He also knew he was a mob favorite. What did Sonny know? Those Muslims again. "You see any Moooslems," Sonny asked Willie Reddish just back from Clay's dressing room. "You see any guys with bullet heads, dark suits?" An *S.I.* colleague, Bud Shrake, would later see Sonny move toward the ring with "real tears in his eyes." There had been demented Clay psychodramas at the weigh-in (tactical con, said Muslims and entourage, "absolute fear," remembered Sugar Ray). While dressing, Clay's eyes stayed fixed on the water bottle; he feared being poisoned. Rudy (later Rahman) was in charge of the water. Abruptly, Clay went over, emptied the bottle.

In the ring, Sonny was all wasted energy, stumbling moves and wild swings, not the fighter who pawed away a jab, then clubbed home a right hand; Clay jabbed him with impunity, opening a cut on Sonny's cheek. Chaos broke out in Clay's corner after the fifth. He was shouting that he'd been poisoned, "I'm blind!" Muslims streamed into the corner, got in Dundee's way. Near forfeiture, the little Dundee hurled Clay toward the center of the ring. Sweat, rosin, or liniment had gotten in Clay's eyes. With Sonny uncharacteristically tentative in his pursuit, Clay's vision cleared. After the seventh, Sonny did not answer the bell, claiming a pulled muscle in his shoulder. The promise had been Theseus against the Minotaur. What a dreary conclusion: Liston, of all people, quitting, and Clay trying to quit.

Cries of fix were loud. Sonny and the mob had gone for the price. Was it so? Why was Liston tearing up, as seen by a good reporter like Shrake? Had he received the word? We are asked to believe that Sonny got old in a snap, was not the fighter George Foreman saw when he worked as a sparring mate at the end of Sonny's career: "He was the only fighter who ever, *ever*, stopped me consistently in my tracks with one punch, backed me up like a sports car." Sonny always refused to talk about the Miami fight. He would talk about Liston 2, saying: "Yeah, I sit down for that one. It weren't Clay. It was *them*. The Moooslems. I got word, inside stuff, they were going to kill me." Ali would never be sure if he had met the real Liston. "The Liston fights," he said once, "were beeeeg, and he made them little, and me along with them." Was Sonny trying to win? "If he wasn't," Ali said, "he's a better actor than me." Sonny Liston went out on a suspicious drug overdose. The theory was that he went into the drug trade, and the sophistication of that calling had been too much for him; one can almost see him trying to discern the higher calculus of crime. On a rainy morning in January 1971 with Geraldine riding point, her unruly Charles was rolled down the Strip in front of the Vegas casinos, and there wasn't a wet eye in all of Christendom.

Ali surveyed the field and picked Floyd Patterson to be next, once the youngest heavyweight champ in history before Clay, a two-time king of the ranks. Sonny's attitude had lure, Floyd's totally enveloped. In today's TV currency, a couple of funny lines, a passing shtick, a new hairdo, an esoteric hobby turns an athlete into a priceless wit of prized individuality. But Floyd, like Sonny, was the real thing. No stranger or more interesting figure ever worked the landscape of sports; it followed that he had been discovered by the mystic Cus D'Amato, who said he often floated out-of-body on the ceiling. There was something vulpine about Floyd, and it might be said that he had the only careerist approach in boxing annals along with Archie Moore. He was dead set on lasting. While the fans and critics would kick him like a sad-eyed mutt one month and then join him the next in his personal salvation (boxing was spiritual to him), there was always the sense of Floyd sitting in an armchair and squinting through pince-nez at ring fluctuations.

To sit and talk with him was a delight, though at times there were colliding emotions; you either wanted to put your arm around him or give him a therapeutic slap in the face. In a moment, you were adrift in the middle of a Russian novel, in a Chekhovian dacha, oppressive heat, the taste of bitter tea, in the middle of souls looking for clarity in a suffusion of grayness. Let's pass on his childhood, it could make you cry. Leave it with adolescent Floyd slashing an X through his picture and telling his mother: "I don't like *him*." Big names, including Frank Sinatra, were drawn to him. Liberals adored him, crowned him a man of brains and race vision. His pluck was inspiring, a fighter, like a skilled repairman trying to build a skyscraper. His instant shame baffled. After a title match, he always had two cars waiting, the victory car pointed to his hotel, the defeat car pointed out of town; he was partial to disguises.

Physically, Floyd, lithe and small, didn't look like a heavy-weight at all. There was no promise of consequence. He fought out of D'Amato's "peekaboo" style, gloves nearly shielding his eyes, had superb hand speed and cheap crockery for a jaw. He had the eyes of a safecracker with no nerve; quite the contrary, though. He had a stiff billow of kinky hair that seemed pasted down on his forehead. Even after winning, he could be a pointillist of damage done; no bruise, scrape, ache would escape detailed amplification. The press loved him. Floyd might be the lost child of Freud, but he dealt in specifics of the grim trade. Clay was purely thin artifice, a windy fanatic for whom boxing came second, a senseless provocateur. Clay had hand-carried a bag of carrots to Floyd and hanged the tag of "Rabbit" on him. Sinatra called Floyd to his suite. "He told me I could win," Floyd said, "had to win. The whole country was counting on me."

Held in Vegas, the title fight would be the most politically exclamatory of Ali's career. "The kid was never the same after Floyd," Dundee said, tapping his head. "The pressure got bigger and bigger. The fun was gone." That night, Clay looked down at the press and said: "Watch closely. I'm gonna show you real punishment." To show his superiority, Clay did not throw a single punch in the first round. He then picked up the beat, strafing Floyd with straight lefts. He began to taunt: "Come on America, come on white America!" He did what he pleased. Floyd seemed impaired, something was wrong. He was decked in the sixth, got up quickly. After the seventh, his train-er hugged and lifted him to ease the pain in Floyd's back. He went on gamely, and the fight turned quickly into a spectacle of cruelty, nastiness being applied to an invalid. "Get him out of there!" Dundee screamed, sensing the crowd's anger. It wasn't stopped until the twelfth, with Floyd, suffering mightily from the back pain, leaving the ring draped over his seconds.

What the country had seen was a certain kind of bullfight, where unimaginative passes prolong the ceremony too long and subordinate the kill. Seeing Floyd in pain and outclassed, it wanted a quick, clean finish, not a class in how to pull off a butterfly's wings. Floyd gimped to Sinatra's suite the next night to apologize, and bumped into human nature. Frank moved to the far side of the room, away from Floyd, sat down, his back "all the way over there to me. I got the message. I left." Public outcry was instant. Sensing his embryonic mythos once more in ruins, Clay said to the press: "Okay, what's the excuse now? Fix? Carrying him? Give it to me! He took my best punches! My hands are swollen." After what he had done to someone whose only mistake was being an integrator, a Martin Luther King man, he was no longer drawn as an out-of-control kid, a rhetorical belch. He became real as well as an insult to whatever integrity boxing had. He had wanted to feast on acclaim, a tour de force. In the end, he had only underlined a line from the Old West: "The vulture hates nothing more than biting into a glass eye."

Ali was always an extremely busy fighter. He defended his title five times in 1966, once in this period in back-to-back months, and he would surpass that pace again in 1972. No champion besides Joe Louis had ever worked so often before. That meant that he was in training most of the year, and that's a lot of gym wear. It also suggests that a fighter needs money, or he believes no one can beat him and there is too much easy prey to pass up. Ali set up shop abroad. He stopped Henry Cooper again in London in the sixth, turning him into a hose that literally squirted blood. He took on Brian London there ("boxers aren't prawns," Brian had a habit of saying, meaning pawns) and dropped him in the third. Then, on to Germany for Karl Mildenberger, who said, "blacks do not like left-handers." No fighters like southpaws. But Ali did not punish him for the remark. Karl confused him; it was a dull affair, almost a slow-motion polka before Ali stopped him in the twelfth round. An understandable schedule; a

man needs a holiday sometime, especially when they weren't exactly looking for him back in the American office. It was the first of
those post-Patterson bouts, against George Chuvalo in Canada, that
he saw public sentiment intrude upon his economics.

"After all this is over," he complained, "I'm lucky if I clear two
thousand." It was far too little for a long night. Ali had hardly anything to say about George, amiable, instinctively civilized, a good
candidate for butler school. He was looked upon as a dumb fighter.
Do you berate a busboy for his failure to prepare haute cuisine? He
just had no ring syllabus, or grasp of anatomy; a kneecap is not a belly,
and your right hand is not your head. "If I hurt him, he'll quit,"
George said. Good to the body, bad to the head, Chuvalo stayed on
him the whole fifteen. Afterward, Ali was left with one hand in a
bucket of ice, the other holding his side, and to make a point he held
up his red genital cup cratered with dents. "For this kind of money?"
he said. "I'm as dumb as he is." Not dumb, George. If anyone was
looking, George had shown the map to beating Ali—come for long
work, stay on top of him, suck the air right out of him.

When he engaged Cleveland Williams on November 14, 1966,
Ali was a celebrity and a polemicist more than a fighter. Called "The
Big Cat," Williams had once had a punch equal to Liston until he was
shot by a state trooper and lost a kidney. If ever the Muslims had an
example of what happened to passive blacks, it was Williams. You
could smell the desolation and sweat of his life, feel the hot sun and
the deadened clank of hope in him. Hugh Benbow, his manager,
abused him verbally in his auctioneer's voice; he, as well as his name,
was right out of William Faulkner. He said of Clay: "They oughta
shoot him at dawn. Title don't belong to no coward. Cleve, you take
this gater-mouth nigger out, and I'm gonna own all of Texas." Cleve
turned, and Benbow said: "You, too, Cleve." Ali seemed bemused by
Benbow.

Broken in spirit and body, Williams was an open firing zone. Ali was technically of a piece. Cleve stood there like a man wishing for a bus to hit him, and it did again and again. Down three times in the second, he struggled to his feet for a final time in the third, with Ali standing over him and letting you choose whether he was transmitting compassion or his own final perfectibility. The press gave him high marks for his work and silence, and wrote about the Ali Shuffle, a scissoring leg dance that he had unveiled for the first time. Legend has it that this was his greatest fight, a look at the real Ali and what he was robbed of when he was exiled. Little was mentioned of Cleve being barely ambulatory, or how he lived in squalid quarters. A masterpiece? If you enjoy watching a game of solitaire.

Signing to fight Ernie Terrell in Houston early in 1967, he quickly reverted to Clay the impaler. Terrell was a laid-back, six-six guitar player, a friend and former sparring mate in the early days. Ernie innocently called him Clay at the signing; that's what he had always called him. "My name's Muhammad Ali!" Ali shot back. From then on, he lost touch with normalcy. Ernie was lower than swine, a racial insult. Never letting up, he poured out the very soul of the Muslim program; an unambiguous renunciation of integration. It was overkill against a man who couldn't care if Ali had antennae for ears. "I'm going to give him the Patterson treatment," Ali said. "Only it's gonna be worse. I'm gonna make him suffer, make him call me by my name."

Ordinarily quite passive, Ernie finally summed him up: "He starts a fight early. Tries to get under your skin. Maybe that's his best talent. I got nothing against him, or his religion. But he's an extremist, and they all twist things. He's always been a liar. He's just a punk, can't think for himself, and he'll always be a punk. He's not a complete fighter, never was when I worked with him. He doesn't want a glove near his face. He lives in fear of that face. We'll see."

Terrell was defensively sharp, expertly fielding Ali's punches early with his gloves. Ali smartly chose a new line, punching openings through Terrell's gloves with left and right uppercuts, the textbook choice of parry against a tall man. Ernie tried to keep him on the ropes; and something key happened in one exchange there. By the fifth, Ali dropped his speed gear and planted for punching. He opened a gash over Ernie's right eye. It was his fight from then on; when would it end? Not for ten more rounds, chorused by his brother Rudy: "Make him say your name!" Dundee told him to shut up. Ali to Dundee: "*You* shut up!" Ali added: "He's gonna suffer." How far could he go with the meanness, with the crowd screaming for the ref (deaf and blind) to stop it, and Ernie a gory sight? In the thirteenth, it so happened, a black man tried to get to Ali's corner and got clubbed by an Ali aide as he shouted: "You rotten scum."

Apologists for Ali ignored his performance, refused to critique his malice, or see it as a serious character flaw; potential martyrs have no flaws. Ernie would claim he had double vision, that Ali had scraped his eye along the rope and had thumbed him three times, forcing Ernie's left eye into the bone. The bone was smashed, and the eye muscles hooked on it. Like many fighters, Ali could be adept with his thumbs. The press was foaming once again. Wrote Jimmy Cannon: "It seemed right that Cassius Clay had a good time beating up another Negro. This was fun, like chasing them down with dogs and knocking them down with streams of water. What kind of clergyman is he? The heavyweight champion is a vicious propagandist for a spiteful mob that works the religious underworld."

On March 8, 1971, according to Muhammad Ali, the planet would stumble in its axis, billions would hold their breaths, including every last ice-covered Sherpa and sand-swept Bedouin, an ecumenical constituency that he claimed as his alone, in contrast to Joe Frazier, "a little old nigger boy who ain't been anywhere 'cept Philly, never done anything for nobody 'cept rich people that back him and politician crooks, never had a thought in his dumb head 'cept for himself." Frazier was up North, yet his shadow rolled heavily over the sun-streaked walls of the Fifth Street Gym in Miami. Celebrities like Sammy Davis Jr. and Elvis Presley, to the sound of whirring cameras, moved in and out of his glow as if seeking reaffirmation of their own rank. "You cool, brother?" Elvis asked, embracing him. "Cool as you." Ali smiled. "And gittin' cooler."

Frazier was training up in the frigid Catskills at the Concord Hotel, sterile and with an emptiness swept by constant wind that bothered him; he could never get warm, loose. He got some bad news from Dr. Finton Speller, the family physician. He had been feeling tired and losing energy. Speller told him he was suffering from high blood pressure, the condition evolving from the anticipation of the fight with Ali and the dogged training. He began to feel better after daily vitamin E and C shots, and then moved the camp back to Philly. Once, according to Ali, he showed up at the Broad Street Gym in disguise to watch Joe work and left unimpressed. "What disguise?" Joe said. "He turn white or somethin'? Wouldn't be hard for him. Hey, who's gonna miss Clay, even if he's dressed like Moses?"

But there was an exchange between the two at Broad Street. The Garden sent George Kalinsky, their photographer, to get some shots that would simulate them in the ring. Ali clowned, Joe kept a fixed stare. When Ali had been in early exile, he had always engaged in sham battle with open hands, and Joe had come to believe that he was trying to measure Joe's strength and reflexes. The adrenaline had pumped at the Fairmount Park incident; this time Joe aimed to transmit a signal. In the ring, with Kalinsky nervous, Joe said: "Let's go at it." Ali was confused, and Joe banged him harder. Ali returned with a shot, and Joe dug a left hook to his belly. "That's it," Ali said, nearly pulling his trunks up to his chin. "Son of a bitch can really hit," Ali announced. After Ali left, Joe said to Kalinsky: "You see his face when I buried that hook in his belly?"

Hecklers piled into Frazier's gym, and Yank Durham, reasoning that Philly wasn't known for generosity to its local names, told one crowd: "You're all welcome. I hear anything I don't like, and you're out the door." A big young guy called him on it: "You too old to throw anybody out a door." Durham said: "I can start with you. If you don't shut up." One afternoon Durham heard the shout of "Uncle Tom." He went over to the guy, grabbed him by his neck, and threw him out to the sidewalk. On some days there was a picket line outside, placed there by black groups who resented that the fight had been given to white promoters. How was the community going to benefit? Durham engaged them: "Blacks never give us a dime when Joe was comin' up. They ridiculed him. I worked all my life. No white give me a thing, no black either. So we're keepin' every dime. Go picket Clay. He'll give you some of his money, I'm sure." A standard inquiry was: "Why you call him Clay? You got no respect for his religion." Durham would shoot back: "See that telephone pole? I don't care if he prays to a telephone pole."

The Uncle Tom epithet tripped so incessantly from Ali's lips, and now from the crowd around the gym, that Joe might as well have been wearing a sign. His son, Marvis, had to defend himself and his father in school. The phone calls came day and night, some calling him a tommin' dog, others vowing that he would never see another day if he beat Ali. The label hadn't stuck with Patterson and Terrell, but it was isolating him to a speck of a man, right in his own town, in his own gym, except for one brave soul who showed up each day with Joe's name tattooed on his back. Frazier had police guarding him around the clock, and it seemed remarkable that he did not teeter into disorientation, that the job ahead stayed fixed in his mind.

It got to Durham finally. One day, without warning, the gym almost empty, Yank picked up a water pail and slammed it repeatedly against a ring post. "It's a damn shame what Clay's doin' to my boy," he said, then kicked the smashed pail with full force up over the ropes.

Young white men, Jews, Italians, Irish, Hispanic, never have to fret much about their racial character. In these times, perhaps always so, young blacks were forced to dwell on the steps to be taken on the wavy line of their existence, of going along or burning down, and this was no time to be neutral. In this regard, where had Frazier failed the test, a young kid run out of town by his mother in fear for his life, while the young Ali, understandably, sucked and slurped the big orange of the Louisville rich and fingered the laurel wreath of wide recognition from hometown whites? Move back three decades, and Frazier had a ring DNA similar to that of Joe Louis, self-effacing, reticent, and worshipped by all blacks. Long after his career, he would say on the subject of Ali: "I don't believe in the separation of races." Where, then, was the justice? "There ain't none," Frazier said. "Not for me. It eats at me, but I don't let on and don't forget. He uses his blackness to kick up a stir, get people excited, maybe convince himself of somethin', then he's gone. He thinks no hurt's left behind. What he ever do for people but give 'em a lot of silly words?"

He added: "He's no martyr. The heroes are them kids with their pieces of body all over Vietnam, a lot of poor blacks. I don't care about his draft thing. His politics. His religion. But he ain't no leader of anything. He stop the war? How do people buy his shit?"

From an irrational rouser for a pseudo Master Race (Bundini said: "Only two kinds of blacks to the Muzzies—niggers and themselves!") and now to a brave, slashing avatar of black thinking, Ali seemed to have a whole nation in stride, the prime figure ready for the gladrags of empty, make-believe sixties radicalism. Young blacks bought the whole hog, not knowing or caring that the Muslims had him in a choke collar and a leash, taking no notice that he had, with great arrogance, betrayed another hero of large appeal, Malcolm X. Black magazines, confused about whether they were MLK passives or Stokely Carmichael's troopers, slew Frazier's blackness at every turn. In *Soul on Ice*, Eldridge Cleaver had his say on Ali as a race dragon: "A slave in private life, a king in public—this is the life that every black champion has had to lead." He called Ali the first "free" black champion, a "genuine" revolutionary, "the black Fidel Castro." Ali led an "autonomous private life" and was a "serious blow" to the white man's self-image, "a champion who denied white superiority, could not fulfill the psychological needs of whites."

Joe Louis and Sugar Ray as slaves? Sugar bowed to no man, led a private and public life the envy of most whites. There had been no greater symbol than Joe Louis, even for many whites who were with him against Billy Conn. He towered over the racially criminal times with nobility and, while on symbols, he was the physical repudiation of white supremacy. He was a slave only to a bad golf score, to which he lost thousands, and a terrorizing IRS (so rank and callous that it made the injustice toward Ali look like a prank). Hounded by the IRS, his mind often sizzled by cocaine from "friends" to ease his worries, Louis had to be hospitalized for clinical paranoia. When he regained his balance, he went under the sinecure of Caesar's Palace in Vegas as an official greeter to high rollers. A saving, not a demeaning role; Mickey Mantle years later would have the same function in Atlantic City.

Inwardly, Ali admired Louis, but expression of his feelings came hard. His ego would not allow space for anyone (except for Sugar Ray, a middleweight) who might be as large as himself. He could be unkind to Louis, serving him up as a model to be pitied and not emulated, or did he see in Louis the future that was always possible? He often ridiculed Louis's shuffling, the slow cadence of his speech,

turning him into a freak without dignity; years later he would offer
Louis $30,000 to stay with him for ten days before a fight with Ken
Norton. But mostly Joe was poor, old sick Joe. "He's gotta stand
round," Ali said, "like a statue in a place full of Roman ones. If I go
down, it's gonna be in a big jet goin' to visit some head of state. If I
ever end up lookin' sick, ain't *nobody* gonna see me in public. I'm
leavin' the ring with *all* my faculties—and all the money. I'm gonna
take every quarter out of this game, then sit back and collect the
interest."

The big jet was in reference to the death of Rocky Marciano.
"Look at Rocky," Ali said. "He's gotta go 'round diggin' up chump
change in Nebraska, wherever. Gets himself killed in a dinky old
plane doin' it." Rocky never went for much luxury. If it was cheap, it
was good, a line of thought he picked up from the parsimony of his
manager, Al Weill, who never called him by his name; always just "get
the fighter" or "tell the bum he's workin' five rounds today." Or, perhaps, it was from the tutoring of Charlie Goldman, who often
explained the perils of being a sucker, whether for a right hand or an
open palm. Marciano didn't trust banks, and when he died his family
could barely find a dime and spent years trying to locate his "lost treasure." There was nothing volatile between Rocky and Ali. He had
been an early critic of Ali's style (imagine, Rocky a connoisseur of
technique!), and sometimes muttered something about flag and
country; controversy gave him hives. He was once involved with Ali
in a moronic computer fight, and Rocky showed up with a toupee
and quite serious; he won. "Too much," Ali responded. "Men in
toupees beatin' me now!" Marciano seemed to sense the pain in Ali.
He told Belinda: "Tell him to stop torturing himself. Get him out of
boxing, forget the whole thing." With the death of Rocky, Ali had lost
an historical playmate, and white America its last stalwart, its obsti-
nate link to a time that surely was no more, and shot glasses were said

to have been raised to his picture above bars, next to Louis, the unde-feated free-swinger of dessicated nose and inviting eye.

Another soon-to-be prop for Ali's historical sweep was Jack Johnson, long dead. He and his father had watched films of Jack in action, and it speaks to his analytical genius that he took away from those grainy strips the one thing that Ole Jack could give him—the art of defense; unglamorous and the hardest gift to perfect in the ring; Jack was a master, Ali would have no equal, picking off punches like lint on a lapel. Ali honed in on Jack while Howard Sackler's *The Great White Hope* was having a good run on Broadway. James Earl Jones reanimated Johnson with a mighty voice that seemed to vibrate the lobby doors. Ali immediately injected himself with the stage power of Johnson, took his intransigence and placed it next to his own. He had seen James Earl on Broadway one day, sprinted up to him and shouted: "The line! Gimme the line!" Jones bellowed with defiance: "Here . . . I . . . is!" Jumping up and down, Ali screamed: "That's it! That's me! You can see it's me! I'm Jack Johnson. Without the white women."

But there was no similarity between their thoughts or actions. They shared only prosecution and hate. Big Jack was a loner and of the epicure school of thought—live hard and let somebody else pay for the burial. To the whites of his time, into the preservation of Nordic purity and dominance, Jack was going eye-to-eye with them, speaking to them of blood and sex and territory. Jack was as personal as the lock pick scratching at the bedroom door, the dreadful promise of untempered polluting sexuality. They drove him out of the coun-try on flimsy pretext. The retaliation against Ali had seemed dry; rustling papers, stamped documents, the system in action like a vise. When it came to black power display, Ali was pallid next to Jack, who faced mob-think with just a confrontational grin and somehow reflected the brutally harnessed energy of his race, all of whose minds carried still lifes of a rope and a high oak tree.

Jack never had the multitudes of followers that lined up behind Ali for the biggest fight of his life. Not just blacks, but young whites whose fathers had looked upon Ali in the extreme as a traitor, at the least merely an hysterical Little Richard. The young people, the largest bulge of population in American history, influential by weight of numbers, were seeking their own cultural voice. An unjust war was their idealistic, surface complaint; the prospect of being drafted was more visceral. These were not boxing fans, they were seekers of the antihero. What mattered was Ali's style, his desecrating mouth, his beautiful irrationality so like their music. His black mysticism only added to his credentials, all in all a true-born slayer of authority and the status quo, a man in opposition to whiney, evil politicians and psychotic generals in the field.

Where did they come from, this mass of angry, mewling youth? They were out of the Beats of the fifties, children of parents with middle class fears and docile lives, with a preoccupation with security and order; nonconformity was a sin. They grew up detesting the noose of the Cold War, people like Senator Joe McCarthy before whom their parents sat as if dumb. Their early spokesman was Jack Kerouac: "The only people for me are the mad ones, the ones who never yawn, or say a commonplace thing, but burn, burn, burn." The kids of the fifties were statistical giants and glutted on a rarefied status that expected every material advantage. "The royalty of the Fifties," Jay Stevens calls them in *Storming Heaven*. They grew up with the superheroes in the comics, who lanced with the forces of evil and injustice, graduated to *Mad* magazine with its knife bent into middle class values. Wave after wave came with their own proclivities that would outrage: rock music, the social deviancy of roles played by Marlon Brando and James Dean, the spirituality of the ethereal poet William Blake, LSD—and now near the death rattle of the sixties, when they would soon return to the suits of the organization man they hated and become ruthless material dandies, they had their own black superhero—Muhammad Ali, who had not the slightest idea of what the hell they were talking about, except there was a mood out there, and he owned it.

Down in Miami, Ali lay on a table as his black masseur, Luis Sarria, never seeming corporeal, just a pair of eyes beaming out in a dark mine shaft, worked his muscles.

"See how fit I am," Ali told me.

"You look terrific."

"Up here, too," he said, tapping his head.

"You'd better be for this one."

"I know somethin'," he said.

"I hope so."

"No, I mean I really know somethin'." He waited for a reaction, then said: "But I'm not tellin'."

"Something in the films of Frazier?"

"Not that," he said. "Don't you want to know?"

"I'm not going to twist your arm."

There was silence, then he motioned me down by his ear. "Frazier," he whispered, "has high blood."

"How do you know?"

"I got spies."

"I don't believe it."

"Suit yourself," he said.

"Suppose you're right. The fight's going to be canceled?"

"Naaaah," he said, "he's too stupid for that. If it's me with high blood, forget it."

"How bad is it?"

"Bad enough," he said. "And it's gonna get badder come fight night. He's gonna explode with tension. Blow up. Right there in the ring. When he sees the whole world behind me. All my people. All my young people out there pulling for me. And there he is. Lonely little Joe. All by himself. Whoeee! That's scary."

In the gym during workouts, Ali produced a scripted set piece. Only the gym itself remained free of tinkering. It was always the same: thick, steaming air heavy with sweat; fading fight posters and the counterpoint of sound from gloves working speed bags and heavy bags; the gabby old retired milliners and beach wanderers as aspish as theater critics; the creak of the ring apron sighing under the desperate footwork of prelim boys; sun lasering through dirty windows turning the dusty, whitewashed walls into a dull yellow; spit buckets forming a gruel that could spawn tadpoles. Plants, Ali's straight men, popped out of the crowd on cue, faces wreathed with cigar smoke and anger, predicting doom for him at the hands of Frazier, what Joe was going to do to that face. He'd stop sparring, engage in fake vitriol. "You there," he'd shout, pointing to a guy with no teeth who was getting five bucks for his lines. "You lay off my pretty face! I'll come down there and turn your face into raw meat! Like I'm gonna do to Frazier. Throw that old beggar out!" And his aides would rush into the crowd. Dressed and showered, he'd then take, say, Burt Lancaster on a tour of the Miami ghetto. "A real show," he said to Burt. "But wait till New York, you ain't seen nothing yet."

His mother, Odessa, stopped by on her way to the Bahamas. She couldn't bear to watch the fight.

"Baby," she said, "don't underestimate this Frazier. Work hard. I'm too nervous."

"Don't worry, Mom," Ali said. "I'll be in top shape. He's a bum."

"Sonny . . . he's no bum," she said, kissing his cheek.

Not like the zoos of Philly, Fifth Street was priceless as a one-dollar look into the entrails of boxing, and it would vanish in time, its history gone as suddenly as the old Garden that now conducted boxing in a new high-rise above Penn Station. But the old Garden, a slattern of a building, was irreplaceable as a venue. Where for decades so many inflamed rallies had been held by American Nazis and flaying evangelists. Where Marilyn Monroe sang to JFK, where ballroom dancers and ice queens and clowns seemed endless. Mainly the old Garden had been the temple of world boxing. Kids doing roadwork in the half-light of a Nigerian or Bangkok morning, or kids listening by a radio, like Ali himself, knew it as a dreamlike place of torn flesh and majesty.

The move of Garden boxing signaled, too, an environmental change. The old-style managers, with lunch on their ties, had their patch for doing business, a couple of blocks on Eighth Avenue smeared with grimy windows filled with old school rings, dusty Army greatcoats, of long and stained shot-and-a-beer bars with an Edward Hopper kind of lighting. No more doing business on a sticky phone in a booth, no more dropping in on a matchmaker, flopping down and putting your feet up on his desk. No more characters like Al Weill, who concealed his cigars and never carried more than seven dollars in mortal fear of being "touched up" by indigent managers and fighters. The whole feel was gone. Rapscallions and double-crossers to the bone, the old power now saw their haphazard stealth to be short of the mark. Well-fed lawyers with intricate traps in their attaché cases who saw big money in boxing were up ahead and lay in wait; boxing was in a double-breasted suit. Fighters were properties; managers had become hirelings.

But Yank Durham thought of Frazier as his own. So what if Cloverlay had his contract, merely a matter then of insufficient funds. He had been there through his ring infancy, he had his heart and mind, had hacked his way through all the nonbelievers. He and his trainer, Eddie Futch, had gone first class with the fighter, did things the right way, produced a machine as carefully as he used one of his old welding torches. Yank had got his chance, too, and proved he was more than just an amateur who specialized in turning street layabouts into prelim boys. He was a cagey old schemer, but not like most of the pickpockets on their way out; he had a trust and, though soaring in a fantasy present, the future intruded on the edge of consciousness. If Joe won, then, maybe, there was a fight or two left in him. If he lost, he'd have to set him down, close him out; it wouldn't be easy. Fighters like Joe climbed to the top out of breathtaking will, got there inch by inch, leaving mounting pain on each rung. He'd have enough money to quit. Yank didn't want him hurt, he was not a fighter of longevity. He knew Ali was going to be a mean night. Too mean, the kind of fight that might cut Joe to a scrap, and he'd have to shut him down. His nerves, he said, jumped at the sad prospect.

When Frazier broke camp five detectives rode shotgun with him to New York, underlining how serious they had taken the many threats to the fighter's life. Joe didn't say much, said one, and "he looked so distant we joked that he was sitting there waiting for us to give him the menu for his last meal." Not unusual for a fighter; muteness is helpful when reels are turning so fast in the mind, though some become unusually garrulous, making one wonder what visions they are trying to muffle. The group rolled out of the Holland Tunnel and were joined by a small fleet of New York police for escort into Manhattan. Durham and Joe checked into the City Squire on Seventh Avenue, then suddenly left when the hotel fielded a bomb threat. To protect himself from the crushing mob on the streets, Ali put up at the Garden. On the night before the fight, Joe was now at the Pierre Hotel, and Joe says in his book Ali called him.

"Joe Frazier, you ready?" Ali asked.

"I'm ready," Joe said.

"I'm ready, too, Joe Frazier. And you can't beat me."

"You know what?" Joe said. "You preach that you're one of God's men. Well, we'll see."

"You sure you're not scared, Joe Frazier?"

"Scared of what I'm going to do to you?"

"Ain't nothing you *can* do," Ali said. "See you."

"I'll be there," Joe said. "Don't be late."

With his entourage streaming out before him, Ali went down and settled into his dressing room, a place that he could turn on the quickest whim into dramaturgy. He'd rouse Bundini to the point of crying, jump on one of his comments and purposely misinterpret it. He'd taunt other members, calling up a bungled chore. He'd joke with Pat Patterson, who had his water bottle under lock and key, and try to guess on what part of the body the inventive bodyguard was packing his iron. You never knew if he was going to show up hysterical or with a calm that nearly rocked everyone else to sleep. Now, he just watched Angelo Dundee float in the room as if he were a priest arranging details for a high mass. They never talked over plans; Ali never worked from notes. He lay on the table and drifted into a half-sleep under Luis Sarria's hands, the buzz of Bundini far off: "Oh, mercy, we gotta big one tonight." "Shut that nigger up," Ali mumbled. Butch Lewis, from Joe's camp, came in to watch the taping of Ali's hands. He then shot up from the table, started to pirouette through the room with volleys of punches. He shouted to Lewis: "Take this back to your dumb chump!"

There were only a handful of people in Frazier's room, Durham, Futch, an assistant, Les Peleman, and a Philly cop-bodyguard. Joe was gloved and ready. Durham took him to the far corner of the room, put his hands on his shoulders, looked him straight in the eye and in his signature voice said: "Well, we're here. I want you to know what you've done, boy. There will never be another Joe Frazier. They all laughed. You got us here. There's not another human who ever lived

I'd want to send out there, not even Joe Louis. Win tonight, and the road will be paved in gold. Think of those mammy-suckin' white people and the hot fields soaking up the sweat and hope of your parents. You were made for this moment. Take it, cocksucker." They hugged and laughed. Joe then lay on the table, a dark bomb ready to be rolled into a hangar. "Five minutes!" someone shouted. Joe got up, loosened up with some body rolls and punches. He then knelt in the center of the room and prayed aloud: "God, let me survive this night. God protect my family. God grant me strength. And God . . . allow me to kick the shit out of this mothafucker!"

How do you describe a roar? Like a cataract, maybe if you had ever looked down on Niagara Falls. Otherwise, a roar is a roar, it goes no place in the mind. It is an empty word in text, it is a sensory word, it has to be heard to be given features. As soon as the fighters began their parade to the ring, there was this sonic blast of sound that seemed to bend the plinth of yellow light over them, and it would seldom drop in decibel. If the guy next to you in the press row spoke, you couldn't hear him. The wall of sound sent a current up the back and made palms moist. The whirlpool of race politics that had for weeks spread to so much passionate exchange, the cross section of accusatory idiocy, eddied out of sight. There was just *The Fight* now, the pure and inescapable sorting out, and there was a twinge of sympathy for their stark aloneness and the immensity of performance, of expectations they faced. Burt Lancaster was doing the color for 340 closed-circuit outlets, Don Dunphy, graceful and spare, had the blow-by-blow, and Sinatra was shooting pictures for *Life*. The place was filled with the aristocracy of fame: Elvis, the Beatles, Salvador Dalí, just about everyone, all of them presumably dispatched from the limos that strung around the Garden two-deep like black pearls.

Like certain soufflés, heavyweight title fights disappoint more than satisfy. If it ends quickly, it's a fix (an artifact from film noir and vagrant, inglorious incidents stuck too much in the lexicon of fans and press). Go the distance, and you're a bum with no punch, or you carried him. But a fight has its own reality (similars in style equal a negative), full of snares, letdowns, inertia, and flashing drama when all the parts locked in right—just like life. It wasn't a film with Martin Scorcese on a skateboard with a hand-held camera, with Robert De Niro being pumped like a fountain of blood, his face dissolving into a hurt built by a makeup man. No wonder the *Rocky* series, which pulverized every cliché in the game, has turned boxing into distorting cartoon, heightened the prospectus, the coming visuals to a level unattainable. Rarely, if ever, do two fighters with opposing styles, the long blade and the shattering rock pick, conjoin, and rarely does a fight evoke such pressing magnitude, void of the relentless smear of hype; this one had no forced marketing blare, none of the verbal offal that passes for coverage today; the Garden was sold out five weeks before the event. Scalpers were getting seven hundred dollars a pop on the sidewalk.

Ali was the first in the ring, in a red velvet robe with matching trunks, and white shoes with red tassels. He glided in a circle to a crush of sound, a strand of blown grass. Whatever you might have thought of him then, you were forced to look at him with honest, lingering eyes, for there might never be his like again. Assessed by ring demands—punch, size, speed, intelligence, command, and imagination—he was an action poet, the equal of the best painting you could find, or a Mozart who failed to die too early. If that is overstatement, disfiguring the finer arts by association with a brute game, consider the mudslide of purple that attaches to his creative lessers in other fields, past and present; Ali was physical art, belonged alone in a museum of his own. I was extremely fond of him, of his work, of the decent side of his nature, and jaundiced on his cultish servility, his thermopolitical combustions that tried to twist adversaries into grotesque shapes. It never worked, except perhaps on Liston, who came to think he was clinically insane. It did work on himself, shaped the fear for his face and general well-being into a positive force, a psychological war dance that blew up the dam and released his flood of talent. The trouble was that, like Kandinsky's double-sided painting of chaos and calm, it became increasingly difficult for him to find his way back from one side to the other.

In a green and gold brocade robe with matching trunks, Joe Frazier almost seemed insectile next to Ali in the ring, and he was made more so as Ali waltzed by him, bumped him and said: "Chump!" Far from that slur, Joe was a gladiator right smack to the root conjurings of the title, to the clank of armor he seemed to emit. Work within his perimeter, and you courted what fighters used to call "the black spot," the flash knockout. He was a fighter that could be hit with abandon, but if you didn't get him out of there his drilling aggression, his marked taste for pursuit and threshing-blade punches could overwhelm you; as one military enthusiast in his camp said, "like the *Wehrmacht* crossing into Russia." I was drawn to the honesty of his work, the joy he derived from inexorable assault, yet had a cool neutrality to his presence. In truth, with a jewel in each hand, I didn't want to part with either of them, thus making me pitifully objective, a capital sinner in the most subjective and impressionistic of all athletic conflicts.

A low restless hum, a crepelike hush, and finally the releasing bell. Four inches taller, nine and a half pounds heavier, and with prehensile arms compared to Joe's uncommonly short pistons, Ali disabused the crowd of any idea for a judicious, point-building first act. He wanted to shoot the lights out early, stop him with a cut or turn him into a groggy drifter, or at the very least discourage the jungle beat of that left hook. It surprised but made eminent sense once you saw him unfurl his plan. He couldn't risk trying to dance Joe into dawn. His body was not built for that approach anymore. He was a blend of hitter, when legs were planted, and flyer—but for fifteen rounds? He had to conserve and blast. Time after time, Ali set and laid out an enfilade of shots, a singing sound of leather with a frequency that jolted you forward in your seat. He was working in time chunks, a miser one minute and all leg, buying the bar drinks in the next, and in one furious spree he sent a shower of spray from Joe's face into a silvery dance up in the lights, causing Durham to bolt upward, screaming: "Goddamnit, roll that head!"

Cold and too exploratory, too tentative, but ever shoveling forward, Joe was up too straight. Durham and Futch wanted him down, gloves rotating at eye level in front of a bobbing head and a swaying torso. They had worked on it in the gym when Futch stretched a line of rope from corner to corner, an effort to force his body down and his head mobile. Over and under, over and under the rope, he swayed and popped at a quick tempo; he must have done this repetition two thousand times. They also concentrated on three areas they thought could put them over: the kind of conditioning that Ali had never seen before; a steady hammering of Ali's deltoid high on the left arm that would ultimately drop his jab to half-mast; and a body attack where "I pull his kidneys out, make that pretty head fall into his lap," Joe said. None of it was working. At the end of the third, Yank told him: "You gonna get us both killed the way you going." Ali, up 3–0, returned to his corner and just stood there, declining a seat.

Frazier picked up the pace in the fourth, fifth, and sixth, down low and slinging, and he began to look like the fighter whose punches could mount to fifty-six a round. He was almost dismissive of Ali's razoring jab, which, if you can get under it, was an invitation to a left hook, his money shot. He tagged him in the fourth with that hook, saw Ali's eyes grow big. Ali was still getting off—but not with abandon; Joe was making him pay with an entrance fee. By the fifth and sixth, Ali was down off his toes completely as Frazier continually boxed him on the ropes and snatched at his organs, and he could feel, as he would say later, "the flower wilt" and seep its bold color. It was here that Ali tacked to a new slant. He knew his own body in a fight, knew that if he kept trying to break Frazier's will, trade with him recklessly, he'd be bankrupt; he'd have to try to bag him in a sly game of points.

In the seventh and eighth, part defensive, part theatrical, Ali went after Joe's spirit and the favor of the crowd and the millions watching, and tried to deactivate the ticking bomb of the fight. He wanted Joe to know that he could do nothing to hurt him, wanted him to know frustration, wanted to seize control by stealth. To that end, he became lost in comic theatrics while Frazier blasted him on the ropes. He wanted the crowd to know that the ropes were cozy to him, and Joe wasn't delivering hurt. He'd roll off the ropes and go into mime. Noooooo contest. He'd flick disparaging waves at Joe, the king playing with his fool, especially when he'd tap, tap, tap jabs lightly to the head as if testing for termites, sign language that he could do what he wanted. Frazier kept coming. "Don't you know I'm God!" Ali shouted at him. Ali returned to his corner, sitting for the first time, and behind 5–3. "Stop playin'," Dundee shouted over the din in his corner. Frazier asked Yank: "What's holdin' him up?"

With the ninth, Ali fought one of the best rounds in history and brought the crowd to its feet with a shock and to such a roar that you couldn't hear the bell. Joe's head seemed stuck to Ali's gloves as rights and lefts, cringing rounds of volley, caromed off Frazier's head, then uppercuts, often used against low fighters, that jerked his head up as if it were being snapped up by rope. His face was melting into ruin, his eyes closing like shades being drawn ever so slowly. Joe wasn't just being hit, he was taking beast licks. Just past the middle of the round, Ali nailed up a picture for the ages. In the center of the ring, with Joe rolling in like an angry wave, Ali got off a design of punches that can only be called incomparable, took the breath away from any student of the game. While backpedaling, the worst, most ineffectual punching position, he loosed a quartet of flush hooks like perfectly timed and blurring explosions, the kind of fire patterns talked about but never before seen; these weren't just punches; it was dark, magnetic Goya. Joe was stopped dead in his tracks, just stood there straight up, absolutely stunned and fogged by what he had just felt and seen.

Give Frazier this: if that kind of round, that quartet of hooks, didn't drop him headfirst into a well of despair, what in heaven or hell would—point-blank fire from a gun muzzle? But Ali had emptied his wallet in that ninth. He moved through the tenth with hesitancy, a kid on broken roller skates, and Joe rallied, ever pressing, moving him now steadily to his own right with his left hook, while Ali was far too languorous on Joe's perimeter. He was still making Joe pay up in spurts, and Joe's features looked as if a child had had at it with modeling clay. Joe accelerated the tempo in the eleventh. Except for the ninth, Joe was now beating Ali to the punch, 3–1 in heavy punch traffic, and in the eleventh, ahead 6–4, maybe 6–5, he sought an ending. With both feet in the air (as pictures would show), Joe sent a murderous hook to Ali's jaw, sending him reeling along the ropes and, eyes open wide, searching for balance; had the hook been to the chin, the true, sensitive button for a knockout, Ali would have been gone. With his jaw bubbling up, Ali rode out the round, moved with a wobble back to his corner as Dundee and assistant Chickie Ferrara rushed out.

Ali was composed for the twelfth and tried to take it to Joe again as Joe advanced behind a hail of clubbing of his own. "He was empty—tired, man," Joe said later. "I could feel it. But I couldn't pull his wings off. I didn't want just to beat this guy, I wanted to destroy him. Hit me, I hit you. I didn't give a damn." Booed for trying to buy time in earlier comic posturing, Ali tried a new angle for time, laying on Joe like a sack of mud after exchanges as Joe repeatedly pushed him off for punching room. In the thirteenth Ali was up on his toes jabbing, trading then clinching, holding his own, a style that paid off. For in the fourteenth, Ali's movement was his best in the fight, stinging Joe with jabs and spinning out as Joe tried to burrow into a firing zone. Frazier's face was a mess now. But visual decomposition isn't—or shouldn't be—a factor on the scales of ring justice; if so, Marciano would never have won. Put the other man in a dark room, make him bleed to the point of intervention, or drown him in points, that's it. Punch-stats, so lazily abused today as measurement of a close fight, mean zero.

Going into the fifteenth and final round in a fight that caused two hearts in the crowd to stop forever, call it 7–6 Frazier, 8–6 Frazier, or 7–7 and nobody would skull you with a chair. Each had to break the tape with fury. Ali, sensing crisis, opened with a left and right that sent spit flecking from Joe's mouth. Joe pushed forward, located him with a nice right, and there it was—bam! The crowd, on its feet from the ninth, couldn't get any higher as a Frazier left hook lifted Ali into the air. He landed on broken, stumbling wheels, careened back to the canvas, his red tassels jumping, his head bouncing in the air, with the ref Arthur Mercante counting. How he got up from that blackjack—who knows? He staggered to his feet, his right jaw now double its size, as if he had a bad toothache. Ali searched for life in his legs. Worn out and with a pitiable face, Joe could not drop him; the most dramatically fought fight in history, its most skillful, was over. Fans swarmed toward the ring.

The crowd beaten back by Garden police, the results could now be heard with decorum. Mercante came in 8–6–1 Frazier, the middle judge 9–6 Frazier, the final call 11–4 Frazier; this latter view from a head certainly made for a flying chair. Ali didn't flinch, said to

Dundee: "Let's get outta here." Mercante said: "It was the most vicious fight I've ever seen. I've never seen so many good punches thrown so often." As Ali left, Joe's brother Tom, tears in his eyes, screamed at him: "Crawl! Crawl on your knees over here to Joe Frazier!" Ali wouldn't be coming out to the press conference. He was getting dressed to go to the hospital for X rays. Jerry Perenchio, the copromoter along with Jack Kent Cooke, walked into a scene in Ali's dressing room that dropped his jaw. He had seen a lot in show business. No doubt he had had, with no boxing savvy at all, vision for this fight, saw in it an amalgam of high-test performance and Hollywood glitter. Memorabilia was not a craze then. But when Judy Garland's pump went for a high price, he saw the future. His idea was to try to gather items from this memorable night—robes, gloves, trunks— especially if they had blood on them. Was he now on such a search? He said he had gone to the room to congratulate Ali. The quarters were empty and dim. He couldn't believe his eyes. On the rubbing table was Ali, and before him on her knees, her head in his lap, arms wrapped around his hips, her long hair spilled over his torso. . . . No, it couldn't be, not after fifteen rounds with Joe Frazier. There was no movement, though; the woman seemed to be in silent grief. Jerry spun back for the door. Ali said: "You know who this is?" Jerry drew closer. Ali turned her head toward the promoter. Diana Ross! "Diana," Ali said, "meet the man who paid me two and a half million to get my ass whupped."

Nothing near being so tenebrous in Joe's quarters. He was spending the last adrenaline of the fight that had been a tourniquet for the pain, the last rush still directed at Ali. "It was wild," Les Peleman said. "He was still out there in the ring." Tears ran down his face as he kept walking in frantic circles, shouting: "I want him over here! I want him to crawl to my feet! Crawl, crawl! He promised, promised me! Crawl to me, crawl! Why aren't you here?" Durham embraced him, led him sobbing to the table. "Easy now, easy," Yank said. Dr. Harry Kleiman entered with his black bag. Joe lay sprawled, his chest heaving, his face a frieze of a lab experiment that was a disaster. Kleiman traced a light through eyes that were busted shutters as he looked for concussive signs. He felt gently for shattered bone. "Can you gimme somethin' for the pain, Doc?" Joe asked. Kleiman shook out several tablets. Joe asked: "Did he fall?" Yank said: "You dropped him in the last round. They took him to the hospital." Joe thought, then said: "Yeah, yeah, that's right. They took him to the hospital?" Eddie Futch advised: "You should have some ice on that face, Joe." He eased himself up, went over to a sink filled with ice, and kept burying his head into it. Yank, his face exhausted, dark circles under his eyes, pulled on a champagne bottle. Like a child, he asked: "Can I have some, Yank?" After a long shower, he hobbled out like an old man; his aides took a long time getting him dressed.

The next day Ali was public again; the X rays were negative. He wanted his legions to know that he didn't lose, it was a bad decision, and that he had only trained for a six-round fight. He had shown remarkable heart and endurance, now with cameras grinding he was trying to steal the fight back from Joe, issuing some subtle, dippy call for a referendum, and he was succeeding. Privately, he was of another mind: "We been whupped. Maybe I'll get some peace now. We all have to take defeats in life." Joe watched it on television at the Pierre, had Ali's comments read to him as he lay in bed. "It's not like I even won," he said. "He's robbin' me. Like nothin' changed!" He struggled to his feet. He tried to lift the TV set, to hurl it across the room. He was too weak. Durham guided him back to bed, saying: "Now, now, Joe. You know he ain't got any sense." Nevertheless, Frazier continued to seethe. A commission doctor came by, suggested he be moved to a hospital in the Catskills. "What?" Joe said. "So he can make more headlines, show how he beat me so bad I gotta be put in a hospital?"

Joe slipped out of the Pierre, went to St. Luke's Hospital in Philly. For twenty-four hours, Dr. James Giuffe had him lay in a bed of ice. Joe dreamed a spirit had taken his hand, said he would be okay. "I could feel his touch. He was right there." They told him the next morning there had been no visitors.

His life hung out there for several days. His blood pressure was in another galaxy, and he had a kidney infection. Day and night, every five minutes, doctors scurried in and out of his room. They thought they would lose him to a stroke. Durham was in London on business, and quickly hustled back. But for a time, only Joe Hand, a cop and stockholder, sat out the nights with him. "Let him live," Joe said to no one in particular. Joe stayed in a deep sleep, almost a coma. When he awoke, he mumbled over and over: "Don't say a word, Joe. Don't let Ali find out I'm here." At one point, four doctors lingered ominously over his bed. He awoke one time, and said: "All the money I made for people, and you're the only one here, Joe." Hand tried to comfort him; what could he say to a man on the brink? Finally, Joe broke through, like he had through Ali's mechanized jab, and he began to stabilize. One doctor sighed and said: "It was close." Joe stayed in St. Luke's for three weeks.

Frazier had no reason to cower, to shrink from what he had done in that fight. He had nearly paid with his life. He won with the kind of conditioning that, to attain it and keep it at such a keening level, would destroy most men. He had won with a fortitude only surpassed by men in war. And he won with left hooks that often seemed, to play loosely with poetic license, capable of dazing a rhino. "Damn evil thing," Ali said, for a moment throwing out the ad copy. "Underestimated it." Mostly, now, he spent volumes of breath on turning a funereal end, so carefully constructed with his brag and vow, into a wedding. Aside from that last left from Frazier, he ignored the crucial—a defeat by strategic misstep or gamble. By dropping

into farcical pantomime (no points for showy hubris in the ring during a shoot-out) to coax distance from his legs, he had squandered at
least two vital rounds. No matter, for even with a loss the irony was
that he had undeniably produced the masterpiece that he had sought
so long. When he put on gloves, the word inauthentic never again
could spill out of a critic's quiver.

Seven months after the first fight, Bryant Gumbel, the editor of
Black Sports, grafted on the temper of the day and stripped some
more flesh from Frazier. He was a mediocre writer and thinker, excellent qualifications for the large success he would have on television's
Today Show with a shallow, hard-worked ultra-sophistication, a cool
broker of opinion next to Howard Cosell's weaselly conniving.
Gumbel never let a bandwagon pass without jumping on it or trying
to blow out its tires, depending on the mood of the day; the ultimate
limo liberal. Durham said: "He's got soft written all over him, a country club black." Gumbel said he walked home after the fight with
tears in his eyes for Ali; a hired, weeping pallbearer for the times and
its temporarily stalled hero. Strapping up his backbone, he wrote a
piece meant to further Ali's campaign for victory by proclamation, to
blur Frazier's definitive prize: "Is Joe Frazier a White Champion in
Black Skin?"

Talking about other champions, he alludes to Floyd Patterson as
the "go-boy" of the whites, blithely sniffs at Joe Louis, and finds that,
given the times, he can exonerate him as a model rep. He even man-
ages to put some gloss on Sonny Liston, casts him as a "victim of soci-
ety . . . hurt and angry . . . this was the black man of his day." Was
Sonny laughing, punching a cloud; short of a body, not bad, this
behavioral reincarnation. But Frazier catches no slack. To Gumbel, he
is pro-establishment, the *E. coli* bacterium of the sixties. Joe calls Ali

by his birth name, Clay. He consorts with an enemy like the South Carolina legislature, where he spoke, saying: "We must save our people, I mean white and black. We need to quit thinking who's living next door, who's driving the big car, who's my little daughter playing with, who is she going to sit next to in school. We don't have time for that." He added that he was hurt that "so few blacks had had a chance to speak here in over a century."

That was far too passive for the likes of Gumbel; guilt by association was the gig, and it is doubtful he even saw or read the fairly long, sincere speech. Gumbel then pulls out some questionable associates. Undiscerning when it came to pictures, Frazier posed with Mayor Frank Rizzo, the Comissar of Philly police known for brutality—and Richard Nixon, the Old Nick of sixties evil. Gumbel would go on to a fat, privileged life in TV, with an ego and ambition that not even a mother could love, let alone colleagues.

Before the fight, Eddie Futch had summed up what was ahead for Frazier if he beat Ali. "Joe's such a decent guy," Futch said. "But when he beats him, Joe is going to go down as one of the most unpopular black champions of all time. I've seen it before, when Ezzard Charles, an excellent fighter, beat Joe Louis. When Ali's defeat is a certainty, the bitterness is going to be indescribable."

Now, two years later, Ali and Frazier were preparing for the middle frame of their trilogy. Yet the 12-round non-title bout floated toward New York like a melancholy fog, aided by the new stomp of marketing that could not mute facts. Though it was still going to be a big night, the edge was gone. The old Ali-killer Futch, through the steady work of Ken Norton, had beaten Ali again, in March 1973, with some help from Ali. Harold Conrad said the morning of the fight he roused Ali from bed—with two women. The Norton fight sent Ali to the hospital with a broken jaw. Belinda, having to karate her way into the ring, ended up in the same hospital with emotional trauma. Dundee claimed Ali's jaw was broken in the second round, and that it was miraculous that he finished the fight; always an angle for his public in Ali's camp. "That's ridiculous," Futch said. "It happened in the eleventh. Anything to deny your fighter his day. No man alive could have gone so many more rounds with a broken jaw. It would have been turned into splinters."

In the meantime, Frazier had lost his title, in January 1973, to George Foreman in Jamaica, a poorly selected opponent if there ever was one. If someone had consulted the holy dictionary of styles, big George would have leaped out as an unfortuitous choice. Might as well have placed Joe up against a wall. He was too small for George, who, before future modification, was a reclusive, semihomicidal sociopath in study. George had no arsenal of punches, and giving him Joe—always there, not hard to locate—was like throwing meat under the door. To the surprise of only those who thought Joe was invincible, Frazier was clubbed to the floor six times in the opening two rounds. But what was more interesting was what went on behind the scenes. Nobody in Joe's camp wanted Foreman—except Joe, who approached the bout with a camp full of doubts about what was left of him and concern for his well-being. His attitude, highly anomalous for him, was that of a yacht owner ready to dive into the sun and fun. Yank was worried about him and had sought to cut his gloves off for good.

"I think it's over, Joe," Yank said. "Too much damage. I don't want to play with your life. You shouldn't either. You got a nice family."

"I gotta hear this from you, too?" Joe said. "That's all I hear at home from Florence."

"Joe, you got enough money," Yank said. "Look at me. Don't turn away. You got enough money. Damn it, give it up. What's to gain?"

"I'm world champ," Joe said. "You think I'm gonna walk just like that? All the work and sweat. Climb a mountain this high, pain all the way, and come down by plane. You hittin' that juice you used to make?"

"I'm not gonna be around forever."

"You wanna walk then? Walk out on me?" He thought for a second. "You sick?"

"Naaaah, just some high blood."

"You takin' the medicine? Take the pills!"

"When I think of the shit . . ." Yank said.

"Take it every day," Joe said. "We'll be all right, Yank. I'm in good shape. Just keep takin' them pills. Promise, Yank?"

"Yeah, cocksucker," Yank said.

Futch was puzzled by Yank's diminishing zest for life, but he agreed about Joe. "He had lost something," Futch said. "Ken Norton had worked with Joe for three years, and Joe always handled him, and here in Jamaica Norton was taking it to him. So I told him, 'Ken, you're not working with him anymore. Have a nice vacation here.'" Norton said: "He seems to have lost his drive." Eddie nodded, for there was no intensity in Joe. Away from the gray-iron grasp of the gym and weather in Philly, he had been lulled by the soothing balm of the island. "The atmosphere," Eddie said, "was one big party and distraction. I changed what I could." He also had an eye on Durham. "For the last year," Eddie said, "he'd say time after time . . . 'Eddie, if something happens to me, promise you'll take over Joe. Look after him.' I told him that he was just a young man, about fifty-two, and that I was sixty-three."

Ali's fight with Joe Bugner, from England, was of considerable interest because he was now open about his dealings with women. It would be a desultory victory over the distance, significant only in that Ali had a floor full of women at his Vegas hotel the night before. It was 3 A.M. when Harold Conrad came down to the casino, shaking his head and saying, "I don't know how he does it. He's a cum freak."

Two nights before Norton III—a fight Ali squeaked by in a decision that angered many—he seemed to break a record of sorts when he bedded five women to win a bet. Sex was once demonized in the ring. When fighters trained near woods—hard for women to reach—managers used to check for footprints after fresh snow overnight. Fearing arousal, the handlers looked at sex talk not only as dangerous in camp, but also as subversive. The sexual act was tantamount to Samson losing his locks; worse, it mellowed out the primitive.

After his loss to Foreman, Frazier also took on the earnest Bugner, a one-man rehabilitative stop for name fighters. Frazier had just enough to win against a heavy that traversed the ring like a trolley with scheduled stops. Yank brought up retirement again. "Damn it, Yank," Joe said, "you too nervous. I see your eyes every day, and they say quit. Let me be. Just stay on your medicine. I'm worryin' more about you than fightin'." Back in South Carolina in August of 1973, Joe was working on his vast spread that resembled a plantation when he got the news. Yank was down with a stroke, and dying. He raced his Harley to Charleston, took a plane to Philly, but he was too late. As Red Smith wrote: "Those organ tones are still." Fighters don't find point men like Yank, who preferred the high road but, if he had to, wouldn't back down from a game of chicken on the low road. Except for formal learning and no interest, he had the stuff to be a first-rate politician.

"Eddie," Joe called Futch. "He's gone. What are we gonna do?" Eddie had been the genius behind Yank, the wizard of tactics and preparation; not even Joe was aware of how deep was his contribution. Never wanting to court press favor or shorten Yank's shadow in any way, Eddie whispered to Yank, who passed it on to Joe. Yank took the heat and the praise and loved being out front just a shade more than the sound of his voice, a velvet treble that he sharpened with work on tape. Critics faulted Durham for Joe's lack of evolution, for seeming to be the same fighter who first walked into the gym. That overlooked the obvious, that he was set in a mold, performed to his body type, endomorphic, and could never be other than he was. Durham straightened out his footwork, sharpened his natural rhythm, and built him into a windmill volume puncher. Without light legs and with a disposition for battle, an intractable aggressor without fear, he could have been ruined so easily in lesser hands. Joe was stunned by his passing. He stood over his body, saying: "Yank, Yank, I told you to take the medicine." As an afterthought he added their term of endearment: "Cocksucker." An incident later underscored their bond. After the Mathis fight, they each bought gold-plated guns, not for protection, but as a symbol between them. After Yank died, Joe's bodyguard Tom Payne showed up with the same gun; he had married Yank's widow. "Where you get that?" Joe asked, and then he fired Payne.

Cloverlay immediately put Futch in charge, with no complaint from Joe. He was a marked contrast from Yank, reserved, soft-spoken, and a ring scholar. His two interests were keeping fit and a love for the work of nineteenth-century poets that he had studied over a lifetime. He had begun as a lightweight in Detroit, became close to Joe Louis, who insisted that Eddie be a sparring partner because of his speed and cleverness. A heart ailment eventually ended Eddie's career, not his work with fighters. Perhaps, because Ali had passed Louis in memory or because he really did see what others didn't (including me), he broke Ali down thusly, his view differing from popular analysis: "You may not believe it, but there's a lot of things Ali can't do. He throws a sub par uppercut. His left hook is adequate, not that great, mainly because of his eighty-two-inch reach. He wants no part of inside fighting. On the plus side, his speed is remarkable for a heavyweight, and he is difficult to corner. He's bold, and not afraid to change his game in a blink. His chin and heart are absolutely superb.

Underestimate them and you're in harm's way. His jab and straight left are punishing."

Ali knew how smart Eddie was and often tried to lure him into his camp, motivated, perhaps to deprive Frazier or to have the security of Eddie's presence. Why else? He surely wouldn't have listened to him.

As the return bout with Frazier approached, Ali had finally vacated the Fifth St. Gym in Miami for the backwoods atmosphere of Deer Lake, Pennsylvania, a seventy-two-acre spread for which he paid $200,000. Here, Ali the set-director emerged to a new, expensive level. A growing maturity, he thought, demanded a more serious man. The camp reflected to what lengths Ali would go to keep his mind fresh and interested, how deeply he could sink into a role. The production costs for this were heavy. He was a one-man economic boom in the Pennsylvania Dutch country. A three-hundred-foot artesian well was drilled, builders swarmed over the place, and antique dealers, breathing heavily in anticipation, made trip after trip up to his mountain outpost. The place became sort of a rustic salon for local merchants.

Valid and old were two words that Ali would drop in a second. The camp had two bunkhouses for his retainers, his own cabin, a good gym, and a mess hall run by his aunt Coretta, all of them made with logs. There were no benches outside. "I decided they're not valid," he said. "I want my people to sit on rocks and logs, *real* logs." One of his favorite items was an antique quarry wagon. "Look at that," he said. "Steel! Wood! Soooo strong. It's worked soooo hard." Another was an 1896 bell (cost, $2,500) that he took joy in ringing each morning at 4:30, rousting the malingerers out of bed as he started his roadwork of four miles, cutting through the lit eyes of possums and rabbits. "It's a valid bell, isn't it?" he often asked. Ali's log house was darker than the other buildings. A big boulder, painted very black, stood in front of it, and its white lettering read: JACK JOHNSON. Joe Louis had one on the grounds too, thirty-five tons of black granite, so did Sugar Ray, and there was thirty-five tons of Rocky Marciano sandstone. "My father," Ali explained, "painted the names." There was even a monument to Sonny Liston.

Cash had also painted a sign of kitchen rules for Coretta: "IF YOU must stick your finger in something stick it in the garbage disposal. DON'T criticize the coffee you may be old and weak yourself some day. PLEASE WAITE Rome wasn't burnt in a day and it takes awhile to burn a roaste." Ali searched for an anchor here, far away from the usual training sites of hotels with chandeliers, pretty women, and heavy carpeting where "you get soft." After roadwork, on some days, he'd cut down trees, eighty-five in all since he had been up there, rather proud that he had busted one ax and dulled five others. "I'm borrowin' my strength from the trees," he said. A curious resident was Gypsy Joe Harris, who was on hard times. Was he tutoring Ali about his pal, Joe?

"He don't ask, never," Gypsy said. "He knows Joe like a book."

"How come you're here?"

"He gives me something to eat and a warm place to sleep. Ali's good that way. Knows how to help."

And Joe?

"I'm in and out with Smoke," Gypsy said. "I don't know why."

Ali and the members of his camp sat by kerosene lamps at night, amusing each other, talking about how right the move had been from the smog of Miami. "All them cars," one said, "cause all that smog." Ali said: "Is that right? Cars cause smog?" One day he had a visitor named Tombs, an undertaker from Atlanta. He wanted Ali to make an appearance for Ralph Abernathy, the movement heir to MLK, now in choppy straits. "He can't even pay the phone bills," Tombs said. "Well, you know how Ralph is." Ali nodded, but preferred talking about undertaking. He asked: "Don't you ever get scared working with all those dead people?" Tombs said he was an old hand, then got on the subject of how beautiful black was, especially black women. "Not all of 'em," Ali said. "Some of them not so fine." In this period, Ali was heavily into UFOlogy and spent some nights looking endlessly up at the clear, sparkling sky.

"I saw the Mothership last night," Ali said one day. "Don't go making any reservations. Black folks only. They carry three bombs. Nothing like we got. Their bombs blow a hole in the earth miles deep. It's nothing we can fight or shoot at. They're fast, too. Move by vibrations. Move 39,000 miles an hour. The Mothership has thousands of smaller ships."

"They've been seeing UFOs for centuries," I said.

"Elijah Muhammad discovered them forty-two years ago," Ali said. "Give him credit for once. He's sooo smart. Them others were fakes. Not the Mothership. I saw it."

One night there was a faraway barking of dogs. Ali jumped to his feet, saying: "They're here!" A security firm that specialized in attack dogs was bringing some to Ali, who planned to use them to get himself mentally ready for Frazier. "After their attacks, meeting them head-on," he said, "it knocks a lot of fear outta you. When a man starts out steadfast, he puts the fear into the other man, and it weakens him. I'm going to grab these dogs, throw them around, rassle with them." Three German shepherds were brought into one corner of the ring. In the other, Ali was fitted with a protective sleeve, and in the other hand he had a plastic bat. One dog after another, teeth bared and snarling, raced and leaped toward Ali, tearing his sleeve to shreds, as he screamed incoherently: "Joe Frazuh! Joe Frazuh!" The empty gym had the sound of wolves fighting over the carcass of an elk. An odd quiet then fell over the gym, with the dogs panting in one corner, and Ali saying: "Wow!" Leave it to Ali to find such an unusual mind-over-matter tool to build confidence.

Ali soon left the silence and snow of Deer Lake for Manhattan, where he was to appear with Joe and Howard Cosell. He had appeared with Frazier earlier on *The Dick Cavett Show*, a meeting in which Joe kept silent as Ali repeatedly called him "ignorant." Futch did not want Joe to see Ali again and only agreed because Cosell promised ("on my heart, Eddie") to sit between the pair. If he had a heart, it was as small as the olives in his tall martinis that stood like sentinels in front of him as he held court and rubbernecked the room for notice. He was a tinhorn poseur, a formerly dismissable amoeba in the lawyer chain who found TV and one day would think he was worthy of being a senator. Those who came after him would imitate and amplify his cheap theatrics, then liken him to the Edward R. Murrow of sports. He became the pioneer for their license to break through their puffed hair and crayon content and to be real journalists. A model who, with faux outrage and oily, uninformed syntax, could not lay the slightest claim to even the more base rudiments of the craft.

Guess where Joe and Ali sat? Right next to each other, making it a live wire of sorry possibility. Joe, still angry about the Cavett show, while they were watching Ali's jaw swell on film, said: "That's what he went to the hospital for."

Ali parried: "I went to the hospital for ten minutes. You went for a month."

"I was resting," Frazier said.

Ali responded: "That shows how dumb you are. People don't go to a hospital to rest. See how ignorant you are?"

Frazier erupted. "I'm tired of you calling me ignorant all the time. I'm not ignorant. Stand up, man!"

Up on his feet and glowering down at Ali, Joe said again: "Stand up!" Ali jumped up and tried to pin his shoulders back. They fell to the floor, each trying to gain a wrestling hold. Handlers, shouting at each other, pried them loose. "I had to get up," Ali said. "The way he was standing up there it looked like he would break my jaw." Joe, in a fury, left the set. Futch went to Cosell, who had his "television moment"—in other words one in which he would be the star, be talked about, be the presenter of unsuspected incident and drama. "You promised," Futch told Cosell. "You are a corrupt individual, do you know that?" Eddie turned away abruptly, with Cosell claiming his separation from culpability, the canned words of a small-time eviction lawyer.

When fight night arrived, there was a tentative expectancy in the big crowd, not like the first fight, when excitement filled the air with the smell of cordite. There was no title at stake here. Ali and Frazier had both lost, might even be on the cusp of disintegration as fighters; the "showdown" element was diminished. Their animus was sensed, though few knew the depth to which it had gone. There was the usual parade of stars, Wall Street hotshots, and the Harlem superflies dressed in ermine and rose-pink coats of rabbit fur, all of them troubadouring loyalists of Ali. Futch was certain he had renewed the energy in Frazier, got him back somewhat on the third rail of his track, had punctured the bubble of confusion that had enclosed him, placed there by Yank's and Florence's steady petitions for retirement. The residual thrill of their first fight accompanied them to their corners.

They had a new referee in this one, Tony Perez, and it would prove calamitous for both, particularly Frazier. Ali came out strong again, with an economy to his moves, a fluidity to his punches. He drove Joe back on his heels and to the ropes in the second with a lead right. Joe was in trouble, then Perez, thinking he heard the bell, interrupted the action, thus giving Joe time to recover. Frazier groped and floundered through the first four rounds, appeared frustrated and unable to sustain aggression, his punching volume. A major reason for this was Perez's action; he was allowing Ali to hold Joe around the neck. "You gotta stop this," Futch told Perez, who said he would. By the middle rounds, Ali was slapping and straying aimlessly to the ropes, a sign of a tired fighter. Joe made his run in the eighth and ninth with some solid work, but to no avail. By holding him at every turn, Ali never let him wheel out his gunnery. No question who would get the decision. Ali, who worked largely to Bundini's hint earlier at camp: "Champ ain't gonna try to hose him down this time. He's gonna pick the backdoor lock."

Call it ring generalship, or sly craft, or Ali making good use of what he had left. But except for bursts of excellence here and there from each, it was a referee's fight. Perez, by giving carte blanche to Ali's plan, had robbed the fight of its drama. Even Emile Griffith, a nonpartisan and former welterweight king, was moved at ringside to keep yelling: "Let go of his head!" Said Futch: "I don't consider it a loss. Neither does Joe, for certain." Futch's anger never surfaced, but each time, ten in all, that he studied the film he grew angrier. Perez, clearly, had placed Joe (who needed space) in irons. Carefully, as if combing a pet for fleas, Futch counted Ali's stifling "holds," tallying 133. When Perez later met Futch at a boxing dinner, he asked for Eddie's support for a Pennsylvania license. Futch said evenly: "I'll oppose you. Whether you're incompetent or dishonest, either way, we don't want you in Pennsylvania."

Ali attributed the victory to the "valid strength" of his Deer Lake camp. Nothing had been settled or clarified, only signs that the ravagement of their first fight had taken a sizable carving of flesh from each.

In the ring, a mere victory is only important to a fighter and the people who bet on him or have an affinity for him. As in no other sport, how one wins is the delineator of claims to true excellence; a string of numbers behind your name, while beautifying, is only agate on the sports page, no guarantee of quality except to imbecilic statistic gnomes. Figures, like bikinis, show more than they reveal. What was the quality of his opponents? Was the big name capable of moving all chips to the center of the table, or there just to put up another digit, prized by marketing people but not by the serious followers of boxing who wanted a tingle, the legitimate prospect of no-exit encounter. Fighters like Jake LaMotta and the two Rockys, Graziano and Marciano, to name just a few of the time, were not from the ring academy, yet were plungers of high and jolting voltage.

And so, by now, was Ali since he threw his heart the first time at Frazier, whose intent was never doubted. When Ali was ready to meet George Foreman for the title in 1974 in Africa, he got high marks, across-the-board respect for his courage and character as a performer, trailed by cemetery whispers, a genuine concern for his life and limb. George Foreman! A true beast! Why, he can jackknife a heavy bag with one punch! No big deal here; heavy bags become supple over time, and even a Boys Club novice could give it a bend. Ali would never tumble to that intelligence from Foreman's camp. Big George never concentrated Ali's mind like Frazier. He knew the style book by rote. While the press might fret over the outcome, Foreman's youth, size, strength, and punch capability against Ali's descent to mortal— he knew that George had none of the volume of Joe, that he was slow, that his punches came in lethargic, single blows like soldiers in a ragged march and, most of all, he was poorly conditioned and emotionally uncentered. George was not managed or trained properly, either; there had been too many voices in his ear, in and out of the ring.

Foreman was a morose young man, often angry and given to deep pit stops in attitude. His models were Sonny Liston and Jim Brown, the kind unafraid (to Foreman) to "throw people out of windows." Ali first saw him on TV when George won the Olympics in the black-revolt Mexico City Games. He ran around the ring waving a little American flag, and Ali said: "Look at that fool jumpin' around. Who's he tryin' to bullshit? He can punch some. Might make some money with him." They later met in 1969 in a Miami gym. Ali said to him: "Don't move. I'll be right back." He came back with a briefcase. George envisioned it containing hundred dollar bills, or maybe Ali's title belt. He opened the case, revealing a telephone, then said: "Can call any place in the world in a second. Nice, huh? Become a champ and you'll have one." George just looked at him: "Is that it?" Ali replied: "You think I was gonna give you something for nothing." George went back to the heavy bag, with Ali yelling: "Harder! Harder!"

That was about the size of it in Zaire, with Ali in his most cerebral fight, a virtuoso performance of mind over the stone age matter of Foreman, as he urged George to hit harder and harder. All Ali asked from Angelo Dundee was that he made sure the ropes had a lot of give to them, and the ring apron was tightened for speed. The looseness of the ropes would allow him to hang there with his long arms so he could sway and time George's single, awkward blows or to tie his arms up. Dundee had no idea what Ali was planning. Old Archie Moore in George's corner saw it right away, yelling: "Oh, no, you beautiful thief! I see what you're doing." It was the "turtle shell" that Archie taught him years ago. Archie tried to tell George about the scheme in the corner. George waved him off, saying: "He's a tired old man." George had a fatal love affair with his strength and punch. Ali had wanted him up close so he could measure his blows, feel that strength recede minute to minute. By the eighth, Ali took the action, feeling that George was ripe for picking, to the center of the ring and knocked him out; he was champion again with another diamond to his collection.

The result stunned the world and its press, and destroyed George, it seemed, forever. He faded out of sight, declared that he talked with God after a bad outing against Jimmy Young, and ended up, after some hard living, on Houston street corners preaching and being mocked. For years he claimed that he had been poisoned in Zaire, still amazed that his strength had left him so quickly. The hard verities of style were lost on him. There is no more vital calibration. When styles do not fit, they stick out like woolly mammoths in subtropical weather; nothing can save the bout. When they are matched (and it is rare), fighters complement each other with their own superior values, and the event has a chance to be memorable. Well, it might be asked, how was Foreman able to dispose of Frazier so easily? No three fighters illustrate the fixity of the equation of style. Big George would crumple the accessible Frazier every month. He, in turn, with his faith in raw strength, would be baffled by Ali forever. And it would always be life and death between Joe and Ali; ceaseless marauding that must be confronted by artistry at its highest level.

But George, it seems, was the least of Ali's problems in Africa. Because of his long entangled sexual life, the solidity of his marriage was unraveling, and reporters paid little attention. Understandably, for the press was not riveted on the salacious as it is today. Not even the shrill hypocrisy of Ali's words matched against his actions could inspire the press. His comments, perhaps frivolous, about African women did not even pop an eye. He said he couldn't be aroused by them because they were too black, that "they could use some white blood on their mammy's side." Much was churning behind the scenes in Zaire, all of it having to do with Belinda, the imperturbable, so it seemed, Muslim princess. There was the sudden and then ubiquitous appearance of Veronica Porche, a gliding nineteen-year-old Catholic in a long white dress, without the beads of sweat on her near-white face that clung to lesser mortals; with much poise she moved by Ali's side like a queenly ocean liner on the night sea of Kinshasa. Who was she? "My babysitter," Ali said, without the slightest nod to the possibility that she might be dysfunctional to his black-is-best image.

Not so to Belinda (now named Khalilah), who knew that she was under siege. From the outside, she was a wife of perfect obeisance. Privately, she'd have her say to a point, but Ali insisted on servility. Steadily, they became more like brother and sister. She was actively opposed to Ali continuing in the ring, and once had a spat about the subject while sitting in a surrey at Deer Lake before Zaire; she feared for him. Herbert Muhammad, who had arranged her marriage to Ali, knew about this, how easily Ali could be persuaded and how unprofitable it could be. Herbert and Don King, the promoter who did what Herbert told him, introduced Veronica into the mix to checkmate Belinda. Prior to the fight, Belinda scratched Ali's face in a bitter argument, and from then on she could be seen wearing a Foreman button. Also present, in between Veronica and Belinda, was a young girl (known and accepted by Belinda) who was totally off the screen and is even today; a mystery woman who will later provide a uniquely penetrating look at Ali—Ali the angel, Ali the user.

The archipelago of the Philippines, seventeen hundred islands strung out like an arrowless bow, was America's first Vietnam, where one-tenth of the population died in what Gore Vidal calls the first "genocide in modern history before Hitler." After a dustup with Spain in Cuba, America flexed its young imperialistic muscle—not without thought. President William McKinley, urged on by Senator Albert Beveridge, who envisioned the United States as the "trustees of civilization," spent a whole night pacing the floor only to decide that God had convinced him to free Filipinos, to take them from Spain. Without much intervention from Spain, America in 1900 found itself smack in the middle of a fierce guerrilla insurgency that wanted only independence. The Filipinos, when not docile, were renowned as fighters. America would lose thousands of troops in regular bloodbaths, and the .45 caliber would be invented to stop the Filipinos because ordinary weaponry didn't discourage them. In the end, the Philippines fell to American colonialism, where garrisoned soldiers and installed bureaucrats referred to the natives as "niggers."

By 1975, the islands were independent, after having shown uncommon courage by the side of the Americans against the Japanese at Corregidor, Bataan, and all through the action. Manila had been reduced to a semblance of rotten teeth during the war, yet all the moral intensity and reconstruction money went to Japan, a fact that made Filipinos bitter and contributed to the rise of the tough-talking Ferdinand Marcos. He was going to bring an end to American puppetry and quasi-colonialism that was still, along with the earlier rule of Spain, gutting a sense of themselves as a freestanding people. It was often noted that Filipinos had one foot in medieval Spain and the other on a Hollywood backlot. In the loose confederacy of the Pacific Rim, the Philippines was seen as the mask of Asia. Filipinos had put on so many foreign masks that when it came time to dispose of one, it had become part of their faces; in some ways, their experience was not unlike that of American blacks. Encircled by the Pacific and South China Sea, the islands were great jagged wounds suppurating in the hot sun, a reminder of how colonialism shreds and corrupts when its acquisitive grasp is released.

Approaching from the air, the country seemed abundant with riches: blue mountains, emeralds of ripening rice terraces, great pools of water that changed color with reflections of the sun. Down on the ground, during a quick look at the land out of Manila, it was no less so, with its flowering poinciana trees, working caraboa, black forms like wood carvings in the fields. When the jet broke out of the clear sky into the thick smog over Manila, you could tear up the postcard, replace it with billowing smoke, baking tin roofs that shot up piercing arrows of light, a city that was sure to yield a Malthusian night terror. As the plane came to a stop, masses of Filipinos came in waves toward it. "Look at that, will ya?" Ali said, a man who certainly knew the quality of crowds.

By now kids had somehow swarmed the jet's wings like ants on remnants of a chicken bone. The heat and sun were enough to blast one back from the cabin doors. It wasn't just hot there, it was as if a central flamethrower was in use that dispensed heavy wet heat that crumpled the spirit instantly. Foreigners, finding it hard to adapt, stayed by the pool, or in bars; air conditioning was like an I.V. load. A motorcade was rushed into place by the plane, and Ali, squinting, hands in front of his eyes, left for the city, on a route that took him through the grim outskirts where people lined the streets and threw flowers at his limo. "See how they love me?" Ali was heard to say. "Never been a champ like me. You think even John Wayne come here and be greeted like this? No way." This was his kind of venue, deprived masses made for his social caterwaul.

In a press corps of about eight hundred, from all points of the world, no one could honestly guess at the quality of the fight ahead. Even after his brilliant gamble in Zaire, how much at age thirty-three did Ali really have left for what would be a totally different fight, without compromise or a place to hide if their patterns of attack held and Frazier was still, as he liked to say, "put together like a tough piece of leather." But this was going to be the endgame of the trilogy and, considering the blood factor between the pair, the probability of the momentous in some form could not be ignored. Back in his Philly gym, Joe once more had worked toward the dangerous edge, not seen since their first fight. "I'm gonna shoot it all over there," he said. "This is the end of the line." Under Futch, he was working again like a farmhand. His feet were in synchrony, his punching volume way up, and Futch had raised his time on the heavy bag from three minutes to five, a long, draining pull for an aging fighter. Futch had a clear vision for the fight. First, he was determined to deter any intrusion from a referee, and Joe would be physically ready and have a single focus on Ali's belly button; he hadn't punched to the body much in their first two meetings.

Up in Deer Lake, serenity was the mood. Belinda was not there, nor was Veronica, only the mystery woman who searched the night sky with Ali for alien ships. Once, he put his boy, not much older than a year, on his knee and said: "One day you'll go to Venus or Mars. You're gonna be a good man when you get big. Speak three languages. Talk to your brothers all over the world. You'll be smart. Not like your daddy. You'll be able to read good. Use your brains like I do my fists." A soft moment that seemed to adumbrate Odessa's often buried influence on him. He had nothing to say about Elijah Muhammad, who died in February of 1975. He died intestate, but left over $5 million to his squabbling sons, including Herbert and Wallace. Not bad for a young man who, after a white guy (he said) pressed a black ear into his hand, would found an erstwhile movement of irregular energy. With that kind of money, why did Ali have to buy him a house in Phoenix and absorb his hospital expenses? " 'Cause he's a nut," Cash said. "The old man took him to the cleaners, and they still not done." In the ensuing struggle for power, Ali would align himself with Wallace, who had an orthodox Islamic world view rather than his father's storefront hustle, though he was not void of unearthly power, according to Ali: "Wallace, he disappears in rooms."

Two hours after tenderly designing his son's future, Ali went into his packed gym for a workout, and if there was any doubt of his mellowing toward Frazier it was dispelled. He hit the gym like a kid bent on chasing the boredom of a late summer afternoon; burn the insect or slowly dissect it of wing and leg? Of all the meanness, racial and personal, directed at Frazier over the years, this one was without duplication. As soon as he climbed into the ring, the crowd chanted his name, and he moved to the edge of the ring as if he were going to explain the finer parts of a seminar. Gypsy Joe Harris, back in Frazier's good graces, stood next to me and watched as Ali let the crowd fall to a hush.

"Who am I?" he finally asked. "You know who I am?"

"The greatest!" Bundini shouted. "The king of all he see!"

The crowd began to chant, responding like one of those crowds that used to greet some Duke of Doo-Wop: "The greatest! The greatest!"

It continued until Ali spread his hands for silence. "Gorilla," he then said. He waited, then came at them with a louder "Gorilla."

"Joe Frazier!" a guy in the back shouted, looking like an arriviste Hell's Angel.

"No!" a young white woman with a pasty face, blond hair like straw, and the decolletage of a barmaid shouted at ringside. "The ape man! Ape! Ape!"

Ali stared above the gathering into infinity, his mouth angry, eyes blank, then screamed: "Joe Frazier should give his face to the Wildlife Fund! He so ugly, blind men go the other way!" Bundini slapped his thighs, the comic in love with his own lines. "Ugly! Ugly! Ugly!" Ali went on, then added: "He not only looks bad! You can smell him in another country!" He held his nose. "What will the people in Manila think? We can't have a gorilla for a champ. They're gonna think, lookin' at him, that all black brothers are animals. Ignorant. Stupid. Ugly. If he's champ again, other nations will laugh at us."

"Call us pig farmers!" the Hell's Angel bleated. "Can't have it!"

"Jist niggers!" a black guy screamed, tossing a grenade from the rear that extracted a sad expression from Ali. "Ain't that the truth," he said. "Jist niggahs and freaks. They gonna say that 'bout me?"

"Nooooooo!" the crowd roared in unison.

"Right on!" Ali agreed, then prepared for his parting shot. "Gorilla," he said. "Ugly and smelly!" He then dropped low, on his haunches, splayed his feet, knuckles waving by his knees, and turned his nose flat and gross as he mimicked an ape. He jumped frantically around the ring, snorting and puzzled like an ape. The crowd chanted his name, mindless, nearly out of hand and, with Frazier not there to trample to death, it pushed toward the ring. Ali held his hands up, then dropped one finger to crush his nose again and said: "Settle down now. Be back in a few minutes and show ya how I'm gonna destroy the niggah."

"Smoke ain't gonna like this," Gypsy said, shaking his head.

Did he have to tell him?

"Why you think I'm here?" he said. "Smoke wants to know everything."

According to Gypsy, he reported back to Joe, who was getting dressed after a workout. A neat man, he was meticulous about the way he dressed and appeared. Music was playing, he splashed lotion on his face, and he was in a high mood.

"What you got, Gyp?" Joe asked.

"He ready to be a corpse," Gyp said. "Not much left. The right hand slow. If you ask me."

"He never looks good in training," Joe said. "Was he hangin' on the ropes like usual?"

"Yeah, you know how he is. Lets them big guys tear at him."

Joe looked at Futch.

"He won't be there in Manila," Futch said.

"What else happenin'?" Joe asked. Gypsy did a little shuffle with his feet, looked at Eddie.

"Well?"

Joe listened to the abuse Ali had poured on him, then said: "Ya hear that, Eddie? He's always after your manhood! Anything else?"

"Well, Smoke," Gyp started. He hesitated, and Joe snapped at him, saying: "Gimme it!" Gyp said: "It was a big crowd. Couldn't move in the place. He hopped 'round like an ape. Said you not fit to be champ. And you smell so bad they can smell you in another country."

Joe turned, gunned a hole in the thin wood of the wall, then flipped over his desk. Futch tried to calm him. Joe, rubbing his hand, finally said: "Eddie, listen up! Whatever you do, whatever happens, don't stop the fight! We got nowhere to go after this. I'm gonna eat this half-breed's heart right out of his chest."

"Joe . . ." Futch said.

"I mean it," Joe said. "This is the end of him or me."

A land of *palabas*, dramatic spectacle, it was said of the Philippines. Nothing was small there except the people. The squalor was immense, made worse by pounding heat and sun, relieved only by the monsoons, which drove against the islands like sheaths of warm metal. Outsize disaster had a regularity, overloaded island ferries going down with two thousand aboard, whole settlements even in the city washed away in an instant by floods, and always the promise of even worse from coughing volcanoes. Certain religious ceremonies—though increasingly viewed in the land as exhibitionistic machismo—portrayed a hunger for more suffering, with parades of bloody self-flagellants and crucifixions. Even the torture commandants of Marcos, it was said, had found new, diabolical ways into the human spirit; for the very special, a special room in the Malacanang Palace that contained the blackest practices. Yet the Filipinos were seen around the world as a remarkably peaceful, passive, fatalistic people, a myth according to one dissident priest who carried a gun while serving mass in what was known as the Church of the Black

Nazarene in the noisy Quippo section, its statue of Christ black from the bombing ash of World War II.

"Do not believe what you think you see or read in tourist books," the priest said. "We are a gentle people but behind the smiles and our endless patience there is a fuse of violence that can go off at any time. One thing is that we know how to survive. We survive better than any people on earth. We suffered the Japanese, having even to bow to them on the streets. We suffered the Americans, who taught us how to be corrupt. The Spanish before them turned us into worthless peons. Centuries like this are evil to a culture, hard to escape. We will outlast Marcos, too."

Manila did not provide the usual backlighting of film noir, endemic to boxing but for a long time hardly evident. Instead, the city, sagging under the weight of millions from the provinces, threw up the feel of tropic-gothic, a place, as Graham Greene once said of Saigon, that "held you as a smell does." It was not hard to imagine Sydney Greenstreet, in a white suit stained by sweat, rolling his girth through an out-of-the-way, dark shop on a rumor, looking for the obsidian glare of the Maltese Falcon. The city was a crossroads of sorts, teeming with gem dealers and smugglers, weapons merchants, Arabs shopping for indentured slaves, homosexuals trolling for little boys, GIs from nearby Clark Field feverishly searching for the action that, unfortunately with each new posting, spread unfairly the label on Manila as the oral sex capital of the world. What other name could its powerful religious head have but Cardinal Sin?

Rumors moved as fast as the drinks by the pools and in the lavish hotels that Imelda Marcos, a queen with an "edifice complex," was raising at an alarming rate to attract tourists, principally waves of Japanese. There were whispers of the "Bionic Boy" sequestered by Imelda and Ferdinand, a wastrel-seer picked up for his occult powers; the palace apparently creaked with Imelda's palm readers, séances, and the president's own claim of clairvoyance and out-of-body experiences.

"Will I ever be poor again?" supposedly was one of Imelda's favorite palm inquiries. Ferdinand had his own interest—Yamashita's Gold, vast war loot said to have been left behind by the Japanese general. One rumor passed on to me by a Filipino cop was of the skeleton factory, where people murdered by cops were taken. Bones were boiled, marrow separated, steamed and blow-dried, then looped through with wiring before shipment to foreign scholars and labs. The skeleton chop-shop never stayed in the same place. I spent, given my curious propulsion toward the socially abnormal, a good part of the night with the cop looking for one in every fetid crevice. "We'll know it by the smell," he kept saying. We found one shop but it was empty, abandoned, with only a sweet excrescence faintly in the air and a splinter of bone the cop picked up in a corner.

It did not surprise that President Marcos agreed to an interview with myself and Peter Bonventre of *Newsweek*. That was the whole purpose of the fight, access and exposure to the rest of the world, to show that Manila was no more an outlaw city, that foreign investment was secure, that martial law, for all its connotations, was a cleansing instrument; Martial Law with a smile. For that opportunity, Marcos's share was $5 million toward the promotion, $4.5 million to Ali, the rest to Frazier. Guns by the hundreds of thousands had been peaceably given up by Manilans. Rumors were considered subversive—and punishable by death. A 12 P.M. curfew, obeyed only by the poor, was in place. Young women were no longer kidnapped from the streets, taken into concubinage, or sold abroad. No tanks in the streets. He was a cool customer sitting there in his white *barong*, made of pineapple fiber, with a jutting pompadour and a face like a folk art engraving. It was all rather boilerplate masquerade, a show, an interview done at the request of the home office. Behind the smiling coercion, though, were the mothers searching for missing children and those skeleton factories.

Marcos had a high opinion of himself as a sportsman and a man of fitness, and at age fifty-six considered himself the most athletic head of state in the world. An aide later boasted of it, too, so I asked him if I could watch him go through his routine. No problem, and two days later, standing around like a court idiot, I attended a Marcos workout, wishing that I had kept my mouth shut. "I make my decisions early in the morning," he said, "while jogging in place in the bedroom." He played a fast game of *pelota*, moving like a jumping coffee bean. He did ten laps in the pool, then, just when I thought he would ask for a game of chess or pick up a piece to demonstrate his famed sharpshooting, he was off to his golf course, trailed by a platoon of aides; several carried automatic rifles, another a holster and a .45 that belonged to Marcos. There were scattered claps to his reasonably good strokes. He was asked his preference in the fight. "Lady Imelda," he said, "is in love with Ali." He laughed: "She has a taste for the feminine in men. I'm partial to Frazier. There is a danger about him." I remarked on Ali's reception at the airport. "If he was Filipino," he said dryly, "I'd have to kill him. So popular." He then said: "That's a joke now, of course." A big bird, perhaps a buzzard, began to annoy him by dropping down uncannily for four or so holes, say thirty yards in front of his shot. Marcos suddenly requested his .45, then aiming, the muzzle flashed, the bird bounced. He pushed on, stepped over the bird without notice.

"Quite a wingspan," I noted.

"Not anymore," he said curtly.

I wondered if there was a school for dictators, so confident was his stride and manner, with the detachment of a minor conquistador. Hard to believe then, but years later the diffident Filipinos would rise up in the streets, chase him into exile, and sack Malacanang. He had, of course, never been the strongman in opposition to America, just a greedy colonialist himself, with his public anti-American patter and fever for the people's treasury and a royal dynasty that would go on to Imelda and then to his son Bongbong. But Imelda got out of hand. Having been ceded too much power in governance (she had been more effective as the beauty with a motherly heart, the Eva Peron of Asia), she became treacherous inside the corridors and finally, at long last, alienating to the public with her extravagance; she'd buy a $5 million diamond on the spot. With his reign near an end, Marcos summoned the chess champion Eugene Torre to the palace; he had sometimes flown Bobby Fischer in for head-to-head matches. Marcos wanted save-the-day strategy from Torre, who told him: "Easy. Sacrifice the queen."

Marcos was with Ali and Frazier only once before the fight, during a press affair at the palace. It was a sumptuous dwelling, with marble that echoed to the step blending with rich, crafted wood, and prominent was a portrait of Imelda set in Mikimoto pearls. Marcos stood between the pair when something was exchanged between them, and Frazier said loudly: "I'm gonna whup your half-breed ass once and for all!" He then abruptly took his leave. Marcos seemed startled for a moment; he was not used to the naked vow of violence, just the delivery of it. The president had met Ali on a previous occasion, was complimentary of Veronica's beauty. She had been introduced by Ali as his wife. In Chicago, Belinda read of the moment in the papers. Embarrassed and angry, she flew immediately to Manila. Ali had also said that "even if [his] children died in a fire, nothing is gonna stop this fight." Once in Manila, Belinda went to the Hilton Hotel, wrecked his suite with Ali gazing on in silence. A few hours later she flew back to Chicago; their marriage was over, and Belinda would get $2 million and their houses.

The fighters trained at the Manila Folk Arts Center, facing the bay and built "for the people" by Imelda. Building was a huge part of her collectomania, as clinical as kleptocracy, and she was an overseer with merciless schedules. One of her hotels, now as numerous as the frangipani trees, was put up so hurriedly that it collapsed on workers. She would later build, in an effort to make Manila the equal of Cannes as a magnet to the stars, the Manila Film Center. With a twenty-four-hour breakneck schedule, it too descended on tired workers, killing hundreds, many with ghostly limbs dangling out of the concrete. Not enough to stop Imelda; she had them chainsawed, then had the place exorcised. Her most splendid creation was for a visit by the Pope, the Coconut Palace (made of 100,000 coconuts), filled with ivory and jade. The Pope refused to take up residence there. "Quite a place," Ali said of his training site. "There must be a lot of money here."

The Marcoses' attitude must have been contagious. That thin line that separated Ali's usual burlesque from insufferable ego seemed to disappear. It crossed over, without doubt, into a disturbing sense of his own power, not dissimilar to what the Marcoses had come to believe of themselves. After running, he'd sit in the predawn on the Hilton steps and say to the hundreds of Filipinos who had run with him: "Don't judge us by ugly Joe Frazier. He's the black who's gone. Watch me! How pretty and smart. There's a new black man in America! All of them like me." At his workouts, he castigated Filipinos for working at menial jobs for a few pesos, while praising President Marcos, the source of all their misery in a brutal web of oligarchy. One day, he abused a shy little Filipino reporter who asked a perfectly clear question. "You don't speak very good English," he chastened him. Ali as Pygmalion? Ali slowly repeated the question (visibly shrinking the fellow into a little nut of shame) with his own brand of fractured syntax. Conspicuously supporting Ali at all times was his brother Rudy, now known as Rahman, a surly presence. His habit was to flick beads

of sweat from Ali's shoulders, or wail: "Preach! Preach!" When he saw
no pencils wiggling, he shouted with a glower: "Take it down, do ya
hear? Write down everything he says!"

His brother was one of thirty eight in Ali's entourage for this trip,
about six or seven who could qualify as workers, and they all could
write his room number with confident flourish on checks. He had
picked up a new addition, a body servant from Malaysia named Bala,
his latest favorite. "He's so obedient," Ali said. "Always saying 'yes sir,
no sir.' He'll go fetch anything for you. Even take your shoes off for
you. I pay people who won't do that. He's civilized." Otherwise,
there were the all too familiar faces: Gene Kilroy, the chief of logis-
tics; a couple of quack doctors worthy of being defrocked; Luis
Sarria, the meditative masseur; the Texan Lloyd Wells, who got the
women and had no other job until he was put in charge of hotel bills
and rooms. "These are professional hangers-on," Lloyd said, in admiration of the staggering bills. "We got the best in the business."
Jeremiah Shabazz, Herbert's muscle and spy; the decent Wali
Youngblood, the taster of Ali's sweat from which he believed he
could divine conditioning; the inimitable and garish Cash, who liked
to say: "Without me, there ain't no Ali." Throw in assorted boyhood
friends, groupies, and grifters, and you had a floating Casbah around
the world.

It was astonishing how unsubtly some of them seemed to live
through him, *become* him. Out of the ring, the struggle for Ali's favor
went on like one of those old European wars, and no one was spared.
"Look at the big trainer, Angelo," one said. "He doesn't know a cue tip
from a bucket." Youngblood, an assistant trainer, used to moan: "I
build Ali up to condition, and Wells tears him down," a comment that
hinted that Wells was in charge of more than accounting. Ed Hughes,
who was in charge of massaging Ali's scalp, said: "Man, I'm not like
the rest of these crabs in a can." In Munich later, when he fought

Richard Dunn, sand started to dribble from Ali's heavy bag. Two workers, like wild insects, dove to clean it up, elbowing each other, with one saying: "Get away from me, boy. I'm handlin' this mess."

In Japan, some of them would be thrown in jail for shooting pictures of nudity in a gender-neutral bathhouse, a sacramental ritual to the Japanese. A crisis point would evolve in Munich. Ali was weary of the bills, gathered them together. He picked on Bundini first. "You, Bundini!" he shouted. "How many phone calls can you make in a day? How many meals can you eat?" Shabazz, munching on a sandwich, shouted: "Amen!" Youngblood, a Muslim, complained: "Too many sausage eaters around here." Ali asked: "Who you mean?" Wali didn't speak. "You make a statement," Ali said, "then don't tell me what you mean. What kind of friend are you?" Youngblood was furious, took off his jacket.

"Come on over here, sucker," Ali yelled. "Come here and I'll throw you out the window."

They all stood there frozen like blind men in Calcutta, sensing that their tin cups were about to be smashed. Ali then calmed down after a long silence and said: "Look, fellas. I don't mind you eating. You want three steaks, get three steaks." He started to get riled again. "I feed you niggers," he said. "I take you all over the world. You see places. You learn things. Never been anywhere in your life. You treat me like this?" But he could never be the constable for long in his little town. "Look, just call long distance once a day, not every minute. Stay on the phone five minutes, okay? I understand. I get homesick myself." He was very sensitive to his gang, patiently adjudicated their quarrels, played them off against each other, and it gave rise to the thought that he might need them more than they could ever suspect. "Nobody," he liked to say, "has ever had a crowd around him like me. Not John Wayne, or Frank Sinatra, or Elvis Presley."

Two figures of perverse fascination were Bundini and Herbert, one for his histrionics and the other for his louche presence. Nominally an assistant trainer, Bundini was a pinwheel of character colors, a three-card monte dealer who could no doubt work the short con (like the pigeon drop); a piano player (usually lit up) in an old whorehouse; a stump preacher to whom the birds would listen; a philosopher manqué; whoever you wanted to see or pay for (he was adroit at getting reporters to go into pocket). His dossier was expansive and romantic—con man, merchant marine, entrepreneur of backroom crap games, close friend of God (he called Him "Shorty"), prodigious drinker, and now for years Ali's emotional witch doctor, who supplied him with verbal dexterity and in a wink could go into a clairvoyant swoon as if the locusts were an instant away from darkening the sky.

Bundini could rev Ali up into a zooming state of indignation, or make him laugh uncontrollably. His was the loudest voice in a ring corner often heavy with pandemonium, his words often drowning out any wisdom Dundee might convey. When Ali was cross, he could reduce Bundini to choking sobs; he had the fastest cry in the West. He felt one with Ali, and he had the peculiar habit of licking the champ's mouthpiece. If Ali had ever seen that example of bonding, he would have surely slapped him—once again. Out of the blue, he would bust him for no apparent reason, except maybe he grew tired of the noise beating in his ear. In Africa, there was a tiff over a robe that Bundini, proudly, had commissioned for him. Ali didn't like the robe and slapped him for his impertinence. To the Muslims, he was the infidel, the transparent opportunist (some nervy critique there), and fouler of the holy air. Years back in Miami, they spread a tale about him when he married a white woman. He went to the marriage bureau with his intended, and the clerk looked up and asked: "What kind of license? Hunting or fishing?" Herbert was now looking at Bundini by his T-shirt stand in the Hilton lobby. "I find it all rather regrettable," he said, frowning at the peon trying to turn a buck.

Herbert had little use for Ali's entourage. "You don't have to be brilliant to hustle Ali," he said. "He's a setup." Who would know that better than he and the Muslims? Over the years, Herbert turned out to be the most proficient harvester of Ali's sweat and pain. He got 50 percent of Ali's earnings, and cut Don King, the promoter of many of his fights, 50 percent. King, no soft touch himself or stranger to the bent deal, gave it up to stay in business. He'd go anthropomorphic about Herbert, sometimes with a crazed look in his eyes, and likened him to every overfed animal in the kingdom; out of breath, he settled on Herbert being the king of wayward swag—everyone else's.

Herbert was a subatomic particle in Ali's life, a certain lethal kind that cannot be seen even under a powerful microscope, their existence known only by their effects. With Herbert, sometimes you thought you saw something, but look back and all you had was a three-piece suit, a hat, brim up and down over his eyes. Others thought of him as a pudgy member of the old *Our Gang* cast, and still others viewed him as an insatiable King Farouk. Far too jolly company for a description of the son of Elijah. He fancied white women and rich cuisine. He was the hatchet man for his father and was in New York, perhaps only a coincidence, when Malcolm X was killed. The entourage gave him a wide berth.

Ali paid obsequious homage to him, the body in constant bow to the grave digger. Herbert held up the publication of Ali's autobiography, not content with his subdued role in it; he was forever caught between wanting recognition—and invisibility. He was the architect of the book, and Richard Durham, the Muslim propagandist, was the writer; the editor was Toni Morrison, who it was rumored fingered the pages wearing gloves. I was doing a profile of Herbert in Munich. He wanted no part of it, with punctuated emphasis from Durham while we shared a taxi to a workout. "Stay away from Herbert," he said. "Do yourself a favor." Why? "You want some bad-ass trouble?" Durham asked.

Joe Frazier looked upon Ali's group as an expensive, distracting grotesquerie. He was a parsimonious caretaker of his money, watched every centime, and had no need for subjects or paid validation. He knew how to sit alone in an empty room. As much as he could, he kept his space from Ali. Except for one time near the fight when Ali—where did he get the energy for such juvenalia?—waited for him to take the air, such as it was, on his hotel balcony. Down below, Ali grabbed the security guard's gun and clicked off several rounds up at Frazier; hotel guards didn't carry live ammo. He raved at Joe: "Go back in your hole, Gorilla! You gonna scare the people! Come out again, and I'm gonna kill ya before time!" Joe turned lazily into his room. He just shook his head toward his visitors. He then looked into a mirror. "Am I a gorilla?" he asked. "Am I? He don't know how this hurts my kids."

Eddie Futch confronted Don King over the selection of the referee. But King would rather face public and media jeers than the wrath of Herbert for a bungle; Herbert, through King, wanted every edge. He had three refs and some judges waiting as guests for Futch's choice. Marcos had invited members from each camp to visit. Right off, Eddie could see the president was proud of this fight and that he wanted no hitches. Afterward, Futch collared the principal administrator of the fight and said: "Look, this event puts the Philippines in the world spotlight. You need a ref who can control the fight, or else the world will laugh at you." He told him how Tony Perez had marred the second fight. He got a Filipino referee and judges, while King argued that Filipinos were too small to handle big men, not the best line of attack. Futch extracted even more: Ali's trunks, per ring specifications, had to be worn below his belly button, and the ropes tightened (so Ali would have no mobility on them). "I want that belly button in plain sight," Eddie warned again. Chalk up King's defeat to inexperience, for he was not yet the Satan of loopholes. "Eddie fucked me," King would moan at ringside.

The sun doesn't just rise in the Philippines. It shoots up with discouraging abruptness, sends hot spears to the eye. The old man had declared a national holiday for the fight that was to be at 10 A.M. The streets had a disorienting emptiness, where usually there were masses of brightly colored umbrellas and tourists going to Intramuros to photograph the old Spanish fort, still nicked by bullet pings and shell fragments from World War II. It was so quiet that, through imagination, you could hear the cocks crowing on the hot breath from Tondo, home to a half million squatters whose hungry kids often foraged through garbage; could hear the beaten trudge of long gone troops across the bay at Corregidor and Bataan; the murmur of servants at the airy oligarch mansions in Forbes Park; the baby hookers giving up the night at the scented bars of Ermita.

Near fight time, bells rang out from the great and ornate cathedrals of Manila, where inside one of them the stentorian Cardinal Sin must have been meditating on the degeneracy of modern taste and the flamboyance shown with the fiscal purse by that slip of an egoist in Malacanang. Without a quiver of breeze from the South China Sea and in the glazing, jiggling heat, thousands were moving toward the Araneta Colosseum with buckets of sweet and sour *adobo* (chicken, pork, and rice) and containers of iced San Miguel beer. They came by tinny but dogged jeepneys (decorative, converted American jeeps from the war), known to careen the streets like Ping-Pong balls, they came by *kalesa*, worn, ribbed small horses and creaking wagons, and by sparkling limos. Those who didn't have the price (two dollars to two hundred) would sit by the millions in front of old TV sets with drunken pixels. A half hour before the fight, the clamp of eerie silence fell again on the streets.

Packed tightly and sweating, the crowd of 28,000 seemed to vacuum all the air out of the arena, a rather scholarly swarm who recognized breeding in fighting cocks (the sporting preference) as well as in heavyweights. Manilans, so buried in American culture, leaped to the jazzy, insolent Ali, then slowly, perhaps remembering old Spain, swerved to their dolorous roots of the underdog, and half of them concluded that the much put-upon Frazier was more deserving. I oozed into a good seat in the second row, below Ali's corner, and right behind the sparse pate of Herbert, who had a bottle of mineral water in front of him and a concealed flask of gin. In tropical haberdashery he was ready for the safari distance. But were the fighters? What would the malarial heat and cubits of human sweat that stuck to the wet patch of light like goo do to their power plants of adrenaline? Ferdinand and Imelda, the mother of "my little brown people," looking a trifle upstaged, took their seats in roomy, studded (no, not with diamonds) monarchial chairs. Ali leaned on the ropes, looked down at Herbert, and said: "Watcha got there, Herbert? Gin! You don't need any of that. I'm gonna put a whuppin' on this niggah's head." The bell snapped Ali to attention, and he swirled to the center of the ring, his unerring launching zone.

Once more he didn't disappoint. Arrogant and contemptuous of Joe's worth, he planned as in their first fight to run the table early. And again for the first three rounds, Joe sought no cover, again too straight in the air, plagued by that old cussed cold motor, and he stayed in the mouth of streaming leather that had the sound of Buddy Rich on drums. Joe's legs buckled a couple of times in the first and looked unstabilized at periods of the second. "He won't call you Clay anymore!" Bundini boomed. With his head jerking up, Joe was seeing more of the arena rafters than Ali. He was being tagged by back-to-back lead right hands, a sin of damnation in the moldy papyrus of the ring. I surveyed the Marcoses to see if they were pleased at getting their money's worth. The little pocket gun seemed dour; Imelda, with a languid wave of her fan to keep the mascara stiff, was as cool as if she were taking tea on the palace balcony. In front, Herbert released a cocky laugh and stayed on the mineral water; some people never learned a thing about Frazier.

A departure in tone showed up in the fourth. Joe's motor was moving him into new terrain. Ali drew blood from Frazier's mouth with another lead right, and Joe tossed his head like a balky horse as he kept snorting and rolling in closer, ever so closer. Joe Flaherty, not far from me and noting the blood, said: "To the lions, the sticky stuff is nectar." Ali sensed a change, and at the end of the round he was miffed. "What you got in that niggah head?" he asked, slapping a glove angrily to his chest. "Fuckin' rock!" He never liked rounds, when he was humming, to be in doubt; an Inca in charge of human sacrifice, upset at bungling the flow of the ritual. In the fifth, no longer tapping dangerously at the surfaces of his game, Joe began to find Ali consistently. The champ, who knew every hatch of escape, couldn't get free of his own corner, had become a bug that couldn't lift up out of the honey jar. Angelo's inkspot eyes were bright with the flicker of concern. "Get back to the center of the ring!" he yelled. "That's where you gotta live!"

Came the sixth, and here it was, that chilling moment that you always looked for when Joe Frazier was in a fight. Most of his fights had it written large: You can go just so far into that desolate, dark place where his heart pounds, you can waste his perimeters, see his head hanging in the public square, then suddenly there he is, a somber cloud mass blotting out the sun. He stayed on Ali's chest, the blood from his mouth sticking to the champ's light crop of pectoral hair. Joe shoveled into his kidneys, his liver, into his heart region, where fighters have observed the pain is excruciating. With nonstop digging, a wild boar going for a truffle, Joe jerked up out of the pit and sent out—Splat! Splat!—two evil left hooks to Ali's head. Dundee said those hooks were the hardest he had ever seen thrown, and after them, Ali was fighting for his life. Ali's legs searched for the floor, his body fast becoming one of Baudelaire's lost balloons. Crying, Bundini embraced him before he got back to the corner. Herbert broke into the gin.

After much of the same in the seventh and eighth, Ali came out for the ninth with some dance, then his body sighed back to the ropes. "The center of the ring!" Dundee screamed. It takes legs and strength to keep the shop open in the middle. He had no taste or vitality for center work. Plopping on the ropes, Ali was panicked and confused, unable to time the velocity of Joe's punches; one half of you expected Joe to request a scalpel. Between the heat and Frazier, Ali was ready for the launch pad. By the end of the round, Georgie Benton, an assistant trainer, and one of my quislings in the corner, would report later that Joe couldn't believe his eyes, saying: "What *is* holdin' this mothafuckin' fool up!" The assault continued through the tenth. After the round, Ali sat on his stool, head bowed, nearly doubled up, his eyes rolling with exhaustion. Tears streamed down Bundini's face as he begged: "Go down to the well once more! The world needs ya, champ!" Ali would later say he almost didn't make it out for the eleventh, it was the "closest thing to dyin' I know." While he sat there, his face a forlorn long shot of Death Valley at the end of an Antonioni lens, Herbert tried to struggle up to the corner, shouting: "You a niggah like him! You gonna quit. Get your ass out there! You hear me?"

Joe trapped him in a corner in the eleventh, and blow after blow carpeted Ali's face, sending spit popping out of his mouth. "Lawd have mercy!" Bundini shrieked. I had the fight 6-4-1, Frazier. Futch thought it was close, but figured the body attack had been so devastating, the best he had ever seen a heavyweight deliver, that he, too, found himself gasping. No words, he said, could describe the sound of the flamenco on Ali's body. Agreed; the aural effect was horrendous. Everything had worked for Eddie, from the tightened ropes to the Filipino referee, Carlos Padilla, a brisk workman who whipped the pace to the acceleration of fatality, quickly moving Ali off every time he tried to hold and gulp for air. Going into the twelfth, for Ali the scant chips remaining would have to be shoved to the center of the table like never before. Did he even have any chips? I didn't think so, not this time, so barren was the visual above me.

When thinking of that precise moment, it's a sharp reminder never ever to leap to a conclusion too far out in front of the evidence. For in the twelfth (Great Scott! By George! Great Balls of Fire! Whatever you need to register the incredible), Ali started to part the Red Sea of Frazier's face, adding a third and fourth wind to William James's famous psychological theory of second wind in humans. He was back in the center of the apron, sluggish but effective, and determined to win or lose it all in his favorite clime. Ali was stopping Joe with those long lead rights again, not giving him a chance to get off his shots. Now, Joe's face began to lose definition and, like emerging islands from the sea, massive bumps rose up around his eyes, especially the left. At the end of that round, Joe said in his corner: "I can't pick up his right." Was it the result of that blind left eye that he claimed only gave him half a ring his whole career? Who knows?

In the thirteenth, Frazier began to flinch and wince from Ali's one-note slugging. Joe's punches seemed to have a gravity drag, and when they did land they brushed lazily against Ali. The champ sent Frazier's bloody mouthpiece flying seven rows into the audience, and nearly pulled the light switch on him with one chopping shot. "My

God!" Angelo screamed, not sure if his eyes were betraying him. "He ain't got no power."

The fourteenth was the most savage round of the forty-one Ali and Frazier fought. It brought out guilt (not felt since Joe wrecked the face of Chuvalo) that made one want to seek out the nearest confessional for the expiation of voyeuristic lust. Nine straight right hands smashed into Joe's left eye, thirty or so in all during the round. When Joe's left side capsized to the right from the barrage, Ali moved it back into range for his eviscerating right with crisp left hooks, and at the round's end the referee guided Joe back to his corner. Eddie Futch was a man in thought. "Never fade a guy who's sneaked his own dice into the game," Yank liked to say. But . . . he remembered their fifteenth round in the Garden; did Ali have another round in him? If not Joe might win it. He looked at the swollen, purple slit of Frazier's eye. In the old days, trainers—not Eddie— would use a razor blade to pop the balloon and release the pressure. Not with this eye; it was beyond help. He remembered, too, the several fighters he had seen killed in the ring. There was a sudden commotion in Joe's corner. The lover of the Lake Poets was signaling to stop the fight.

"No, no, no!" Joe kept shouting. "You can't do that to me!"

"Sit down, son," Eddie said. "It's over. No one will forget what you did here today."

With the only strength they had left, both fighters stumbled toward their dressing rooms to a continuous roar. When Ali hit the passage leading toward his room, he was draped around the shoulders of his handlers, his feet dragging, his face one of terminal exhaustion. The first thing they saw in the room was a dead man, part of his head blown away. The cop on duty there had been twirling and fanning his gun in front of a mirror, accidentally offed himself, and now he was in a heap below the mirror, with a Jackson Pollock scatter of blood on it. "Is he dead?" Ali asked, barely able to speak. "A dead man. Get me outta here." An omen! His handlers moved him to a sofa in another room.

Tears trickled down Joe's face in the other room. He was being embraced by Eddie when Bob Goodman, the press liaison, entered, asking: "Joe, can you talk to the press?" Joe agreed, and Goodman went to Ali and asked: "Champ, you up to the press?" Bundini went ballistic: "You insane? Look at him!" Ali was a clump on the sofa, his skin a gray color. "Joe's out there," Goodman said. With that, Ali raised his head and asked, as if incredulous: "He is?" He added: "Get me my comb." Ali would be a long time coming out.

After the press conference, Joe retired to a private villa for rest. He had been sleeping for a couple of hours when Georgie Benton entered with a visitor. The room was dark. "Who is it?" Joe asked, lifting his head. "I can't see. Can't see. Turn the lights on." A light was turned on, and he still could not see. Like Ali, he lay there with his veins empty, crushed by a will that had carried him so far and now surely too far. His eyes were iron gates torn up by an explosive. "Man, I hit him with punches that bring down the walls of a city. What held him up?" He lowered his head for some abstract forgiveness. "Goddamn it, when somebody going to understand? It wasn't *just* a fight. It was me and him. Not a fight." He dropped his head back to the pillow, wincing, and soon there was only the heavy breathing of a deep sleep slapping off the shoreline of his consciousness. He was correct. No mere fight, whatever the talent, could reach such carnal roots and produce such full-bodied greatness, the kind that Ali would maintain long years later had carried him to parts unknown in himself and had had no portfolio equal. Thoreau said: "Know your own bone." They did—and then some.

That night Ali was led by Imelda Marcos up the winding, red-carpeted staircase as the guest of honor at Malacanang Palace. Soft music drifted in from the terrace. She led him after a while to the buffet table, flared by huge candelabra that threw an eerie light across his face and a body that had survived the ultimate inquisition. The two whispered as she filled his plate. Never before had he seemed so pitiably unmajestic. He lifted the food slowly up to his bottom lip, scraped raw and pink. His right eye was half closed, purple going to black. His skin was dull and blotched. He chewed his food painfully, then suddenly moved away from the spray of light as if he had become aware of the mask he was wearing, as if an inner voice were laughing. He shrugged, and the moment was gone.

If ever there was going to be an epiphanous moment in his life, his body might now be the profound courier. It was evening, the next day, in his Hilton suite, his body bent and listing to the right, so badly had his organs been seared; he had been urinating blood since the fight. "Everything in me is on flame," he said. "He stood there gazing at the sun bleeding a dark, tragic red (no sun so fits a land, its dramatic sunsets unrivaled), eased down over the brown water of Manila Bay. His right hand hurt and was swollen, his eyewhites streaked with blood. He looked at his right hand, tried to make a fist but couldn't. "What this man do to me?" he asked with a rasp as he guided my hand over a ridge of bumps on his forehead. "Why I do this?" He searched the horizon as if looking for an answer. "It was insane in there," he said. "Couple of times like I was leaving my body. The animal could've killed me. That man weren't human in there. I must be crazy. For what?" He took in the sunset again, then said: "This is it for me. It's over." Had the body, at long last, trounced the ego?

NOCTURNES

Six years earlier, in 1983, when that chicken leg jiggled like a baton in his hand, it was still possible to exclude him from brain damage. No one knew for sure, and those from the old entourage loudly brushed off his condition (as if they could not face that they had been so close to an interstate pileup) as a thyroid problem or hypoglycemia. Now, in 1989, there was no turning away from it, though his current doctor was trying. There was the feel of a damp offshore mist to the hospital room, a life-is-a-bitch feel, made sharp by the hostile ganglia of medical technology, plasma bags dripping, vile tubing snaking in and out of the body, blinking monitors leveling illusion, muffling existence down to a sort of digital bingo. Propped up slightly, Ali lay there with a skim of sweat above his lip and on his forehead, with a tremor to his arms and head; one of his metaphorical, helpless flies caught on a melting sugar cube.

Images and echoes filled the room, diffuse and speeding, shot through with ineluctable light and the mythopoeic for so long that no one (enemy or friend) could have guessed on the dizzying arc of the ride that he would land here in a little hospital on Hilton Head Island, South Carolina. Sonny Liston once said, while gnawing on some ribs, "He way up there now. Like an eagle. Where he gonna land, how he gonna land?" Leave it to Sonny to insinuate, in his own way, the law of probability to Ali's streaming contrail. He was, after all the social fuss, a fighter, not stone shaped by a Medici court sculptor. Keep your eye on the wear and tear, Sonny was saying, not the ancient poets singing Greek verse to him. Ali knew the margins of dominance had compressed perilously. But his talent was so persuasive, his ring wisdom so minutely cataloged. As he often said, all he would ever do is grow old. What was he doing here? After so many realities, it was not easy to inhabit this final one, this blinking out of neurons so precious that they were called the "butterflies of the soul" in early brain science.

The fights with Frazier had done true damage to Ali, and Manila had been the last life-altering choice of his long, long trip in a game where longevity is a killer. Every organ, every centimeter of bone in his body wanted mercy. Looking at him on the hospital bed, I was reminded of his face during the latter rounds in Manila, his eyes closed with the pain of exhaustion, his whole frame coming down like one of those old buildings erased by implosions. No one will ever know how he was able to revivify himself; he didn't even know. William James's second wind, though valid, won't do for that kind of effort. A guess: somewhere in the twelfth round, not expecting it, by now barely capable of noticing it, he must have picked up a faint signal from Frazier, maybe a sudden and dramatic give to Joe's body that had not been there before, that startled him into a semblance of freshness and urged him to shoot the moon with his last fragments of resolution.

"If you wanna know," Frazier would say, "who won the three

fights, well, just look at him now." Joe, no doubt, was the major figure in the evidence of how he came to be here at Hilton Head, yet
there was more, a career-long miscalculation of odds. In one way,
he was superbly prepared for fights most of the time, working on
his body like Duke Ellington, filling in holes and spaces, hooking
his rhythm section together. In another, he was incorrigibly self-
destructive, chose to ignore the physics of the brain. Gym work puts
a lot of wear on a body, especially for Ali. For a show of invincibility,
tossing meat into his maw of an ego, he'd hang on the ropes and let
huge men have their way with him; protective headgear, when it
comes to the brain, is no protection. Why did he spend round after
gym round on the ropes? For the public show, yes, but he had
become cavalier, bored, and his rope habit expressed a growing lazi-
ness. And, too, in the second half of his career, sexual hedonism was
militating constantly against the anchorite in him.

The number of punches he took in the gym (needless) and live
bouts (especially in the second half) are incalculable, but were far too
many for a fighter with his style, though the volume from Frazier
would have been unavoidable even by an early Ali. Above all, Ali
knew the fatal extraction so common to the ring. The images never
left him. Why did he have a love-ridicule feeling about Joe Louis? He
flinched from Louis's condition, his presence a too sharp reminder of
the danger, a mirror of what could be. He had other examples every
day in his camp at Deer Lake. Hardly a day passed without a small
procession (to whom he gave a meal and money) of the ring indigent,
old and broken, like medieval supplicants from a ghostly past. Never
far from him were Johnny Juliano, an obscure fighter who did odd
jobs, and his brother Rahman. He'd look at Johnny and see his wasted brain, and say: "I'm not gonna be Johnny Juliano. No way." He'd
look at Rahman, with his peculiar habits, and say: "My brother hardly fought at all. And not even he's right in the head."

Howard Bingham, his closest friend and a non-Muslim, was in the hospital room, his eyes fixed on Ali tethered to the bed, a scene as incomprehensible to him as it would seem to others who followed the champ's radiated glow, such was the prognosis of his life after the ring. Ali had known the road away from this, the "road out" that Archie Moore had preached. He knew what the currency of earthly immortality was: get out in time on your own terms, which added an uplifting, stirring Homeric touch. If the fall was too messy, the national psyche, so hooked on the bread-and culture circus of film stars and athletes, would rush to the collision of the gifted and fate and then recoil; there was no suspense, no shot in the arm in the mundane. There was a reason why Rocky Marciano, who left undefeated, was so cherished; he was the model American winner who took it all and beat the system, and so by a curious social osmosis, those who loved him were one with him—winners all.

Ali never looked for long back on Manila, or much else, neither the deadly repetitiveness of his kind of training nor the draining frequency of his fights. The temptation is to put his carelessness into the column of commonplace greed, yet it's not that simple. Ali had always collected people and things that seemed to reinforce his state of mind of the moment, but he dispensed much more than he gave to himself; he was not a flighty, addicted acquisitor. With money, there was something much deeper. He now had a vague fear of being broke, and a growing concern, having been so loose with his treasure, that he might not be able to provide for the well-being of his children. The other piece to his seeking life extension in the ring was his attraction to power and celebration. He had fun with his chamber fools, but beyond that was the world that adored him. He had, on the interior, become inseparable from his persona, infatuated with the thrall he could elicit, the range of his cultural reach.

With only the conviction of his vanity and a shave of what he once was as a fighter, he pressed on, fighting four times in 1976 against mostly deficient tradesmen, and on occasion was aided by the generosity of awed scoring; officials only seemed to watch what he did, not his opponents' work. Ken Norton could have received the decision against him late that year in Yankee Stadium and not caused a riot. He fought twice in 1977, was severely punished by Earnie Shavers. In 1978, he lost and regained the title against an ordinary Leon Spinks. Who was going to intervene, end the self-abuse? Murmurs in his camp, behind cupped hands, suggested guilt and worry. Ali had no Yank Durham or Eddie Futch. Where was Herbert, working on his Swiss bank inventory? For years, those in close knew Ali followed Herbert, acted on his every word. Herbert, in turn, always denied he held such control, said Ali only listened to Ali; it is remarkable what a man can come to believe when his end of the take is a hundred percent. Allowing for a laggard or stunted conscience, it was patently obscene to send Ali up against Larry Holmes in 1980, his former stablemate, young with a deadeye aim, who would go 48–0 before losing. Ali was supposed to earn $8 million, but reportedly received only $4 million. What mattered was that Herbert took the fight while knowing that Ali would be sorely tempted and could not afford to pass it up.

Ali had retired in 1979, worried about his condition. He had been in the ring twenty years, and had fought roughly 15,000 rounds, live and in the gym. The average fighter's career is less than three years, and even with success rarely does it go beyond six. Seven months into retirement, his mystery woman got a call from him. He was married to Veronica and living at Hancock Park in Los Angeles. He said he had bills of thirty to thirty-five thousand a month. "I gotta fight again," he told her. She said: "Please don't. You're going to get hurt." He knew it had been over since Manila, and he'd been caught in what Hegel called the "bad infinite" of his ring life, of repeated diminishing cycles, the torture of losing weight, the hard, hard oiling of mushy reflexes. Greatness hadn't trickled out of that splendid caramel mold of a body, it had poured out and along with it some of his image. Worse, he had begun to slur his words, sometimes had trouble speaking. "I'm gonna fight Holmes," he said. "No, Muhammad, don't," she said. He was, she worried, on the edge of debilitating injury

Fighters know how to suffer. They demagnify pain and seldom talk about it. Though some fighters have been called "bow-wows" within the sport, thresholds of pain are hard to detect in fighters. Being called a dog, while not good for business, seems a bit much, like libeling the courage of the water boy at the Charge of the Light Brigade; after all, he did show up. I have often suspected that the best fighters are sadomasochists who abjure pain in their words while they secretly warm to it. Old trainers used to tell me that they had known fighters who got hit so much that it became pleasurable, that they even ejaculated; no empirical evidence, for certain, but the history of orgasm pursuit, through Krafft-Ebing, suggests that no stone has ever been unturned.

Eyes, nose, ears, larynx, kidneys, they all take horrific beatings. But their faces tell where fighters have been, the potholes over which they had to rattle, from the small arenas with the single light bulb and a backed-up toilet in the dressing rooms to the flooding light of the big time. Or, at least, that was the route for years until the species became gunned out, and now big money is instantly at hand for the kid of reasonable talent who can be hyped into the cosmos until the cable wires sing. I have seen lips nearly sheared off, eyes so closed they would resist a pneumatic drill. But the face that truly captivated belonged to Chuck Wepner, who went fifteen sluggish rounds with Ali; it was a face embroidered by a tipsy church lady. There were rivers of scar tissue. When he fought Sonny Liston and took too many stitches to count, the press asked Liston if he had ever seen anyone braver than Chuck. Sonny replied, "Yeah, his manager." Who could blame Wepner's wife for threatening to leave him if he didn't take his picture down from behind the bed?

The Victorians, of all people, can be thanked for the concentration on the head in boxing, namely the Marquis of Queensbury. The Marquis, preoccupied with all questions of manhood, got Oscar Wilde sent up for a homosexual fling with his son, and on the side invented the padded glove for boxing. The days of the bare-knuckle fighter were over. They fought a lot of rounds in those days (seventy-five sometimes) but had long rests at their whim and did far less damage than today. Queensbury thought gloves would spare knuckles, quicken the pace of fights, often marred by grappling. With the easily damaged pterodactyl wires of the hand given a cushion, the gloves put all the focus on the head as a target and elevated sharpshooting, though the Gothic buttresses, Doric columns, and Baroque portals of the skeleton would remain under siege. If you think of the body as a Renaissance cathedral, then its cupola is the brain, where the simple art of touching your nose is a complicated process.

What happens to the brain when foot-pound pressure descends on it? Neurons are little batteries that conduct billions of electrical transactions, essential to thinking, remembering, walking, all motor skills. It used to be thought of, the brain, as a dull meat machine, now it is seen by brain science as a magnificent computer that is the frontier of everything, this being far from what the Egyptians saw; in mummification, they scooped it out, thought it was worthless; the heart was the center of magic. The brain floats in a cerebrospinal fluid. When the head is hit, the brain oscillates, wearing down much in its path, twisting the brain stem and swiping out neurons. A deft brain science writer, David Noonan, once queried an annoyed Larry Holmes on the subject. Holmes said, "Call a doctor. Anything can happen in life."

Holmes did not want to fight Ali. He had nothing to gain from the bout, except widespread censure for cutting down a legend; his large end of the purse forced him to it. Time after time, members of Ali's entourage would corner him in a restaurant or in an elevator, and the deep-felt request was always the same: "Don't hurt him, Larry." Holmes had no belly for the job, promised he would try his best, and you can almost see him, a great precision puncher, pondering his tray of scalpels for the one that would get the job done and allow him to remain a humanitarian. Ali seemed stuck to the ropes, where, with his creaky reflexes, he could get hurt bad. Below him, looking up, was Joe Louis in a wheelchair, drawn and weak and soon to die. Returning to his corner, Holmes complained: "What's wrong with him? He's like he's doped. He won't fall. I'm hitting him with everything and he won't fall." And he never did; Ali could not answer the bell for the eleventh, just sat there exhausted, his head dangling like the broken head of a child's action figure.

One year later, December of 1981, just when you believed sanity had claimed all parties for good, Ali came back once more for a small-change bout against Trevor Berbick, an earnest plug, in the Bahamas. By now, there was a distinct tremor to Ali's hands; it had begun after the Holmes fight. He stepped into the ring, goaded by ego or money, who knows, fat jellied on his middle, his hand speed sighing and wheezing like a busted old fan; tropic rot on the trade winds, and the knell for ten rounds came from the counterfeit sound of a cowbell. As Dave Anderson of the *Times* wrote: "He needed a trip to Nassau to learn that he was forty." The end result reminded of the discovery by a young scholar early in the century of an Etruscan warrior. When he opened the sarcophagus, he did not see a skeleton, rather a body with all its limbs in place as if freshly buried. In a moment it dissolved. The helmet rolled to the side, the breastplate collapsed. The body had lain inviolate for centuries, and now, with air contact, all was gone, and only a golden plume of dust hovered near the torches.

On the hospital bed in Hilton Head, Ali opened his eyes, his lips parting like manhole covers, and asked the nurses: "You die here . . . they take you home?" The nurses rolled their eyes and smiled, struck by his innocence; it had nothing to do, they knew, with morbidity. He was not joking, either. The practical aftermath of death seemed to stimulate his curiosity on these days. Nothing urgent, mind you, just something that began to get in your mind when watching 15,000 cc's of blood move in and out of your body for five hours. But the procedure was not dangerous and there was no discomfort, except for the heavy tedium for someone who had spent his entire life in chaotic mobility. The nurses noticed his blood pressure, slightly rising. They believed he had to urinate. He couldn't bear being helped to urinate; the idea of women aiding him made him anxious. His eyes were closed. One called out: "Come on now, Ali." His breathing was barely audible. "Stop it," the nurse begged. "Please." She knew he liked to feign death. He didn't move, then suddenly his head gave a small jerk, then his eyes bucked wide open, and he said, "You thought I was dead. Got no funny people round me anymore. Have to make myself laugh."

Hospitals had always frightened and bored him; most of all, they got in the way of life. He now decided to tell a joke: "Abe Lincoln went on a three-day drunk, and what's he say when he wakes up?" He held for a beat, then said: "I freed whoooooo?" He laughed. "Stop it, Ali," a nurse warned. "You'll drive the needles through your veins." Ali calmed, then said: "I'll never grow up, will I?" That was some of the problem. No one had ever wanted the toy to be real, or obsolete like everything else. He was in better form than the night before when his head had nearly flopped into the dessert. He was like a faraway signal that came in and out, and often he asked, in the airports during the trip down, when people alighted by his rigid, stoic body like birds pecking for proximity to fame: "Where am I?" Dr. Rajak Mendenica, full of cheer, came into the room. He had had a lot of famous clients. His office contained photos of a senator, a Saudi prince, and an ambassador, all of whom signed their pictures with hearty appreciation for his cancer work on them.

But there were questions of a commonsense variety. The very expensive procedure he was using on Ali was called plasmapheresis. The blood cleaning removes the immune complex, which in turn removes toxins. It was a solid treatment for a blood problem and would provide an energy bounce for any patient. Did Ali have a blood condition? "He's been poisoned by pesticides," Mendenica said with confidence. The comment startled. It was contrary to an earlier finding by Dr. Dennis Cope of U.C.L.A., who found that Ali had "Parkinson's syndrome, secondary to pugilistic brain syndrome." In short, he had taken too many head shots. Certain that Ali would recover completely, Mendenica said: "I find absolutely no brain damage. The magnetic resonator tests show no damage. When I became his doctor, I watched a number of his fight films. He did not take many head blows." Film would have shown him precious little of true impact. Was he kidding?

"No," Mendenica, an émigré from the Balkans, said. "I do not see many head blows. When I first began work on him, he was in bad shape. Poor gait. Difficult speech. Vocal cord syndrome, extended and inflamed. He is much better. He just travels too much." Earlier, a mention was made in Ali's room about a comment by Floyd Patterson, who was critical of the treatment. Ali insisted on hearing what Floyd had said. "No brain damage?" Floyd had said. "Next you'll be hearing Ali was bit by a cockroach. He'll drop dead in a year." Ali thought a moment, then said: "Floyd means well." Floyd's comments were now being given to the doctor. "He's rather ignorant," he replied. "I'm going to have to call that man." But Mendenica had other more serious problems. Marshall Tito, once head of Yugoslavia, had been so grateful for the doctor's treatment that he arranged funding for a clinic in Switzerland. When Tito died, Mendenica's funding was cut off, and he was left with the bills and a criminal indictment by the Yugoslavians and the Swiss. Ali would testify for him at the Swiss trial. The good doctor may have known his blood, but he was at a loss in the webbing of the brain; once more, as in the ring, Ali was in the wrong hands. As Ali left that night, he was asked about the treatment. "Sheeit," he said wearily. "Nothing helps."

After Manila, Joe Frazier, with his head shaved to a glistening point, heavy and slow, met George Foreman in June 1976. In training, Futch noted that Joe spent long parts of sessions on the ropes, where he'd go for rest, lie back and pick off punches, and often miss the one you did not see, then it's over; this is where careers end. Eventually, fans grow tired of a fighter's survival and want the seriously new to sweep out the old. George wasn't new, but at least he'd dispatch a barnacled name once and for all. George dribbled him, then stopped him in the fifth, with most of the crowd shouting Ali's name. Frazier came down with hepatitis, and five years later came back to fight to a draw against a barrel of congealed rust named Jumbo Cummings. "No, I don't approve," Futch said, refusing to work with him, opening the split between them that had been dormant after Manila. Joe was fond of saying: "I got mugged by the ref in the second Ali fight, and Futch took Manila away from me." He particularly resented what Eddie had said after the third fight: "Ali's too strong for him now, and Joe's too small." When Joe later took some of his fighters to North Carolina, Eddie was there and Joe just gave him a curt nod of acknowledgment.

Frazier's life settled into the Broad Street Gym, a local fixture in the rough precinct where he had begun. His life fell into a groove, working with his fighters, checking into hotels, minding clocks and schedules. He had bought the gym from Cloverlay for $75,000 along with the remaining fighters under contract to the syndicate. Among his first fighters was a then-promising Duane Bobick, a white heavyweight; nothing more arouses ownership interest, and Faustian pacts are made in the endless search for one. Joe was getting him ready for a workout and slipped a right hand glove on his left hand. Accidental, but Bobick looked at him with disgust and said: "Yeah, and you want to be a trainer?" Bobick disappointed; white heavyweights invariably break your heart. But Joe learned that you can't be friends with fighters, that he'd have to grow a new, tough hide in a new, subtle game. He'd adopt the method used by Yank Durham on him, clever but definitely not subtle. Yank insisted on obedience and punctuality, no lip and industry; even Yank's voice scared Joe.

Frazier began to train his son Marvis; no problem with the dogma there. Marvis was a heavyweight, a good boxer who Joe tried to turn into a prototype of himself. Eventually, he'd get out of the ring with $1 million in total earnings. But Joe was having trouble with other young fighters. They didn't want to be told what to do, when to do it. He lost a couple of good amateurs to others, and didn't like it much; so much for loyalty, they didn't even allow him to make an offer. He had not charged managers for training their fighters in his gym, now he would. "You don't go to General Motors," he said, "build a car and say it's yours. Same thing at my gym. If you come here and learn, I want to make money back." He had a young phenom, Bert Cooper, "a natural hitting machine." Big things were ahead, then he lost Cooper to coke and the streets. Joe began to despise drugs, and would find how close to home they could touch.

One of his prizes was Chandler Durham, a light-heavy and the son of Yank. He threw himself into the shaping of Chandler. "The boy could fight," says Burt Watson, Frazier's business manager. "But Joe just couldn't bring him into line. He called Joe names, and Joe took it. He thought he was Joe's equal. Joe would shake his head and say: 'Your daddy's spittin' in the grave at the things you're doin'. Chandler, too, was gobbled up by the environment. Chandler was a friend of Joe Jr., whom Frazier guarded like a Doberman. Joe Jr. was five-five, 147 pounds, and everyone who saw him not only thought he was a duplicate of Joe, but also found him better; his ring record was 15–0. "He positively walked through people," says Watson. "One of the greatest talents I've ever seen." Frazier knew it, his heart pounded with recognition of himself; he was alive, back at the hunt again. Until Joe Jr. slipped into a haze of drugs, with Frazier cruising the night streets in his car, looking for him, desperately trying to break his fall; he couldn't. Joe Jr. got into trouble and was sent to prison for three years. Mentally, it leveled Joe to his knees.

Marvis was the opposite of Joe Jr., listening to his father's every word. Joe once told him: "If the speed limit is thirty, you do twenty-five. If you're ever stopped, step out of the car with your hands up. If you're with buddies, tell 'em to cut out the laughing and pay attention to the officer. Say yes sir, no sir." Marvis was stopped and got out with hands up. The cop just looked at him, asking: "What're you doing, son?" Marvis said: "What my daddy told me." Who is Daddy? Smokin' Joe Frazier. The cop said, laughing: "Get back in the car . . . and give him my best." Always practical, Marvis knew that he did not have the motivation and the destructive instinct of his father, and he sensibly left the ring early after being bopped quickly by Mike Tyson; he became a preacher. Florence, Joe's wife, was never keen on Joe fighting, let alone Marvis. The two argued often over Marvis as a fighter and Joe's nightlife, and the final break came when Joe told the family he had had two children by another woman. "When a marriage is gone," Joe said, "it's gone. Hey, I wasn't easy. I know that."

A Gullah himself, Burt Watson first met Joe in 1990 at a wedding. Aside from his gym, Frazier owned a limo business and was filling in for a driver with a hangover. The two became fast friends, hit the clubs every night until Burt couldn't handle it anymore. "I was showing up loaded at work, bent out of shape," says Burt. "So I couldn't keep up with him anymore. I jokingly told him: 'Hire me, or leave me the hell alone.'" Burt joined him as business manager. Joe fired the remaining people from Cloverlay, saying: "These are people who have not done me justice." Frazier's name had not been in circulation. Burt got him on the autograph circuit, where he'd make three thousand dollars a session, packaged him for commercials, got him into the money flow. "We worked together for ten years," says Burt, "and I was his shoes and his pants. But nothing seemed to make him happy."

Joe had a reputation as a two-fisted drinker around town. "Sure, he drank," says Burt, "but, you know, I never saw him drunk. Four or five of us would be in a place, and he'd take all the drinks, a wine, a vodka, whiskey and brandy, then put them in one big glass and belt it down. He called it his Man or Mouse drink. Joe was a real accessible guy. There's not a legend you can walk up to and be friendly. I saw Dr. J. out one night, and if you got near him you'd get your leg broke. Not with Joe. Some places were rough. I'd say, 'Let's get outta here . . . I don't care how good your left hook is.' Nothing to get a call from Twenty-third and Columbia, the roughest area in Philly, and there he is sitting there and buying drinks for people with no teeth, with wigs on and twirling guns. Nobody gave him trouble. He has the body of a freak, very hard. I accidentally ran into him in the gym, and I saw stars." What about his eyesight? "He couldn't see past my fingers. I had to be right on top of him. In the gym, he worked the light and heavy bags with bare fists. You know how that feels? He once got an inch and a half cut on his hand, not in the gym, and he just poured booze on it. He's settled back now, though. Thank the good Lord."

Watson could never understand Joe's attitude about money. He was an easy touch in the gym, even loaned guys five thousand dollars, then complained about only making eight thousand one long day for doing autographs. "Joe," Burt said, "I bring the money in the front door, and you send it out the back." Says Burt: "One time Joe was peeling off a few bills for a guy in the gym. The guy went for the whole roll, but turned the wrong way. Right into Joe's left, and there he was on the floor moaning and unable to walk." The pair traveled constantly, and Burt remembers an afternoon when a trooper stopped them in North Carolina. Joe promptly showed him his license and registration.

"Are you Joseph Frazier?" the trooper asked.

Joe nodded.

"Do you know you were speeding?"

"Yeah," Joe said. "Doin' a 120."

"Where you from?"

"West Philly," Joe said.

"Spell it," the trooper said.

"That's not my job. I get paid for beatin' people up."

Joe took the ticket, got back in the car, mumbling: "Smart mothafucker."

When a lion no longer hunts or roams, the smallest insects begin to eat it alive, reducing and devouring. Frazier, Watson observed, was being torn up inside. He couldn't let Manila or Ali go. "On a five-hundred-mile trip," says Burt, "that can get mighty tiring, hearing about Ali. We were on our way to Florida once, and I happened to pay a small compliment to Ali. Joe squealed a turn into a gas station. I got out, looked up and he's speeding away. Where was he going? I was in the middle of nowhere. Do you know, I waited two hours there. Finally he comes back and says, 'Get your ass in here. Some things best left unsaid.' This was, mind you, almost twenty years since

Manila. For a long time, I didn't understand what was eating at him, then I did. Ali doesn't know how deep he cut into Joe. You don't do to a man what he did to Joe where we come from. You never have to wonder what Joe's thinking. He never mopes or gets depressed. He says what's on his mind. To Joe, it was total betrayal by Ali. The acclaim Ali gets eats at him. Joe is the only legend still disrespected. Ali robbed him of who he is. To a lot of people in this city, Joe's still ignorant, slow-speaking, dumb and ugly. The tag never leaves him. Ali can't even talk, and he's still the prize. I saw it at Joe's Hall of Fame induction in 1989. Ali was there."

Watson adds: "It was Joe's night, and here it was all about Ali. The crowd acted like it wanted Joe to go away. He just couldn't shake Ali, not even in the museum display where their paychecks from the first fight were together, their gloves, everything. Watching the evening progress, Joe just lowered his head and shook his head. It hurt. People have only seen one Joe, the one created by Ali. If you're a man, that's going to get to you in a big way. It would me. Look at Philly, murals are all over the place. Dr. J. Patti LaBelle. Marion Anderson. Frank Rizzo. Where's Joe? What's worse, they wanted to erect a monument to a fighter to reflect the struggle of the common man. What do they put up? A statue of Sylvester Stallone, Rocky, not even real, when they have a total example in Joe Frazier. You tell me. A movie character big as life next to the sports arena. Part of it is racism and disrespect for Joe. Funny thing. Joe is like Ali now. Doing all the talking. Odd. If I could get them together, Joe wouldn't forgive, and Ali, in his condition, wouldn't know how."

Burt remembers the coldness of Frazier at the Night of a Thousand Stars, a ceremony for athletes at Radio City in New York. Everyone was there: Joe DiMaggio, Willie Mays, Dr. J., Wilt Chamberlain, Mickey Mantle, and so on. "I was helping Joe get dressed," says Watson. "So many names there. And there was Ali, over in a corner by himself, no one talking to him. DiMaggio looked over, then quickly turned away. But Joe kept a view of him out of the corner of his eye. You know those vests for formal dress? Ali had it in his hand and was trying to tie it around his neck like a tie. I wanted to help him. But I couldn't, not with Joe there. So I finish with Joe, and show him his place in line. I go back, and Ali's still trying to tie the vest around his neck. I gotta tell ya, I almost lost it, looking at him. I went over and said: 'Here, lemme help you, champ.' I put the vest on properly, then his jacket. He mumbled something and left. Had Joe seen that, I'd've been out of a job."

Watson got caught in the financial crossfire between Joe and Florence, and got fired for it. "I hold no grudge," says Burt. "He's a lonely, bent guy in some ways, close and then not close, cheap and then not cheap. He trusts no one. Ali's influenced Joe so much he's determined the man he is today. A couple of ghosts, if you ask me. One is still in the ring in Manila, the other doesn't even know there was a Manila. It was a bad reckoning for both, that day."

Frazier had years before tried to break a sword on the head of Eddie Futch, too; not easy to do. Eddie had opposed his return with Jumbo Cummings and drew Joe's anger when Eddie, as just an adviser, told Joe that Marvis was too green to face Larry Holmes. Joe told others: "He never did anything for me except collect fifteen percent of my purse. Eddie can't train nobody. He was just there to wipe me down." This was not about Marvis, Eddie knew, it was the Frazier-Ali thing, that last round in Manila that Joe wouldn't forget. Eddie bided his time.

In Vegas for the Marvis-Holmes fight, they went on a radio show together. Eddie refused to confront him, then Joe got bolder and bolder, until Futch opened up on him. He told him of his relationship with Yank Durham, how Yank followed what he said on all matters. "But Yank was my friend and your manager," he said, "and I never wanted to take credit. I made more money than you think." By now, Frazier was off balance, he was hearing new information. "And why did you call me every time a decision was needed?" Eddie asked. Joe backed off, and they just skirted the edges of Manila, neither now wanting to escalate the argument. Even so, when Frazier was in a mood usually brought on by a comment about Ali, he would excoriate Futch. He had been too soft to have been in charge. Yank would have sent him out for the fifteenth in Manila. "Don't talk to me about Eddie Futch," Joe said. "He became a big hero with the press. Such a caring man. Don't talk to me about him." Nobody had; it was as if he had been talking to himself.

Frazier seemed to have become increasingly unpopular in Philly. Marvis and Joe's daughter Jacqui, a lawyer, handle his business, and they have alienated the local press and organizations with their demands attached to access and money. For his part, he feels the press gives him no respect. He was much ridiculed over an action he took concerning a land deal Cloverlay made long ago. Joe had received $80,000 from the syndicate as his share of the sale. Now, he was claiming in a suit that he had been robbed of the land. He sent letters to seven hundred homeowners, for years entrenched in a township, saying that he owned the land and wanted payment for it. They had a lot of fun with that one, some of them parading with signs reading: "Hey, Joe, we won't go!" It was a frivolous action that reinforced the idea that he was none too bright.

In 1998, at 3:30 A.M., he was arrested for driving under the influence. He was acquitted the same year. Then he filed a civil suit against the city for racial profiling. At trial recently, Joe took the stand. "What have I done to deserve this?" he asked. "Philadelphia police and I have grown up together." He began to sob. He said he had had root canal surgery earlier in the day, and he was taking pain medicine, cough drops and Listerine to keep his mouth fresh. Handcuffed, he said, he was made to kneel for thirty minutes in back of the police car, causing pain and aggravation to old boxing injuries. The cop said he had bloodshot eyes, "slurred speech" (an upset there; did he expect to hear an ancient Greek orator?), and was incoherent. "He swayed back and forth," the cop said. "It appeared he was going to fall over." A witness for Joe testified that he "stumbled" because he had had a toe amputated. The jury, six whites and two blacks, returned with a defeat for Joe, quickly short-circuiting a sellout of the Merck Manual of Symptoms to potential DWI candidates.

Burt Watson was asked if Joe might have been drinking. "I don't know," Watson said. "He has a lot of serious health problems. I don't think he drinks much anymore." He was also asked about Gypsy Joe Harris, how he later emerged in Frazier's life. "Joe," he said, "always had a soft spot for Gyp. He felt bad about his life. Homeless. Just short of being totally blind. He was kicked out of the gym over and over for having drugs and booze. He finally kicked cocaine, and Joe let him back in to help train fighters. Joe said: 'The first time I see a bottle . . . you're out.'" Did Joe help him with money? "I guess so," Burt said. "But sometimes Joe never looked to help people close to him. Anyway, he was kicked out again, and several days later he was seeking to get back, and he died of a heart attack just steps from the gym door, damn near in Joe's arms." Frazier should have been thankful to Gyp. If it was true that Joe had been blind in his left eye his whole career, that Gypsy knew and never sold him out as he so easily could have done out of bitterness over his own aborted career. With one word, Joe would never have come to be haunted by Ali or Manila, would have been sentenced for life to chopping heads off of cattle.

In the late eighties, Ali was in Utah in political support of conservative senator Orrin Hatch, which meant he showed up in a crowd and waved; he was certainly not politically literate. He had the urge to move while staying at his inn, went outside, looked up at the jewelry of the big night sky, and began walking. He could see the cars, not many at 3 A.M., crawl toward him on the blacktop, until their headlights would fill up his eyes, and they'd swoosh by and vibrate his body. It was "scary" out there, he said. "So dark. A wolf out there? Wild dogs? Can't see anything. Gotta look down at the white line in the middle of the road. Soooo quiet, it's really scary." On the way—where was he going?—he'd kneel and pray for his mother, or do exercises. Five miles out, he turned back for his hotel, arriving with the sun coming up. What was he doing out there? Any guess will do. It may not even have happened, could be he just wanted to tell himself a scary story.

What he was doing with Orrin Hatch, a politician who at one time would have put him in Leavenworth on bread and water, was not much clearer. Ali's life now, beyond the circus, seemed a cratered dreamscape. And out of each crater popped a manipulative figure to lead the most dedicated of followers, an unorganized manipulator himself (any scheme used to gather his attention), into a newer reality. The old entourage was a child's diversion, a game compared to the new ones that jerked his strings. Arthur Morrison, among others, comes readily to mind, Ali's deal-a-minute sidekick for a while, who ended up in a Manhattan court trial for making threatening phone calls to former girlfriends and bomb threats to institutions, including a police station. Ali, the seeming professional friend of the accused, did not testify for him, though he would for many others, including Mike Tyson. Ali and Morrison had been together in cologne, shoe polish, and powdered milk business, all of which lost money—other people's. But Morrison dropped Ali's name while on the stand, repeatedly bringing up their unproductive trip to Iraq in 1990 to secure the release of hostages held by Saddam Hussein as human shields. Arthur was found guilty and sentenced to seventeen years.

But Morrison was a piker next to Richard Hirschfeld, the reason why Ali was out there allied with Senator Hatch. Hirschfeld was a fast talker, a lawyer who liked to play with a yo-yo, had extensive Middle East connections, and was generally viewed and passed off by himself as one of those endless men with the secrets in Washington, almost an international Harry Lime in *The Third Man*—without the false penicillin. The SEC knew him well. He had been in front of its tribunal a number of times for allegedly improper business dealings, and in 1986 was permanently barred from practicing before the SEC. He was a close friend of Mohammad Fassi, the Saudi sheik who had shot to fame with a wild divorce and his talent for painting genitalia on the statues on his Beverly Hills lawn. He was also a good friend and lawyer to Ferdinand Marcos, whom he secretly taped. Marcos had been driven from the Philippines, and now, according to Hirschfeld, was mounting an invasion of the country. He took the tapes to Capitol Hill. Marcos claimed a breach of lawyer-client association and extortion. Nelson Boon, a partner with Ali and Hirschfeld in an auto factory construction, said: "Hirschfeld uses Ali as a prop, a door opener to big operators."

In June of 1988, the *Washington Post* ran a news account of Ali, out of nowhere, talking to one of its reporters on the phone. He appeared to have a hard grasp of politics, current states' rights issues, and federal judgeships being contested. Noses of reporters who had known Ali for a long time began to twitch, particularly that of Dave Kindred, a columnist for the *Atlanta Journal*. How could this be? Ali had had the political insight of an infant. Kindred investigated. What or who was behind the new Ali, the wily Washington lobbyist who seemed to have the ear of everyone from Strom Thurmond (their only common ground was Dr. Mendenica) to Orrin Hatch and Arlen Specter? Specter's wife even baked Ali a double-chocolate–mousse pie. For a while, Ali was known only as a

brilliant phone presence to the senators—that is, until he began to
show up on Capitol Hill.

When he materialized, the senators, confronted by the empty shell
of Ali, sought running room, guarding their flanks with comments like,
"Well, he's just quiet," or "sometimes he doesn't take his medicine."
One of Sam Nunn's aides, noting Ali's listlessness and Hirschfeld's rat
terrier presence of aggressive quizzing, wondered: "Is Ali being carted
around like a puppet?" Senator John Warner's press secretary, Peter
Loomis, said: "Hirschfeld did all the talking. Ali was yawning. He could
barely focus his eyes." Ali and Hirschfeld had spent the entire summer
on Capitol Hill. What were they after, or more likely, what was
Hirschfeld after? Ali had had a suit seeking $50 million in damages
from a "wrongful conviction in the 1967 draft evasion case." It was
defeated, and now Hatch and others, like W. C. Fields with the Bible,
were looking for loopholes to remedy it. Some of the senators even
suspected that Hirschfeld, who reportedly could do a flawless impression of Ali, had impersonated Ali in their prior telephone conversations. When confronted with these suspicions, Ali vascillated on the
alleged fraud. "I don't know nothin' 'bout politics," he said. Then, on
the Capitol steps in front of the press, he later denied the allegation
and said he had trust in Hirschfeld. "I have no bosses," he said. "I'm
the boss." Hirschfeld also denied the allegations. From the day he
joined the Black Muslims, that has to be one of the big self-delusions
of all time. Through Ali, Hirschfeld had sought the damages and to
make himself an indispensable broker to the Republican Party.

Thomas Smith, a Detroit lawyer involved in the auto factory deal,
cut to the center of Ali, saying: "Ali baffles me. I don't know how I
feel. He's gullible and easily led by Hirschfeld. At the same time, I
perceived Ali laughing at everybody. He's so aloof. He doesn't care
enough about people. Ali seems to be in a world by himself, and he
looks out of it at you once in a while." Wilfred Sheed, in his long ago

book on Ali, had him pegged right, too. "He wants to tell everything, and he wants to hide everything. There is evidence to support every Ali theory. This is confusion of Ali's creation. He insisted that today's truth is better than yesterday's. . . . He likes to take a piece of make-believe and will it into reality." He was getting a lot of help now, from his fourth wife, Lonnie, a graduate of Vanderbilt and daughter of the traveling companion to Ali's mother, certain quarters of the press, and a lawyer-writer Boswell who seems insistent on making the public believe that, next to Martin Luther King, Ali is the most important black figure in the last half century. Whew!

When, in fact, he was the double of Faye Greener, in Nathaniel West's novel *The Day of the Locusts:* "None of them really heard her. They were all too busy watching her smile, laugh, shiver, whisper, grow indignant, cross and uncross her legs, stick out her tongue, widen and narrow her eyes, toss her head so that her platinum hair splashed against the red plush of the chair. The strange thing about her gestures and expressions was that they didn't really illustrate what she was saying. They were almost pure. It was as though her body recognized how foolish her words were and tried to excite her hearers into being uncritical. It worked that night; no one even thought of laughing at her. The only move they made was to narrow their circle about her."

Kindred noted the similarity to the lives of Marilyn Monroe, Elvis, and John Lennon, all "passive and vain," who relinquished their lives to others in so many places, saying they'd be right back and then forgetting where they put those lives. Ali was just wandering when he and Veronica divorced. She got the big house and $750,000; Ali the dining table inscribed in Arabic. Herbert said he told Ali, above all, to get a prenuptial agreement, but "she talked him into tearing it up." At this time, it was becoming apparent Ali needed someone to take care of him. With Lonnie, he had married a "new boss." At first he had the habit of taking off in his Winnebago, stopping in college towns to set up a card table and hand out Muslim pamphlets; very unprofitable. Understandable (when one nourishes the soul), among the fifty most marketable athletes, the market has an aversion to billboards in decline. All of that would end with Lonnie and her tight circle of pushers.

Serious effort was made to reestablish him as a seminal figure, a legend worth some money, for advertisers and investors looking for a name to front businesses. Why they would go to him was baffling; his business history of failure could be a model at the Wharton School of Finance. But this was a subtle game, involving groupie writers. He had to be kept on the move: lucrative autograph sessions, $200,000 for appearances, to deflect emphasis on his health. To the press, Joe Louis had been for years a poor, broke, venally used mummy. Now, to some of the press—mainly in New York—the image evolved of Ali as just a man afflicted with Parkinson's, not a careless fighter who had had his brain cells irradiated in the ring; rather neat. If you needed a good picture that speaks to the new channeling, it was there in a photo of him taken in a New York magic shop: Ali dressed up as the medieval trickster Merlin. The circus had been lunatic in the early days, but now, with heaving and puffing, a new one was going up with meticulous calibration. Ali would be on the road over two hundred days a year.

There was no telling where he would turn up next, rigid and glazed of eye, the "man of peace and good will." He showed up in Vietnam at long last, he showed up at the bedside of a London fighter named Michael Watson, doing the Ali Shuffle for the brain-damaged kid. He was found in Syria deep into fasting, flanked by doctors who were monitoring him and saying: "He's much better. He's off the thirty pills he takes a day." In Egypt, he was said to have made out a $750 traveler's check to a street urchin. We even had word of his ascension to the higher reaches of the paranormal, while traveling with Thomas

Hauser through Pennsylvania. Ali suddenly contorted in pain. According to Hauser, a close member of the circle, Ali said, "In two days there's gonna be a plane crash in South America." We are told that two days later a Surinam Airways jet went down, killing 168. Nothing, really, according to Lonnie: "He predicted the Pan Am crash in Scotland." Ali, thanks to Lonnie and minute reconstruction, was on the boards again—the indomitable legend, nearly effervescent to select writers.

There were a couple of places Ali didn't show up. Not of a piece physically, it was perhaps understandable that he made no effort to relieve the poverty of Bundini Brown or see to the meager wants of the poor and dying Luis Sarria, the one man who never asked for anything from him. He did show up at the hospital to see Bundini as he was dying from a fall. He could only move his eyes. Ali leaned down to his ear and said: "We had some good times, didn't we?" Bundini's eyes scraped up and down. And, most of all, he was for years out of touch with the supposed love of his life, Aaisha Ali, the mystery woman who had performed the role of a fifth wife (simultaneously with Belinda), had given him a child, and had been left to blow to pieces in severe hard-luck winds. Aaisha's little tale reveals all the gentleness, trickery, and spite of which Ali was capable in his dealings. Ali never acknowledged that he was married to her, a point that does not upset her. Nothing much does, except the lupus that has made her an invalid.

Aaisha was once Wanda Bolton, a pretty little high school junior, age seventeen, on her way to being a doctor like her brother and, presently, to Brazil on an international scholarship when she met Ali on a visit to Deer Lake with her brother and mother. It was meant to kill time, a little summer diversion that would end with estrangement from her father and deep regrets in her mother. Ali had just lost to Ken Norton and was getting ready for their second fight. He was talking to some fans when he picked up Wanda's face and stayed on it. "Have you ever seen a fighter as pretty as me?" he asked. "Look, not a single scar." His eyes captured her, they seemed controlling. He wasn't pretty, she thought; his "head was too square." She adds, "But there was this aura, he had an inner beauty." Ali said to her: "You like an Indian princess. Come on, we're going to the movies." They went to see *Charlotte's Web*. On return, they went horseback riding, sat after a while, and talked. Wanda said she was going to Brazil. He said he had been waiting for a blue-jeaned country girl like her for a long time. "You won't be going to Brazil," he said. "I have special powers. You're meant to be with me."

Wanda went home, "chalking it up as a wonderful memory." Soon he was on the phone wanting her to go to Manhattan. No, her mother would not go for that. He called her mother at work and talked her into it, cinching the deal when he said her older brother and friend Kim could come, too. "I hadn't even had a date in my life," she says. They went to Herbert Muhammad's apartment, and Wanda thought it strange when Herbert said: "She'll give you many sons." She says now, "Herbert had the same influence over Ali that Colonel Parker had over Elvis." After that, he was at the Bolton house frequently, the two of them sitting on the porch and eating ice cream. "He had dental work in Miami," she says, "and he wanted me to go with him. I did, too. But there was no way my parents would allow that. With a thirty-one-year-old boxer! No way. But he was clever. He hired my brother, Kelly, as a bodyguard. He told my mother that 'we're doin' a documentary' on how religion affects people. I was to give the Christian perspective." Parents want experiences for their children; the trip was tough to pass up. "I was filled with a sense of adventure, and very much in love."

Everyone was put up at the Fontainebleu Hotel, Ali's favorite; mother, brother, a couple of classmates. She says: "We were all living in a warm, golden glow. None of us cared, or even realized it was really like a shadow. Often a cold and distant one of Muhammad Ali." Ali put a full-court press on her mother, who watched things closely. Wanda roomed with her friend Jacqui. Ali kept going out with her mother on shopping trips, insisted she get her hair done. With Jacqui in Ali's bedroom, she was giving him a foot massage when he pointed to a bag filled with money. "Count it," he said. "There should be four thousand. Put three hundred on the dresser. I want you to keep the rest. Buy some things to take home. I have to think of something to explain the money to your momma." Wanda and Jacqui only bought a couple of tacky watches. Ali said: "You two are so innocent. That's what makes you so special." They went to the dentist together. Ali left her outside, until he spied a young jogger talking to her. They had an argument.

"Men, you can't trust them," he said angrily. "That little nigger wanted you. It was your fault. He seen your legs in that short skirt."

She said that everyone wears miniskirts.

"No woman of mine! Dress like a decent Muslim woman, it wouldn't happen."

"I should have stayed at the hotel," she said.

"Don't get smart with me," he said. "See, you give a woman money, and right away she's bossin' you around."

"Here, take your money back," she said. "Money isn't a thing to me."

"I'm sorry," he said. "I get upset about other men." He paused: "You know the real reason I didn't want you in the dental office? I'm scared to death of needles. The Greatest, scared of getting a shot." They went into the office. He asked if his daughter, Wanda, could go with him. "She's got a bad fear of getting shots." In the chair, he said to Wanda: "Now come to Daddy. Hold Daddy's hand . . . you're going to be just fine. Ain't nothin' to be afraid of."

Ali's favorite game, says Aaisha, was Power. Once, in the lobby, Ali said: "Watch this. I can get them to do anything I want." A group of sleek, rich women raced up to him, wanting his autograph. "On one condition," he said. "Kneel down and kiss my hands." Aaisha says: "I was shocked. These million-dollar Miami women did it! It's hard to tell this story. It makes him sound cruel, humiliating. He was simply seeing how far his power could take him." Another game he played was to carry little Wanda around the hotel on his shoulders, saying: "This is my illegitimate twelve-year-old daughter."

When it came time for Wanda to go to Brazil, she was torn between her mother's dream for her and the man she loved. She called Ali: "I can't go." He said: "You'll never regret it the rest of your life."

She says now: "I have no regrets. But I have a deep shame and regret for the pain I caused my mother. Having her child make a terrible mistake. By the time my mother put it all together, I was pregnant." She embraced Islam instantly, was taught how to sew, cook, and take care of a man and children. She was called Wanda X, and Elijah would later name her Aaisha. When her mother heard of the pregnancy, she was furious. She went to Deer Lake, found Ali in the kitchen; the place went silent. She said: "You're going to talk to me now! I feel like throwing you off this mountain!"

"Momma," Ali said, "everything's gonna be all right. This is my religion. I'm making Wanda my wife. I'll take care of her. The child she's carrying will never want for anything."

"She's only seventeen!" she yelled. "Her whole life's in front of her. I don't care about your religion. I don't believe in it. My child is pregnant, and you did it!"

Wanda was accepted by Belinda; they were like sisters. Aunt

Coretta approached Ali one day at the camp and said: "Muhammad, you'd better do right by these girls. They're just babies. I'm ashamed of you, Muhammad. I'm really ashamed of you." Wanda ran with Ali in the mornings. She was a good jogger, kept daily logs, and taught him how to run to get the maximum out of his roadwork. Ali was fixated on having a boy. "But when Khaliah was born," she says, "he was so happy. She was Odessa's favorite." The child who would not want for anything, so said Ali. When Ali fought in Zaire, trouble rose up. Belinda fought with him, Aaisha was hidden away. Old Cash was fond of Aaisha. He said: "Come on, I'm takin' you with me. You're not sittin' in this hotel room." Veronica, the eighteen-year-old beauty queen, was now in the mix. Cash and Aaisha showed up at the lawn party. Ali said to his father: "Are you crazy? What you bring her here for?" Veronica was there, and Aaisha could see he was smitten by her. She was already into the role of pious Muslim, but Belinda and Aaisha knew it was an act.

Back in the States, the pair confronted Ali about Veronica. "I was scared to death," Aaisha says, "but Belinda sat right down and said, 'We know about Veronica, and we don't like it. She's got to go.'" Ali became enraged. Who did they think they were? To him, they were out of line; Muslim wives were docile, not mouthy snoopers. He was going to make Veronica his wife. No, said Belinda, who knew Muslim law, certainly the one that said that there could be no other wife without the other wife's consent. She sprung from the chair and pointed, saying: "No!" It would eventually sort out in Manila after Belinda's angry appearance there. She returned, saying to Aaisha: "If you had any sense, you'll get out, too. He's disloyal, not worthy of a good woman." Aaisha says: "The last I heard . . . Belinda was working in a check-cashing place in Chicago."

Ali never thought Belinda would leave him, says Aaisha, "and I missed her sisterhood." Veronica became pregnant, and Ali was bragging that he was going to have a boy. Aaisha continued to be loyal even after he married Veronica. Because of lupus, pregnancies were high risk for Aaisha. Ali became more and more critical of her. He mocked her height. Why didn't she have leg implants, so she could be tall and queenly like Veronica? Veronica continually drove herself between Ali and Aaisha. He told her that Aaisha was there before her, and if she left Aaisha would be his wife, so get used to it. "I was batted around like a ball," says Aaisha, "and then we had a showdown. I'm not the type to be argumentative, but something had to give. To him, I was being disobedient."

Aaisha said, "Veronica doesn't love you, all she wants is your fame."

"That's what you think," he said.

"No, that's what I know," she said.

"She does love me!" he shouted.

"She's going to be your downfall. She's just interested in being a celebrity and an actress."

Ali said, "She left college for me. That's more than you did."

"Oh, I only had to leave high school because I was pregnant with your child. At seventeen!"

"I've fed you!" he shouted again. "Put clothes on your back, kept a roof for you. You traveled around the world because of me! You gonna do that on a high school diploma?"

"I ate before I met you," Aaisha said. "Traveled with my family. Yes, you have taken me around the world—in more ways than one."

In Japan, Aaisha began to ponder what she had lost, a probable medical future and her lost adolescence. Ali's leg was battered by the wrestler Inoki in a ludicrous grab for money. When he hit the elevator of the hotel, veins swollen, he collapsed. Aaisha held him in her arms, and the doctor with them gave him a shot to thin his blood. They got him to the hotel room all right, then he passed out on the bed. It was time, Aaisha thought, to put this madness behind her. This wasn't her world, all this extravagance and peacock living. Could she live without him? "I had to save," she says now, "what little was left of me." She stayed on for a while, then one day, with Khaliah, she went back home, leaving everything he had given her in Chicago. His constant warning replayed in her head: "You leave me, you'll end up a nothin', a nobody that no one will want. Anybody who'd leave Muhammad Ali is a fool." Eventually he bought her a little two-room house in Bala Cynwyd, Pennsylvania.

They would meet a year later in the Edwardian Room at the Plaza in New York. They had agreed that she should start a business, an idea she had for holistic therapy. Ali would fund it. She presented him with sixty pages of research and plans while the two dined. He glanced at then and then ripped them up. "If you really want the business," he said, "you'll get it on your own. You don't want to go to bed with me, why should I make it easy for you?" She says now: "Earlier in the day, I had refused his sexual advances. I was serious about building a new life for myself." She looked at the torn papers, then walked out, with Ali shouting after her: "Who do you think you are to walk out on Muhammad Ali! You're gonna suffer. I'll see to that!"

Her hundred-year-old house was in bad shape. He said he would send money for repairs. In 1983 the furnace went up, leaving Khaliah and her without hot water or heat. They had to sleep by the fireplace to keep warm. They had little to eat. She refused to go on public assistance, or go to her parents. "Backbone," the daughter Khaliah says now, "pulled us through, made us strong." Khaliah was a sick child, went to the hospital twice with life-threatening conditions. When the furnace exploded again in 1984, she finally called Ali. He said: "You want to be independent, you think you don't need me anymore. Get it fixed yourself." He thought a moment, then said, "I'm going broke. I take care of my parents, my brother and his family. Veronica and her family. I can't take care of everyone. I'll try to help you." Says Aaisha, "He never did."

She went to court, and a four-year legal battle ensued. He had high-priced lawyers in California. Aaisha just wanted child support. The proceedings were filled with hurt for Khaliah. A deal was set up where a bank would create a trust on behalf of Khaliah. The money would be invested and the interest would go to Khaliah for support. When she turned twenty-one, the principal would revert back to Ali; not a dime for Khaliah. He was sitting in the corridor. Khaliah went over to him.

"Daddy," she said.

"I can't talk to you," Ali said. "They tell me I can't. Sorry, baby."

"Well, Daddy," Khaliah said, with tears in her eyes. "No one will ever tell me I can't talk to you. You may think I'm too young to know, but I'm not." Ali had million-dollar trusts for the rest of his kids. Khaliah continued, "I know I don't get any money when I turn twenty-one. But all these lawyers are getting rich. But that's all right. I don't want your money. I'll make my own way. I just want you to know that no matter what, I love you, Daddy."

Ali went back to the courtroom and said he wanted to speak. He wanted to fire the lawyers. "He just wanted Khaliah to have the money," Aaisha says. "It was sad. No one listened to him. His speech was thick, his movement stiff. He appeared incompetent. The lawyers and his new wife, Lonnie, totally ignored him, going on as if he weren't in the room." But Khaliah Ali, his bright daughter, would never stop in her love for her father, and in so doing would stand her ground more than once with Lonnie.

Aaisha remembers much about Ali. She knows what he truly thought of Joe Frazier. "He thought he was a pure nigger," she says. "He said that Frazier didn't know how to talk, or look good, and that it was insulting if he became the heavyweight champion." If one moment sums up Ali for her, it was when they went to see *The Wiz* on Broadway. "Ali was always restless in theaters," she says. "He wanted to leave. Then, the Tin Man came on, and he was hypnotized, especially when he began to sing 'To Be Able to Feel.' We went outside, and he said, 'I wish I could feel something. I've never been able to in my life.' He bought a player, got the tape, and ran that song over and over."

At fifteen, Khaliah went to the American Broadcasters Dinner in New York to see her father. Lonnie, she says, would not allow her near him. She had no money, and Howard Bingham had to give her thirty dollars. At midnight, alone and angry, she made her way to the bus station. "Lonnie blocked me at every turn," she says, "but I wouldn't give up. I had a right to see my father." With tenacity, she'd sneak around to see him, leaving scraps of paper with her number on it. "They'd find it in his pockets," she says, "and throw them away. So I began writing my number on the bottom of his shoes. I'd be blocked at every turn by Lonnie and her aides. Look, I'm not the only kid of his who had trouble seeing him. They have to suck up to Lonnie. But I wouldn't bow to her. Never. She once said to me: 'I am Muhammad Ali now.'"

A major blowup occurred in Philadelphia in March 1996 at a gala for the twenty-fifth anniversary of Ali-Frazier 1. Lonnie, Khaliah says, refused her admittance. She only got to the ceremony because of Jacqui Frazier, Joe's daughter, who insisted on her attendance. That night Khaliah was up in her father's Ritz suite. She was wrapping his title belt around her waist. Ali gave her the belt. "Oh, no," Khaliah said. "I was just playing. I can't." He said: "You keep the belt." Lonnie and the people around her began to get nervous. Downstairs, they cornered Khaliah. Kalita Muhammad, an aide, lit into her, saying: "You can't have the belt! It has to go to the Smithsonian. Your father doesn't know what he's doing! You can't have it!" Khaliah says, "They had me convinced to give it up." Back in the suite, she told her father

her decision. "No!" he said, trying to yell. She says, "I was being called all sorts of names by Lonnie and her group."

The argument went on for a while as Ali refused to budge. "You take the belt," he kept saying. Khaliah remembers: "Lonnie was in a rage. I thought she'd throw me out the window. She kept saying, 'You can't give that to her!' Jim Brown was there. Even he was anxious. My father cursed at Kalita and Lonnie. Then he began to cry. When did you ever hear of Muhammad Ali crying? Never. This was a big thing to him." Howard Bingham told her quietly to keep the belt. With everyone still arguing, Jim Brown escorted her to the elevator and out of the hotel safely. He told her: "Your father gave that to you. You can't let anyone take it away from you."

Khaliah was seventeen then. Now, at 26, she says: "There's so much wrong with his situation. They run him to death. For what? He's had his fame. It's about money. He's a substance, an item. Items don't make action. People like Lonnie and others act for it. They take on authority. It's easy to do. They don't respect me. It's easy for them, especially when they're dealing with my father, who's a child himself. I want nothing but time with my father. How long is it going to be before he doesn't know who anyone is?

"I wasn't fond of the way Momma Bird (Odessa) was treated before her death. She lived in a roach-infested place, bills all over left unpaid. But he has to take the blame. He's always let people take control of his life. I went out two weeks before her death. She was on a respirator. Lonnie says to my father, 'We can't afford this, Muhammad.' He's not being treated right, either. He's not being exposed to the advances in Parkinson's. He was drinking coffee. Can you imagine? I'm mindful of my father's lack of integrity. Things were just the way they were. Why do you think he does missionary work? He wants people to know that he's been a good man. That a lot of things happened that he doesn't deserve. That he's credited too much for a lot of things. He's never lived in the world we did, he never did know the ordinary lives people have to live. But I let the past be the past. I live in the present with him. That's all I have—and not much of that."

"Last night," Ali said, "I dreamt of black ravens." He was outside the Hilton Head clinic after that long day in 1989, his voice a monotone, his stare trying to connect two distant points. "What's it mean?"

"I don't know. Just a dream."

"Every night? Ravens?"

"Dreams are like that. There'll be others."

"I never liked ravens," he said. "In my dreams, they angry, cover the sky and screech. It's an omen. That's what it is."

What strikes now is the thick, dominant silence that marked his days, in contrast to the dithyrambic sound that accompanied his passage, when his every public word snared the literati into thinking he had something to say, each word weighed until they grouped and became Ciceronian insight; a one-man theater troupe, given a wardrobe to fit every desired moment. The writer Wilfred Sheed noted back then, "He will have to make twice as much noise after he's through with boxing if he wants to stay famous." But physical disaster—of his own making—has kept his fame intact. He would have become the bore dodged at the party, as he often threatened to become when he was in apostolic and/or sociological thrall; best then to think of lunch or replay an old poker hand, thereby reducing him to the white sound of an air conditioner. The future promised that there would be no more clothes with which to dress him up.

What he was and was not is only of celebrity moment, unworthy next to his talent even in an age now of desperate and flimsy construction of heroes, the pallid figure made towering, assigned value in

a valueless time. As a fighter, a champion—and there is no other measurement for those who ignore the buzz—he was the surface of a
shield, unmalleable, made for mace and chain, flaring with light. He
was the uncommon standard, the true measure that says the Parthenon
should not be able to be scaled by those with just a shoeshine and a
smile. Brilliance, greatness, of such impoverished meaning now, do not
do the job when it comes to what he did with a pair of Everlast gloves.
Funny, though, while watching film of most of his fights, trying to
reassess the breadth and detail of his work, the mind strays from him,
as though knowing that film cannot reclaim the once real. Attention
goes to eerie, gray figures trying to survive and solve him, and it is like
looking, from a high, high view, at the diorama of a lost world.

They were gone now, most of those who peopled the parabola of
his ring life, and memory calls them up, just flickers of thought with
no ordering of place or value. Sugar Ray Robinson: who imposed himself on a room like a rare artifact of pre-Columbian art, making his
last stop in a dinky arena in Pittsfield, Massachusetts, in a rattling station wagon alone with a suitcase showing the stickers from French
liners he used to take. Sonny Liston: blasted even by the NAACP, set-
ting off for the hills of Denver with a backpack of bricks and a jar of
water, when he suddenly braked, snorting, the mucus streaming from
his nostrils, at a shrine of Mother Cabrini. He soaked a rag and wiped
her feet. "They look dirty to me," he said. Floyd Patterson, whose
favorite words were the self-portraying "vicissitude" and "enigma,"
now hardly able to remember that he was once a fighter. Old and
unordinary Cash, Ali's father: dying at the most prosaic of stops of a
heart attack—in a hardware store. One can still hear him jabbing at
his son. "I eat pork. Nothin' wrong with pork. Get these Muslim
loafers outta here, I'll cook you up a nice pork roast."

And the others . . . so many of them: Oscar Bonavena: shot to death
outside a Nevada whorehouse for trying to woo the owner's wife and

take the joint over. Jerry Quarry: the best white heavy since Marciano, constantly trumped by his betters in the division, not knowing how to find the bathroom in his brother's small house, his food having to be cut in small pieces, then dying of erosive brain trauma. Cleveland Williams: having to run down his manager for his money on the street, then being handed a swindling $37.50 as his end, with his manager Hugh Benbow berating him. "I'm ashamed of you." The Big Cat died in an accident coming home from a dialysis treatment. George Chuvalo: a good man with a bad roll, two sons lost to drugs and suicide and finally the suicide of his wife. Archie Moore: the mentally bejeweled fakir, above all, who knew the most and was listened to the least; he lived, like one of his oaks, to a graceful, long age. Bundini Brown, saying: "Next to the champ, I loved the sea best. It makes the world small. I was, you see, a pillar-to-post baby. You know, born on a doorstep with a note on my chest that says 'Do the best you can for him.'"

I thought of my first conscious sighting of Ali. In *Requiem for a Heavyweight*, by Rod Serling, when the young Clay was the opponent of Mountain Rivera, and would send him into the arms of social workers and make him in the final pulling shot of the camera a wrestler in Indian headdress; Mountain's fall from pride and dignity certainly so very far from any wild irony that could descend on the new royalty of Clay. "Great fight, kid," he says to the old and battered Mountain. "You were great." The last striking sense of him that persists and stings comes from his daughter Khaliah. She was at Momma Bird's funeral, and that night sat with her father. She was both sad and happy. For the first time, she had him alone. She thought of all they would talk about. But he just sat there for hours in the dark living room, saying nothing. She sat with him, wondering—what is he thinking? She said nothing. Over and over, he listened to the same song lyrics until dawn broke: "Ain't no sunshine when she's gone, only darkness every day. . . ."

AUTHOR'S NOTE

A large part of this book comes from my own observations, analysis, and long relationship with the principals of this story—Ali, Frazier, and the people who surrounded them. Writing about the ring then, unlike the marketing-driven coverage now, could be done on a highly personal basis. Writers could sit with fighters and their managers for long hours without interruption, leading to the kind of story-telling sessions that invariably added at least some view of the fighter's inner world.

Very little in the way of preparatory reading has been done for this book; most of what is out there is first- and secondhand hero worship. However, a few books were especially rewarding. *Black is Best*, by old colleague Jack Olsen, catches the early Cassius Clay with a sharp reportorial eye and is certainly the finest book to have been done on Ali. Wilfred Sheed produced a keenly observed work back in 1975, *Muhammad Ali*, that also ranks as a piece of boxing literature. The autobiography written by Joe Frazier with Phil Berger was helpful in that it provided a sincere overview of Joe. But the same cannot be said for *The Greatest*, the autobiography of Ali done with the Muslim propagandist Richard Durham. It is a screed of misdirection and fantasy that, along with the film of the same title, is in part responsible for the Ali myth. Conversations with the late Tex Maule, Dick Russell, former *S.I.* colleague, were always enlightening, as were long talks over the years with Sugar Ray Robinson and Archie Moore. Sugar's fine book with Dave Anderson was also quite helpful.

Acknowledgments are due a number of people, particularly my editor, David Hirshey, for his enthusiasm and close attention; my agent, Chris Calhoun of Sterling Lord Literistic; and Sunni Khalid, a student of the Nation of Islam. And, most heartfelt, to Anne Janette Johnson, for the generosity of her time in the preparation of the manuscript; and to my son, Mark, for his strong editorial hand and unlodgeable belief.